PROVI

Books by the Author Translated into English

God, His Existence and His Nature: A Thomistic Solution of Certain
Agnostic Antinomies (1914)

Christian Perfection and Contemplation, according to St. Thomas
Aquinas and St. John of the Cross (1923)

The Love of God and the Cross of Jesus (1929)

Providence (1932)

Our Savior and His Love for Us (1933)

Predestination (1936)

*The One God (1938)

The Three Ages of the Interior Life: Prelude of Eternal Life (1938)

The Three Ways of the Spiritual Life (1938)

*The Trinity and God the Creator (1943)

*Christ the Savior (1945)

The Priesthood and Perfection (1946)

Reality: A Synthesis of Thomistic Thought (1946)

Life Everlasting (1947)

*Grace (1947)

The Priest in Union with Christ (1948)

The Mother of the Saviour and Our Interior Life (1948)

*The Theological Virtues—Vol. 1: Faith (1948)

*Beatitude (moral theology, 1951)

Last Writings (spiritual retreats, 1969)

Books by the Author Not Translated into English

Le sens commun: la philosophie de l'être et les formules dogmatiques (1909)

Saint Thomas et le neomolinisme (booklet, 1917)

De Revelatione per ecclesiam catholicam proposita (1918)

De methodo sancti Thomae speciatim de structura articulorum summae
theologicae (booklet, 1928)

Le réalisme du principe de finalité (1932)

Le sens du mystère et le clair-obscur intellectuel: nature et
surnaturel (1934)

Essenza e attualità del Tomismo

Dieu accessible à tous (booklet, 1941)

*De Eucharistia: Accedunt de Paenitentia quaestiones dogmaticae (1942)

Les XXIV Theses Thomistes pour le 30e Anniversaire de leur
Approbation (booklet, 1944)

Verite et immutabilite du dogme (booklet, 1947)

*De virtutibus theologicis (1948)

---

*Commentaries on St. Thomas Aquinas' Summa Theologica.

PROVIDENCE

By

Fr. Reginald Garrigou-Lagrange, O.P.

Translated by
Dom Bede Rose, O.S.B., D.D.

TAN BOOKS AND PUBLISHERS, INC.
Rockford, Illinois 61105

Nihil Obstat:	P. Jerome Wespe, O.S.B.
	Censor Deputatus
Imprimi Potest:	✠ Thomas Meier, O.S.B.
	Abbot
Nihil Obstat:	F. J. Holweck
	Censor Librorum
	St. Louis, Missouri
	January 2, 1937
Imprimatur:	✠ John J. Glennon
	Archbishop
	St. Louis, Missouri
	January 2, 1937

This book is a translation of *La Providence et la confiance en Dieu*. Republished in 1998 by TAN Books and Publishers, Inc. by authorization of The Dominican Province of France, Paris.

Library of Congress Catalog Card No.: 98-61399

ISBN 0-89555-633-2

Cover illustration by Janssens.

Printed and bound in the United States of America.

TAN BOOKS AND PUBLISHERS, INC.
P.O. Box 424
Rockford, Illinois 61105
1998

To

The Holy Mother of God

Mother of Divine Grace

as a

Token of Gratitude and

Filial Obedience

FOREWORD

Having treated elsewhere of God [1] and of providence [2] from a purely speculative point of view, we here resume the consideration of these great questions in their relation to the spiritual life. The primary object of contemplation is, in fact, God Himself and His infinite perfections, especially His goodness, His wisdom, and His providence. Our activity and our progress toward eternity must be directed from the higher plane of this contemplation. From this point of view we shall treat here: (1) of the existence of God and of His providence; (2) of those perfections of God which His providence presupposes; (3) of providence itself according to the Old and New Testaments; (4) of a trusting self-abandonment to God's providence; (5) of providence in its relation to justice and mercy.

May these pages instil in the minds of those who read them a better understanding of God's infinite majesty and the absolute value of the one thing necessary, our last end and sanctification. Their chief aim will be to insist on the *absolute* and supremely life-giving character of the truth revealed by our Lord Jesus Christ and infallibly proposed to us by the Church. Souls are perishing in the ever-shifting sands of the relative; it is the absolute they need. Nowhere

---

[1] *God, His Existence and His Nature,* tr. by Dom Bede Rose, O.S.B., 2 vols.

[2] *Dictionnaire de théologie catholique,* articles: Providence, Prédestination, Prémotion.

will they find it but in the Gospel entrusted by Jesus Christ to His Church, which has preserved, taught, and expounded it. It has been exemplified in the lives of the best of her children.

TRANSLATOR'S PREFACE

In these days of positive unbelief, agnosticism, and general indifference concerning the supernatural, it is to be hoped that this English translation of the Reverend Father Garrigou-Lagrange's *La Providence et la confiance en Dieu* will serve a useful purpose. In this book the author has proved conclusively to anyone of upright mind that there is an all-wise and designing Providence, who has created all things with an end in view, and this especially as regards human beings. The whole of creation confirms this view. Long ago the psalmist declared that "the heavens show forth the glory of God: and the firmament declareth the work of His hands" (Ps. 18:2). If we believe in the existence of God—and no reasonable being can deny this—then we must say with the bard of Avon that "there's a divinity that shapes our ends, rough-hew them how we will" (Hamlet, V, ii, 10).

The first part of this book is a brief summary of a previous work by the same author, entitled: *God, His Existence and His Nature*. The proofs for the existence of God and a discussion of the divine attributes constitute the basis of Providence. This French work was well received. Within a short time after publication six thousand copies were sold. It has also been translated into German, Italian, and Polish.

In conclusion I wish to express my indebtedness to the Reverend Dr. Newton Thompson for his painstaking care in preparing the manuscript for publication. This indebtedness also applies to the second volume of *God, His Existence and His Nature,* which due to an oversight was not mentioned at the time of its publication.

I also wish to thank the Reverend Dr. Bernard Wall, late of Wonersh seminary, England, for his courtesy in allowing me the use of his manuscript, which I consulted on various occasions. The verification of many quoted passages was thereby much simplified and this enabled me to proceed more rapidly.

Bede Rose, O.S.B.
St. Benedict's Abbey
Mount Angel, Oregon

CONTENTS

PART I

THE EXISTENCE OF GOD AND OF PROVIDENCE

PART II

THE PERFECTIONS OF GOD WHICH HIS PROVIDENCE PRESUPPOSES

PART III

PROVIDENCE ACCORDING TO REVELATION

PART IV

SELF-ABANDONMENT TO PROVIDENCE

PART V

PROVIDENCE, JUSTICE, AND MERCY

PROVIDENCE

PART I

THE EXISTENCE OF GOD AND OF PROVIDENCE

CHAPTER I

GOD THE PRIME MOVER OF CORPOREAL AND SPIRITUAL BEINGS

Before we proceed to consider the meaning and import of the proofs for the existence of God and His providence, it will be well to point out one general proof that virtually contains them all. It may be summed up in this way: *The greater does not come from the less,* the more perfect does not come from the less perfect, since the latter is incapable of producing this effect.

There are in the world living, intelligent beings that come into existence and disappear again; they are therefore not self-existent. And what we say of the present applies equally to the past.

Consequently they require a cause, one that is self-existent. Hence there must exist from all eternity a first Being who owes His being to none but Himself and is able to confer being on others: a first living being, a first intelligence, a first goodness and holiness. If it were not so, the life, intelligence, goodness, and holiness of which we have experience could never have made their appearance in this world of ours.

Already open to common sense, this proof may be further scrutinized by philosophical reason, but no fault can be found with it.

The greater cannot come from the less as from its wholly

adequate, efficacious cause, for the additional perfection would itself then be without a cause, without a reason for its existence, and hence absolutely unintelligible. It is utterly absurd to maintain that the intelligence or the goodness of Jesus, of the great saints—of St. John, St. Paul, St. Augustine —are the result of unintelligent matter, of a material and blind fatality.

This general proof is at once more convincing when we consider the motion of bodies and spirits—motions from which it is shown that God is the first mover of every being, both corporeal and spiritual.

Already advanced by Aristotle, this proof from motion is set out as follows by St. Thomas in his *Summa Theologica,* Ia, q. 2, a. 3:

> There is motion in the world, from the
> lowest order of beings to the highest.

St. Thomas takes as his starting-point a fact of evident experience, that there is motion in the world: the local motion of inanimate bodies displacing and attracting one another; the qualitative motion of heat increasing or diminishing in intensity; the motion of development in the growing plant; the motion of the animal desiring food and going in quest of it; the motion of the human intellect passing from ignorance to a knowledge at first confused, then distinct; the motion of our spiritual will, which from not desiring a certain object comes to desire it more keenly; the motion of our will which after desiring the end desires also the means to attain it.

Here, then, is a universal fact: there is motion in the

world, from the motion of the stone that is thrown into the air, to the motion of our minds and wills. And we may say that everything in this world is subject to motion or change —nations and peoples and institutions as well as individuals. When a motion has reached its peak it gives place to another, as one wave of the sea is followed by another, one generation by another, a phenomenon that the ancients represented by the wheel of fortune on which the more successful were lifted up, only to descend once more and give place to others. Is it a fact, then, that everything passes, that nothing endures? Is there nothing constant, nothing stable and absolutely permanent?

All motion requires a mover

How are we to explain this universal fact of motion, be it either corporeal or spiritual? Is the explanation to be found in motion itself? Is it its own reason, its own cause? To answer this question, we must begin by pointing out two facts. First, in motion there is something new that requires explanation. Where does this new element come from, which previously had no existence? The question applies to past as well as to present forms of motion. Secondly, motion exists only in a movable object: it is this individual motion for the sole reason that it is the motion of this mobile object. There is no displacement without a body that is displaced, no flowing without a fluid, no current without a liquid, no flight without a bird that flies, no dream without a dreamer, no motion or volition apart from an intelligent being that wills.

But if there is no motion apart from a mobile object, is it possible for that object to move itself by its own power and without a cause of any kind? Can the stone of itself set itself in motion without someone to throw it into the air, or without some other body to attract it? Can the cold metal become hot of itself, without a source of heat?

But, you may say, a living thing moves itself. True, but is there not in the living thing a part that is moved and another that moves? If the blood circulates through the arteries of an animal, is it not because the heart by its contraction makes it circulate?

So also in man. If the hand moves, is it not because the will moves it? And if in its turn the will is moved, passing from a state of indetermination to one of determination, must it not be moved by some object attracting it, by some good? And is it sufficient merely for the good to be presented to it? Must not the will direct itself or be directed to it? It does in fact direct itself to the means because it first of all desires the end; but in the case of the first desire of an end, as when we come to the age of reason or when on waking in the morning we begin to exercise our will, is not an impulse from some higher source necessary to start our volitional activity, so as to make our will pass from the state of repose, of inactivity, to that first act which is to be the cause of all the acts that follow? That act contains something new which demands a cause; and the will, not yet in possession of this new perfection, cannot give it to itself. (Cf. St. Thomas, Ia IIae, q. 9, a. 4; q. 10, a. 4.)

Shall we say that this particular motion, whether corporeal or spiritual, has as it cause another motion anterior to it? But, if we consider motion as such, whether realized in this present motion or in the motions that precede, we shall see that it is a transition from potency to act. Now potency is less perfect than act; potency, therefore, cannot confer act upon itself. Once again, if there were not a mover for every motion, the greater would come from the less.

The stone was capable of displacement; now it changes its position; it does not do so without a mover that projects or attracts it.

The plant in its growth passes from potency to act, but not without the action of the sun, air, and moisture from the earth. The animal passes from potency to act when it pursues the prey that attracts it, but only in virtue of that higher activity which has endowed it with the instinct to feed upon this object rather than upon some other.

Man himself passes from potency to act, from ignorance to knowledge; for him it is an intellectual acquisition. But the intellect does not give itself these acquisitions which hitherto it did not possess.

Our will, too, passes from potency to act, to which at times it clings heroically. Where does this new perfection come from? The will could not confer this upon itself, since it did not possess this before.

All motion, then, whether corporeal or spiritual, *requires a cause:* without a mover the mobile thing is not moved. The mover may be within, as the heart is within the living animal; but if this mover is itself moved, it demands another mover superior to itself. The heart that at the moment of death stops beating cannot set itself going again; in this case it would require the intervention of the Author of life Himself, by whom that life was given and who maintained its motion until the organism finally spent itself.

Every motion demands a mover: such is the principle by which St. Thomas throws light upon this great universal fact of motion. The irrational animals perceive, indeed, that there are motions of the sensible order; but, that every motion demands a mover, is beyond their comprehension. They have no grasp of intelligible being or of the *raison d'être* of things, but only of sensible phenomena—color, sound, heat, and the like. On the other hand, being and the *raison d'être* of things constitute the very object of our intellect; hence we are able to grasp the truth, that without a mover all motion is impossible.

Every motion requires a supreme mover

But we must go a step farther. If for every motion either corporeal or spiritual a mover is required, does this necessitate a supreme mover?

A number of philosophers, including Aristotle, thought it possible to have an infinite series of movers accidentally subordinated to one another in past time. For such as these the series of animal generations, for instance, never had a beginning. There was never a first hen or a first egg, but always, without beginning, there were hens that laid eggs; the motion of the sun revolving in the heavens had no beginning and will have no end; the evaporation of water from the rivers and seas has always been producing rain, but there was no first rainfall.

We Christians hold it to be a fact known from revelation, that the world had a beginning: that it was created not from all eternity (*non ab aeterno*), but in time. This is an article of faith defined by the councils.

But precisely because it is an article of faith and not merely one of the preambles to the faith, is why St. Thomas holds that reason alone can never demonstrate that the world had a beginning (Ia, q. 46, a. 2). And why does this truth transcend the natural powers of our intellect? Because that beginning depended on the free will of God. Had He so willed, He might have created the world ten thousand years, a hundred thousand years, millions of years before, or at a time even more remote, without there having been a first day for the world, but simply a dependence of the world on its Creator, just as a footprint in the sand is due to the foot that makes it, so that, had the foot always been there the footprint would have had no beginning.

Although revelation teaches that the world did in fact have a beginning, it does not seem impossible, says St. Thomas, for the world always to have existed in its dependence on God the Creator.

But, if a series of movers accidentally subordinated in the past may be infinite and does not of necessity require a first in time, it is not so with a series of movers necessarily and actually subordinated at the present moment. Here we must eventually arrive at a supreme mover actually existent, one that has not merely given an impulse at the beginning of the world, but that is moving all things now.

For example: the boat carries the fisherman, the sea enables the boat to float, the earth holds the sea in check, the sun keeps the earth fixed in its course, and some unknown center of attraction holds the sun in its place. But after that? We cannot go on in this manner *ad infinitum* in a series of causes that are actually subordinate. There must be a first and supreme efficient cause existing not merely in the past but in the present, and this supreme cause must act, must exert its influence now; otherwise the subordinate causes, that act only when moved by another, would not act at all.

Trying to dispense with the necessity of a source is the same as saying that a watch can run without a spring, provided it has an infinite number of wheels. The watch may have been wound up a thousand times, a hundred thousand times, or times without number, in the past—it matters little; what is necessary is for it to have a spring. Likewise it matters little whether the earth had a beginning in its revolution around the sun; what is necessary is for the sun to attract it now, and for the sun itself to be attracted by a more remote and actually existing center of attraction. In the end we must come to *a first mover that acts of itself* and not through another of a higher order. We must come to a first mover able to give a full and adequate account of the very being or reality of its action.

Now that alone can account for the being of its action which possesses it in its own right, and that not only potentially but actually; a being which, as a consequence, is its very act, its activity, and which, instead of having received its life, is life itself. Such a mover is absolutely immobile in the sense that it already possesses of itself what others acquire by motion. It is in consequence essentially distinct from all mobile things, whether corporeal or spiritual. And here we have a refutation of pantheism. God cannot be confounded with the world, for He is immovable, whereas the world is in a state of perpetual change. It is this very change that demands an immobile first mover, who, instead of passing from the potential to the actual, is His act from all eternity; who is consequently being itself, since action presupposes being and since the mode of action follows upon the mode of being. "I am the Lord and I change not" (Malachias 3: 6). It is false to say that everything passes and nothing endures, that nothing is constant, nothing stable. There must be a first mover who is Himself absolutely immovable.

To deny the necessity of a supreme cause is to maintain that the explanation of motion lies in itself, that a mobile thing can of itself and without a mover pass from potency to act, can confer on itself the act, the new perfection it does not yet possess. To do away with a supreme cause is to claim that, as someone has said, "a brush will paint by itself provided it has a very long handle." [1] This is maintaining always the same thing, that *the greater comes from the less.*

As evidence of this necessity for a supreme mover in the present and not merely in the past, we may take another example, this time from motion of the spiritual order.

Our will begins to will a certain thing: a sick person, for instance, wishes to call in a doctor. And why? Because first of all he desires to be cured, and to be cured is a good thing. He began to will this good thing, and this act of willing is an act distinct from the volitional faculty; for with us this faculty is not of itself an eternal act of love for the good; it contains its first act only potentially, so that when the act makes its appearance it is in the will as something new, a new perfection. In order to find the ultimate *raison d'être* of this becoming, of the very reality of this first act of willing, we must go back to a *first mover of mind and will,* one that has not received the impulse to act, who acts without its being given Him to act, to whom it can never be said: "What hast thou that thou hast not received?" We must eventually arrive at a *first mover* who is His own activity, who acts solely through Himself, since action presupposes

---

[1] Sertillanges, *Les Sources de la croyance en Dieu,* p. 65.

being and since the mode of action follows upon the mode of being.

Only being itself, which alone exists of itself, can in the last analysis account for the being or reality of a becoming, which is not self-existent.

Are we not forced to recognize the existence of this first mover when we are confronted with an important duty to be performed at all costs and without delay, such as the defense of family or country; are we not too aware of our weakness, our powerlessness to proceed to action? What is then needed is action, not words. Who, then, will effect the transition from potency to act, if not He and He alone who has given us the faculty to will and is able to move the will, seeing that He is more intimately present to it than it is to itself?

Similarly, *the first act of our intellect,* whether it be when we come to the age of reason or when we wake in the morning, presupposes a first impulse given to it by the supreme intellect, without whose concurrence we could not think at all. This impulse, by many unperceived, becomes at times strikingly apparent on those occasions known as flashes of genius. Even the man of genius merely participates in intellectual life. He has a part in it, and everything that is by participation is dependent on that which exists of itself and not through another.

Is not the existence of the first mover of intellects forcibly brought home to us when, after failing to see where our duty lies, we retire within ourselves and there eventually get enlightenment? How have we passed from potency to act if not by the assistance of Him who has given us intelligence and who alone can enrich it with new light?

The first mover, therefore, is not in potentiality for further perfection. He is pure act without any admixture of imperfection. Consequently, He is really and essentially distinct from every limited mind, whether angelic or human, these passing from potency to act, from ignorance to knowledge. Here again we have a refutation of pantheism.

Is the first mover of corporeal and spiritual beings necessarily spiritual?

To move intellects and wills without doing violence to them, evidently the mover must be spiritual. *The greater does not come from the less.*

But even the first mover of corporeal beings must be spiritual, for, as we have seen, It must be immobile in the sense that It is its own action, its own being. This cannot be true of anything corporeal; all bodies are mobile; matter is in perpetual motion.

Even if prime matter is supposed to be endowed with primitive essential energies, still it cannot as an agent account for the being of its own action; for such an agent must not only possess action and existence, it must be its very action, existence, and consequently must be absolutely immobile, possessing of itself all perfection and not a tendency to it. Now matter is forever in motion, constantly acquiring new perfections or forms and losing others.

The first mover, therefore, of corporeal and spiritual beings must evidently be spiritual. It is of Him the liturgy speaks when it says:

> *Rerum Deus tenax vigor,*
> *Immotus in Te permanens.*

(God powerful sustainer of all things,
Thou who dost remain permanently unmoved.)

In what then does the immobility of the supreme mover
of corporeal and spiritual beings consist? Not in the immobility of inertia, of an inert body, for that is inferior to motion. It is *the immobility of supreme activity,* which has
nothing to gain, because of itself and from the first it possesses all that it is possible for it to possess and is able to communicate that abundance externally. On board ship the
sailors pass to and fro at their duties, but is it not the captain
who directs them to action by the spiritual activity of his
intellect and will, standing immovable on the bridge? There
is far more vitality in the steadfast contemplation of truth
than in mere commotion.

The immobility of the first mover is not the immobility of
the stone, but the immobility that characterizes the contemplation and love of the supreme good.

The characteristics of the supreme mover

Since the first mover is pure act with no admixture of the
imperfection of potentiality, it follows that He is in no way
perfectible. He is *infinitely perfect,* pure being, the pure and
ever actual intellection of supreme truth, the pure and ever
actual love of the fulness of being ever actually loved.

He is *omnipresent,* because to move all beings whether
spiritual or corporeal, He must be present, since these beings
do not move themselves, but are moved by Him.

He is *eternal,* for He has always by and of Himself all

His being and all His action of thought and love. In one immobile instant transcending time, He possesses His life simultaneously in all its completeness. When the world was created, the creative act did not commence in God, for it is eternal; but it produced its effect in time at the desired moment fixed from all eternity.

The first mover is *unique:* for pure act does not receive existence, it is existence; it is being itself, which cannot be multiplied. Were there two first movers, since one would not be the other, each would be limited and imperfect and would no longer be pure act and being itself.

Moreover the capacity of a second pure act could be nothing more than the first, and would be superfluous: Could there be anything more absurd than a superfluous God?

If such be the case, if there is an actually existing first mover of corporeal and spiritual beings, what practical conclusions are to be drawn from it?

In the first place we must learn to distinguish in life between the immobility of inertia and the immobility of higher activities. The immobility of inertia or of death is inferior to motion. The immobility that characterizes the contemplation and love of God is superior to the movement it may produce by directing and vivifying it.

Instead of dissipating our life in mere commotion, let us endeavor to recollect it so that our activity may be more profound, more consistent and lasting, and directed to eternity.

Secondly, let us frequently establish a contact in the summit of our soul with the first mover of corporeal and spiritual beings, who is none other than the living God, author not only of the soul and its natural acts, but of grace also and salvation.

Let us make this contact on waking in the morning, for then we receive within us that impulse from God that stirs us to action. Instead of going astray at the beginning of the day, let us welcome this first impulse by responding to it.

Let us in the course of the day resume this contact with Him who is the author of life, who was not content merely to urge us in the past, or merely to set us in motion at the beginning of the day, but is ever sustaining us and actualizing our voluntary actions—even the freest of them—in all their reality and goodness, evil only excepted.

Before lying down to rest, let us renew this contact, and all that sound philosophy has just told us about the first mover of corporeal and spiritual beings will appear transfigured, transported to a higher plane, in the Our Father.

"Thy kingdom come": the kingdom of the supreme intellect, by whom all other intellects are directed. "Thy will be done": that will to which every other will must be subjected if it is to attain to its true end.

"Lead us not into temptation," but sustain us by Thy strength; maintain our intellect in truth and our will in the good. Then we shall have an even deeper insight into the meaning of those words of St. Paul spoken in the Areopagus (Acts 17: 24): "God, who made the world and all things therein . . . hath made of one all mankind . . . that they should seek God, if happily they may feel after Him or find Him, although He be not far from every one of us. For in Him we live and move and are." In Him we have our being —not natural being only, but the supernatural being of grace which is the beginning of eternal life. Of this supreme mover, the source from which the life of creation proceeds, we have been able to speak only in an abstract and very imperfect manner. It is He whom we must see face to face when we come to the end of our journey and reach eternity.

CHAPTER II

The Order in the Universe, and Providence

The general proof for the existence of God—that the greater cannot come from the less—we have made more precise by an examination of motion. We have seen how all motion, corporeal or spiritual, requires a mover, and in the last resort a supreme mover; for in a series of actually subordinated causes (for instance, in the series: the earth attracted by the sun, the sun by a more distant center), we must eventually arrive at a supreme mover who does not require to be previously moved, who must therefore possess activity of Himself if He is to confer it upon others. That is, He must be His action instead of merely receiving it. He acts without its being given Him to act. And as action presupposes being, and the mode of action follows upon the mode of being, the supreme mover of corporeal and spiritual beings, to be His action, must also be being itself, according to the Scriptural expression: "I am who am."

We must now speak of a proof that establishes at once the existence of God and His providence—that based on *the order prevailing in the world*. Of all the proofs for God's existence, it is the most popular. Easily accessible to commonsense reason, it is susceptible of greater penetration by philosophical reason; and when it is applied from the physical to the moral order it may lead to the most sublime contemplation. We find it expressed in Psalm 18: 2: "The heavens show forth the glory of God: and the firmament declareth the work of His hands."

The fact: the order prevailing in the universe

The fact is this, that in nature, in those things that lack intelligence, we have an admirable *ordering of means to ends.* "This is evident," says St. Thomas, "since those things which lack intelligence—the heavenly bodies, plants and animals—act always, or at least nearly always, in such a way as to produce what is best" (Ia, q. 2, a. 3).

Finality and order are apparent in the *universal attraction* between bodies. The purpose of this attraction is the cohesion of the universe. It is seen in the translational motion of the sun through space, carrying with it its entire system. It is again seen in the twofold motion of the earth—the rotation about its axis every twenty-four hours, which is the cause of day and night, and its revolution round the sun in three hundred and sixty-five days, which is the cause of the seasons. In this constant regularity of the heavenly bodies in their courses, we have an obvious instance of means directed to an end, as the greatest astronomers declared, rapt as they were in admiration for the laws that they discovered. And many good things in this world would not be realized without the difference of day and night and the distinction of seasons, so necessary for the germination of plants and their development.

If we ascend a little higher and consider *the plant organism,* we see how admirably its arrangement enables it to use the moisture and transform it into sap, in a word, to nourish and reproduce itself in a regular and constant manner. If we but consider a grain of wheat put into the ground, we see that its purpose is to produce an ear of wheat, not of barley or rice.

We have only to consider an oak to see the utility of its roots and sap for the life of its branches and foliage. We have only to examine the collective organs of a flower to see that they all concur in the formation of the fruit which the flower is intended to produce—a cherry, for instance, or an orange. A particular flower is intended to produce a particular fruit and no other. How is it possible not to see in this formation a designing idea?

If we ascend still higher and consider *the animal organism,* whether in its lower or higher forms, we see that as a whole it is adapted for the animal's nourishment, respiration, and reproduction. The heart makes the red blood circulate throughout the organism for its nourishment; then the dark blood charged with carbonic acid is again transformed into red by contact in the lungs with the oxygen of the air. Obviously the heart and lungs are for the preservation of animals and men.

Certain parts of the animal organism are truly marvelous. The joints of the foot are so made as to adapt themselves to every position in walking, and those of the hand are suited to a great variety of movements. A bird's wings are adapted for flight far better than is the best airplane. The smallest cell, which is related to thousands of others, is a masterpiece in itself. Of particular beauty is the harmonious arrangement of the many parts of the ear, for the perception of sound; and again, the very complex structure of the eye, in which the act of vision presupposes thirteen conditions, each of these again presupposing very many more, all of them adapted to this simple act of vision. In the eye we have an instance of an amazing number of means adapted to one and the same end, and this organ is formed in such a way as to produce always, or usually at any rate, what is best.

If now we consider *the instinctive activity of animals,* especially such as bees, we meet with fresh marvels. It would require the genius of a mathematician to invent and construct a bee-hive; and no chemist has yet succeeded in making honey from the nectar of a flower. Yet the bee is obviously not itself intelligent: it never varies its work or makes any improvement. From the very beginning its natural instinct has determined it to perform its task in the same way, and it will continue to do so forever, without in any way bringing it to perfection. On the contrary, man is continually perfecting the implements of his invention because, through his intelligence, he recognizes their purpose. The bee, too, works with an end in view, but unconsciously; yet it works in a way that excites our admiration.

Shall it be said that this wonderful *order* in the heavenly bodies, in vegetable and animal organisms, in the instinct of animals, is the effect of a happy *chance?* What happens fortunately by chance is not of regular or even frequent occurrence, but extremely rare. It is by chance that a tripod, when thrown into the air, falls on its three feet; but this rarely happens. It is by chance that a man digging a grave finds a treasure; but it is an unusual thing. On the contrary, the wonderful order we have been considering as prevailing in nature is an order of fixed unchangeable laws, which are always applicable. It is a constant harmony and, as it were, the perpetual symphony of the universe for those who can hear it, that is, for great artists and thinkers and for the simple, to whom nature speaks of God.

Shall it be said that, amid a large number of useless organisms, a fortunate chance has formed a select few capable of receiving life, with the result that these have been preserved while the useless ones have disappeared? Such is the evolutionist theory of the survival of the fittest. But this would be tantamount to saying that chance is the first cause of the harmony prevailing in the universe and all its parts, and that, surely, is impossible. To be convinced of this, we need only reflect on what is meant by chance. Chance and its effect are something accidental; it is accidental for the tripod, when thrown into the air, to fall on its three feet; it is accidental for the gravedigger to find a treasure. Now the accidental presupposes the non-accidental, the essential, the natural, as the accessory presupposes the principal.

Were there no natural law of gravitation, the tripod would not, when thrown into the air, fall accidentally on its three feet. If the man who accidentally finds a treasure had not had the intention of digging the grave at that particular spot, this accidental effect would not have come about.

Chance is simply the accidental concurrence of two actions that are themselves not accidental but intentional, intentional at least in the sense that they have an unconscious natural tendency.

To say, therefore, that chance is the first cause of order in the world is to explain the essential by the accidental, the primary by the accessory; it implies as a consequence the destruction of the essential and the natural, the destruction of all nature and of all natural law. There would no longer be anything but fortuitous encounters, with nothing to encounter or be encountered—which is absurd. It is equivalent to saying that the wonderful order in the universe is the outcome of disorder, of the absence of order, of chaos, without cause of any kind: that the intelligible is the outcome of the unintelligible: that brain and intelligence are the result of a material, blind fatality. Once again it is to assert that the greater comes from the less, the more perfect from the less perfect. That is the substitution, indeed, of absurdity for the mystery of creation, a mystery that has its obscurities, but that is plainly in conformity with right reason.

The fact, then, that constitutes the starting-point of our proof holds good: namely, there is *order and finality in the world,* that is, means ordered to certain ends; for beings without intelligence, such as plants and animals, always or nearly always act so as to produce what is best. Universal attraction is for the cohesion of the universe, the seed of a grain of wheat for the production of the ear, a flower for the fruit, the foot of an animal for walking, the wings of a bird for flying, the lungs for breathing, the ear for hearing, the eye for seeing. The existence of finality is an undeniable fact, as even the positivist Stuart Mill admits.

More than this: not only is it a fact that every natural agent acts for some end, but it cannot be otherwise. Every agent must act for some purpose since, for the agent, to act is to tend to something determinate and appropriate to itself, that is, to an end. If the agent did not act for some determinate end, neither would it produce anything determinate, one thing rather than another; there would be no reason why the eye should see rather than hear, why the ear should hear rather than see. (Cf. St. Thomas, Ia IIae, q. 1, a. 2.)

Perhaps the objection may be raised, that we do not see for what useful purpose the viper and other harmful animals exist. True, the external finality of certain beings does frequently escape us, but their internal finality is plain enough. We are quite able to see that the viper's organs serve for its nutrition and preservation. Its poisonous effect upon us induces us to be on our guard, and reminds us that we are not invulnerable, that we are not gods. Faith tells us that, had man not sinned, the serpent would not have become harmful to him. In spite of obscurities and shadows, there is light enough for those who are willing to see.

The materialists say there is as much heat or motion or calorific energy in a kettle as in a gier-eagle. Ruskin retorts:

Very good; that is so, but for us painters, the primary cognizable facts, in the two things, are, that the kettle has a spout, and the eagle a beak; the one a lid on its back, the other a pair of wings; . . . the kettle chooses to sit still on the hob; the eagle to recline on the air. It is the fact of the choice, not the equal degree of temperature in the fulfilment of it, which appears to us the more interesting circumstance (*The Ethics of the Dust,* Lect. X).

The materialist does not perceive that wings are for flying, the eye for seeing; he will not recognize the value of finality of the eye. Yet, if he feels that he is losing his sight, he goes to the oculist like the rest of men, and that is at any rate a practical recognition of the fact that eyes were made to see with.

For those who are willing to see, there is light enough in

spite of obscurities and shadows. The finality of nature is an evident fact, not for our senses of course,—for these get no farther than the sensible phenomena—but for our intellect, which is made to grasp the *raison d'être* of things. For the intellect, obviously the eye is for seeing, the ear for hearing.

A means cannot be directed to an end except by an intelligent designer

From the fact that there is order in the world, how are we to ascend to the certain truth of God's existence? By means of the principle that beings without intelligence can tend to an end only when *directed to it by an intelligent cause,* as the arrow is directed by the archer. More simply, a means cannot be directed to an end except by an intelligent designer.

Why is this? Because the end, which determines the tendency and the means, is none other than the effect to be realized in the future. But a future effect, which as yet has no actual existence, must, to determine the tendency, be in some way already present, and this is possible only in a cognitive being.

If nobody has ever known the purpose of the eye, we cannot say that it is made to see with. If nobody has ever known the purpose of the bee's activity, we cannot say that it is for making honey. If nobody has ever known the purpose of the lung's action, we cannot say that it is for the renewal of the blood by contact with the oxygen of the air.

But why must there be an intelligent designer? Why does not the imagination suffice? Because only the intellect knows the *raison d'être* of things and consequently the purpose, which is the *raison d'être* of the means. Only an intellect can see that the wings of a bird are made for flying and the foot for walking; only an intellect could have designed wings for flying, the foot for walking, the ear for hearing, etc.

The swallow collecting straws to make its nest does so without perceiving that the building of the nest is the *raison d'être* of the action it performs. The bee, as it gathers the nectar from the flower, does not know that the honey is the *raison d'être* of its gathering. It is the intellect alone that reaches beyond mere color or sound down to the being and the *raison d'être* of things.

Only an intelligent designer can have directed means to an end; otherwise we would have to say that the greater comes from the less, order from disorder.

But why is an *infinite intellect* necessary, one strictly divine? Why, asks Kant, should not a limited intellect, like that of the angels, be sufficient to explain the order in the universe?

It is because a finite or limited intellect would not be thought itself, intellection itself, truth itself. Now an intellect that is not truth itself always known is merely directed to the knowledge of the truth; and this passive presupposes an active direction, which can come only from the supreme intellect, who is thought and truth itself. It is in this sense that our Lord declares Himself to be God, when He says: "I am the way, the truth and the life." He does not say merely, "I have received truth," but, "I am the truth and the life" (John 14: 6).

This, therefore, is the conclusion to which our proof leads us: a transcendently perfect intelligent designer, who is truth itself and consequently being itself, since the true is being that is known. It is the God of the Scriptures: I am who am. It is providence or the supreme reason of the order in things, by which every creature has been directed to its own particular end and finally to the ultimate end of the universe, which is the manifestation of the divine goodness. This is the way St. Thomas puts it (Ia, q. 22, a. 1):

We must necessarily suppose a providence in God; for, as was pointed out above, whatever goodness there is in things has been created by Him. Now in created things not only in their substance is goodness to be found, but also in their order to some end, and in particular to the ultimate end, which, as we concluded above, is the divine goodness. Hence this goodness in order apparent in created things has also been created by God. Now since God is the cause of all things through His intellect, in which therefore the conception of everyone of His effects must pre-exist, there must also pre-exist in the divine mind the conception of this ordering of things to an end. But the conception of the order of things to an end is strictly providence.

Providence is the conception in the divine intellect of the order of all things to their end; and the divine governance, as St. Thomas observes (*ibid.,* ad 2um), is the execution of that order.

We now understand more fully the significance of those words of the psalm: "The heavens show forth the glory of God" (Ps. 18:2). The wonderful order of the starry skies proclaims and extols the glory of God, and reveals to us His infinite intelligence. The harmony of the universe is like a marvelous symphony, the sweetest and most effective chant of the Creator. Blessed are they who listen to it.

Is there not a great moral lesson in this proof for the existence of God from the order prevailing in the world? Yes, an important one that is taught us in the Book of Job and more clearly later on in the Sermon on the Mount.

It is this lesson that, if there is such *order* in the physical world, much more must it be so *in the moral world,* in spite of all the wickedness human justice allows to go unpunished, as it also leaves unrewarded many a heroic act giving proof of God's intervention in the world.

It is the Lord's answer to Job and his friends. As we shall insist later on, the purpose of the Book of Job is to answer this question: Why so often in this world are the just made to suffer more than the wicked? Is it always in expiation of their sins, their secret sins at any rate?

Job's friends declare that it is, and they blame this poor stricken soul for complaining. Job denies that the trials and tribulations of the just are in every case the result of their sins, even their secret sins, and he wonders why so much suffering should have befallen him.

In the latter part of the book (chaps. 32–42), the Lord replies by pointing out the wonderful order prevailing in the physical world with all its splendors, from the life of the insect to the eagle's flight, as if to say: If there exists such order as this in the things of sense, much more so must there be order in the dispositions of my providence concerning the just, even in their most terrible afflictions. There is in this a secret and a mystery which it is not given to men to fathom in this world.

Later on, in the Sermon on the Mount, our Lord speaks more plainly (Matt. 6: 25): "Therefore I say to you, be not solicitous for your life, what you shall eat. . . . Behold the birds of the air, for they neither sow, nor do they reap . . . and your heavenly Father feedeth them. Are not you of much more value than they? . . . Consider the lilies of the field: . . . they labor not, neither do they spin. But I say to you that not even Solomon in all his glory was arrayed as one of these. And if the grass of the field . . . God doth so clothe: how much more you, O ye of little faith." If there is order in the world of sense, a providence for the birds of the air, much more so will there be order in the spiritual world and a providence for the immortal souls of men.

And lastly, to the question put in the Book of Job, our Lord gives the final answer when He says (John 15: 1–2): "I am the true vine: and My Father is the husbandman . . . and everyone that beareth fruit, He will purge it, that it may bring forth more fruit." God proves a man as He proved Job, that the man may bring forth the splendid fruits of patience, humility, self-abandonment, love of God and one's neighbor—the splendid fruits of charity, which is the beginning of eternal life.

This, then, is the important moral lesson taught us in this sublime proof for the existence of God: If in the world of sense such wonderful order exists, much more must it be so in the moral and spiritual world, in spite of trials and tribulations. There is light enough for those who are willing to see and march on accordingly to the true light of eternity.

CHAPTER III

God, the Supreme Being and Supreme Truth

The proof for the existence of a first mover of corporeal and spiritual beings, and of a supreme intelligence, the author of the harmony prevailing in the universe, will prepare the way for a better understanding of three other traditional proofs for the existence of God. They are those of (1) God, the supreme being and supreme truth, (2) the sovereign good who is the source of all happiness, and (3) the ultimate foundation of our obligations. These we must touch upon if we would have a right idea of providence.

Following in the steps of Plato, Aristotle, and St. Augustine, St. Thomas develops the first of these proofs, called the proof from the degrees of perfection, in the *Summa Theologica*, Ia, q. 2, a. 3, 4a via. Its point of departure lies in the more or less of perfection to be found in the beings that compose the universe, a perfection always limited, from which our minds are led on to affirm the existence of a supreme perfection, a supreme truth, a supreme beauty.

Let us closely examine the starting-point of the proof, the fact upon which the proof is based, and then the principle by which the proof rises from the fact to the existence of God.

The fact: the degrees of perfection

The proof starts with the fact that there are *in the universe beings more or less good,* more or less true, more or less

noble. In other words, in the universe of corporeal and spiritual beings, goodness, truth, nobility exist in varying degrees, from the lowest mineral such as iron with its strength
and resistance up to the higher degrees of the intellectual
and moral life apparent in the great geniuses and the great
saints.

Of these *degrees of goodness* in things we have daily experience. We say that a stone is good when it has solidity
and does not crumble away; a fruit is good if it provides
nourishment and refreshment; a horse is good if with it we
can go on a long journey. In a higher way a teacher is good
if he has knowledge and knows how to impart it; the virtu-
ous man is good because he wills and does what is good; far
more so is the saint, in whom the desire for good has become an ardent passion. And yet, however great a saint may
be, he has his limitations; no matter how much good he has
accomplished, like the Curé of Ars he will experience hours
of intense sadness coupled with a sense of his own helpless-
ness at the thought of all the good that remains to be done.
Indeed, the saints realize most of all their own nothingness.

It is an established fact, then, that goodness is realized in
varying degrees. It is the same with nobility: the vegetable
is nobler than the mineral, the animal is nobler than the
vegetable, man is nobler than the animal. One man is nobler
in mind and heart than a certain other; yet he too has his
limitations, his temptations, his weaknesses, his very imperfections. Nobility has its degrees, but even the most exalted in our experience are still very imperfect.

Similarly, truth has degrees, for that which is richer in
being, as a reality, is richer also in truth. True gold is superior to spurious gold alloyed with copper, the true diamond

is superior to the artificial, the upright mind is superior to the false. Surpassing the mind that possesses a knowledge of but one science, physics for example, is the mind that ascends to the sciences of the spiritual world, to psychology and the moral and political sciences. Yet how very limited is the truth of even these higher sciences!

The more we know, say the great thinkers, the more we realize all that still remains to be known, and how little we do know. So, too, with the great saints: the more good they do, the more keenly they realize the amount of good that still remains to be done.

What, then, is the explanation of these *various degrees of goodness,* nobility, and truth, or of beauty? Does this ascending gradation remain stunted, incomplete, without a culminating point, a summit? Must the progressive ascent of our minds toward the true halt at a limited and impoverished truth, as in the case of our psychology and our moral and political sciences? Must the progressive ascent of our will to the good halt at one that is imperfect, mingled always with some defect, some impotence? Must our enthusiasm at the sight of the ideal be forever followed by a certain disillusionment and, if there is no summit, by a disillusionment for which there is no remedy?

The principle: the more and the less perfect presuppose perfection itself

Following in the steps of Plato, Aristotle, and St. Augustine, St. Thomas explains the fact of the various degrees of the good and the true by means of the following principle: "Different beings are said to be more or less perfect in the measure of their approach to that being which is perfection itself."

By this sovereign perfection does St. Thomas mean ideal sovereign perfection, one existing solely in the mind, or one that is real? He means a real perfection, for that alone can be the cause of the various degrees of perfection which, as we have seen, do exist and which demand a cause.

The meaning of the principle invoked by St. Thomas is that, when a perfection (such as goodness, truth, or beauty), the conception of which does not imply any imperfection, is found in various degrees in different beings, none of those which possess it imperfectly contains a sufficient explanation for it, and hence its cause must be sought in a being of a higher order, which is this very perfection.

For a clearer understanding of this principle let us pause to consider its terms. When an *absolute perfection* is found in various degrees in different beings, none of those possessing it as yet imperfectly contains a sufficient explanation for it. Here we must consider (1) the multiple and (2) the imperfect.

1) *The multiple presupposes the one.* In fact, as Plato says in the *Phaedo,* his disciple Phaedo is handsome; yet beauty is not peculiar to Phaedo, for Phaedrus, too, is handsome. "The beauty found in some finite being is sister to the beauty found in similar beings. None of them is beauty; each merely participates, has a part in or is a reflection of beauty." (Cf. *Phaedo,* 101, A.)

It is not in Phaedo, then, any more than in Phaedrus, that we are to find the *raison d'être* of the principle of their beauty. If neither can account for the limited beauty that is his, he must have received it from some higher principle, namely, from Beauty itself. In a word, every multiplicity of beings more or less alike presupposes a higher unity. The multiple presupposes the one.

2) *The imperfect presupposes the perfect.* The principle we are explaining is brought home to us even more forcibly when we consider that the perfection of the beings we see around us is always mingled with its contrary, imperfection. A man's nobility and goodness cannot be said to be un-limited, mingled as it is with so much infirmity, with its trouble and errors. So also ignorance and even error con-stitute a great part of human knowledge; this merely partici-pates in truth, has no more than a part and that a humble part in it. And if it is not truth, that is because it has re-ceived truth from some higher source.

Briefly, *an imperfect being is a compound,* and every com-pound requires a cause uniting its constituent elements. The diverse presupposes the identical, the compound presupposes the simple. (Cf. St. Thomas, Ia, q. 3, a. 7.)

The truth of our principle will impress itself more forci-bly upon us if we observe that a perfection such as good-ness, truth, or beauty, which of itself implies no imperfection, is not in fact limited except by the restricted capacity of its recipient. Thus knowledge in us is limited by our restricted capacity for it, goodness by our restricted capacity for doing good.

Hence it is clear that, when a perfection of this kind, that as yet is in an imperfect state, is found in some being, such a being merely participates or has a part in it, and has therefore received it from a higher cause, which must be the *unlimited perfection itself,* being itself, truth itself, goodness itself, if this cause is to be capable of imparting to others a certain reflection of that truth and goodness.

Among the philosophers of antiquity Plato has emphasized this truth in one of the finest pages to be found in the writings of the Greek thinkers. (Cf. *Symposium,* 211, C.) We must learn, he says in substance, to love beautiful colors, the beauty of a sunrise or sunset, of the mountains, seas, and skies, the beauty of a noble countenance. But we must rise above mere material beauty to beauty of soul as displayed in its actions; thence from the beauty of these actions to the principles that govern them—to the beauty of the sciences, and from science to science ascending even to wisdom, the most exalted of them all: the science of being, of the true and the beautiful. Afterward there will arise in us the desire to have knowledge of the beautiful itself and as it is in itself—the desire to contemplate, says Plato,

that beauty which grows not nor decays; is not fair in one part, uncomely in another; fair at one time, uncomely at another; fair in one place and not in another; fair to some, uncomely to others . . . a beauty residing in no being other than itself, in an animal, in the earth or skies or elsewhere, but existing eternally and absolutely, of itself and in itself; in which all other beauties participate, without inducing in it by their birth or destruction the least diminution or increase, or any change whatsoever.

The disillusionments that we meet with here on earth are permitted precisely in order to direct our thoughts more and more to this supreme beauty and impel us to love it.

What Plato says of beauty applies equally to *truth*. Transcending particular, contingent truths, which possibly might not be so (as that my body exists at this moment, to die perhaps tomorrow), there are the universal, necessary truths (as that man is by nature a rational being, with the capacity to reason, without which he would be undistinguishable from the brute beast); or again the truth, that it is impossible for something at once to exist and not exist. These truths never began to be true and will continue to be true always.

Where have these *eternal, necessary truths* their foundation? Not in perishable realities, for the latter are governed by these truths as by absolute laws, from which nothing can escape. Nor is their foundation in our finite intellects, for these eternal, necessary truths govern and regulate our intellect as higher principles.

Where, then, are we to look for the foundation of these *eternal, necessary truths,* governing all finite reality and every finite intellect? Where is that foundation if not in the supreme being, the supreme truth always known by the first intellect, which, far from having received truth, is the truth, pure truth, without any admixture of error or ignorance, without any limitation or imperfection whatever?

In a word, the truths which govern all perishable reality and every finite intellect, like necessary and eternal laws, must have their foundation in a supreme truth which is being and wisdom itself. But it is God who is being itself, truth itself, wisdom itself.

Such is this further proof for the existence of God proposed by Plato, St. Augustine, and St. Thomas.

We now see more clearly the significance and scope of

the principle on which this proof is based: "Different beings are said to be more or less perfect according to the measure of their approach to that being which is perfection itself." In other words, when a perfection such as goodness, truth, or beauty, the concept of which implies no imperfection, is found in varying degrees in different beings, this cannot be accounted for by any of those beings in which it is found in as yet an imperfect degree; the being merely participates in it, and has received it according to the measure of its capacity—has received it, too, from a higher being who is this very perfection.

What practical conclusion are we to draw from this ascent? It is expressed in that saying of our Lord: "None is good but God alone"—good, that is, with goodness unalloyed. God alone is true, with a truth and wisdom untrammeled by ignorance; *God alone is beautiful* with that infinite beauty which we are called upon to contemplate some day face to face, that beauty which even here on earth the human intellect of Jesus contemplated as He conversed with His disciples. *"God alone is great"*: that was St. Michael's answer to Satan's pride. The thought of this makes us humble.

Ours is but a borrowed existence, freely given us by God, and He keeps us in existence because indeed He wills it so. Ours is but a goodness in which there is so much infirmity and even degradation; there is so much error in our knowledge. This thought, while serving to make us humble, brings home to us by contrast the infinite majesty of God.

And then if it is a question of others and no longer of ourselves, if we have suffered disillusionment about our neighbor whom we had believed to be better and wiser, let us remember that he too has suffered disillusionment about us; let us remember that he too is perhaps better than we are, and that whatever is our own as coming from ourselves— our deficiencies and failings—is inferior to everything our neighbor has from God. This is the foundation of humility in our relations with others.

Lastly, we must admit that the disillusionments we ourselves experience, or which others experience through us, in view of the radical imperfection of the creature, are permitted that we may aspire more ardently to a knowledge and love of Him who is the truth and the life, whom we shall some day see as He sees Himself. We shall then understand the meaning of those words of St. Catherine of Siena: "The living, practical knowledge of our own wretchedness and the knowledge of God's majesty are inseparable in their increase. They are like the lowest and highest points on a circle that is ever expanding." And the more we realize our own imperfections and limitations, the more we realize, too, that God has a right to be loved above all things by reason of His infinite wisdom and His infinite goodness.

Our final observation is this: the supreme truth has Himself spoken to us: He has revealed Himself to us, as yet in an obscure manner, but it is the foundation of our Christian faith. It is in the name of this supreme truth that Jesus speaks, when He says: "In truth, in truth, I say to you." He is Himself the truth and the life, and by His help from day to day we must gradually live a better life. This far surpasses Plato's ideal; no longer is it an abstract, philosophic ascent to the supreme truth, but the supreme truth which condescends to reach down to us in order to raise us up to Himself.

CHAPTER IV

God the Sovereign Good and the Desire for Happiness [1]

When speaking of God as supreme being and supreme truth we saw that a multiplicity of beings resembling one another in one and the same perfection, such as goodness, is insufficient to account for the unity of likeness thus existing in that multiplicity; as Plato said, the multiple cannot account for the one. Moreover, none of the beings possessing the perfection in an imperfect degree is sufficient to account for it; for each is a compound of the perfection and the restricted capacity limiting it, and like all compounds it demands a cause: "Things in themselves different cannot possess an element in common except through a cause uniting them." [2] This compound participates or has a part in the perfection; it has therefore received the perfection, and can have received it only from Him who is perfection itself, which in its notion implies no imperfection.

From the moral point of view this doctrine becomes of vital importance in reminding us that the more *we realize our limitations* in wisdom and goodness, the more our minds

[1] We here reproduce the substance of a study we have developed at greater length in another work entitled: *Le réalisme du principe de finalité,* Part II, chap. 5, "La finalité de la volonté: le désir naturel du bonheur prouve-t-il l'existence de Dieu?"

[2] St. Thomas, Ia, q.3, a.7, and *De Potentia,* q.3, a.5.

should dwell on Him who is wisdom and goodness itself.
The multiple finds its explanation only in the one, the
diverse in the identical, the compound in the simple, the
imperfect mingled with imperfection only in the perfect
that is free from all imperfection.

This proof for the existence of God contains implicitly
another which St. Thomas develops elsewhere, Ia IIae, q. 2,
a. 8. He shows that *beatitude* or true happiness, the desire
for which is natural to man, cannot be found in any limited
or restricted good, but *only in God* who is known at least
with a natural knowledge and loved with an efficacious
love above all things. He proves that man's beatitude cannot consist in wealth, honors, or glory, or in any bodily
good; nor does it consist in some good of the soul, such as
virtue, nor in any limited good. His argument for this last
is based on the very nature of our intellect and will.[3]

Let us consider (1) the fact which is the starting-point of
the proof, (2) the principle on which the proof rests, (3)
the culminating point of the proof, and (4) what the proof
cannot extend to.

1) The fact of experience: true, substantial, and enduring happiness cannot be found in any passing good

We can ascend to the sovereign good, the source of perfect
and unalloyed happiness, by starting either from the notion
of imperfect subordinate goods or from the natural desire
which such goods never succeed in satisfying.

If we begin with those *finite limited goods* which man is
naturally inclined to desire, we very soon realize their im-

---

[3] Cf. *Summa Theologica*, Ia IIae, q. 2, a. 8.

perfection. Whether it be health or the pleasures of the body, riches or honors, glory or power, or a knowledge of the sciences, we are forced to acknowledge that these are but transitory goods, extremely limited and imperfect. But, as we have said repeatedly, the imperfect, or the good mingled with imperfection, is no more than a good participated in by the restricted capacity of the recipient, and it presupposes the pure good completely excluding its contrary. Thus a wisdom associated with ignorance and error is no more than a participated wisdom, presupposing wisdom itself. This is the metaphysical aspect of the argument, the dialectic of the intellect proceeding by way of both exemplary and efficient causality.

But the proof we are here speaking of becomes more vital, more convincing, more telling, if we begin with that *natural desire for happiness* which everyone feels so keenly within him. This is the psychological and moral aspect of the argument, the dialectic of love founded on that of the intellect and proceeding by way of efficient (productive, regulative) causality or final causality.[4] These, the efficient and final, are the two extrinsic causes, each as necessary as the other. Indeed the final is the first of the causes, so that Aristotle (*Metaphysics,* Bk. XII, chap. 7) saw more clearly the final causality of God the pure act than His efficient causality, whether productive or regulative.[5]

[4] Cf. *ibid.,* Ia IIae, q. 1, a. 4: "Is there an ultimate end to human life?" "Absolutely speaking, it is impossible in a series to continue to infinity in any direction. . . . Were there not an ultimate end, nothing would be desired, no action would have a term, nor would the inclination of the agent find repose."

[5] If, instead of considering simply the end of this natural desire, we consider its ordering to that end—and this demands an efficient, regulating cause (*ordinans vel imperans movet ut agens, non ut finis*)—then the argument pertains to the fifth way of St. Thomas, which is that based upon the presence of order in the world: "All design presupposes a designer." In this sense the passive ordering of our will

Following in the wake of Aristotle and St. Augustine, St. Thomas (Ia IIae, q. 2, a. 7, 8) insists on the fact that *man by his very nature desires to be happy*. Now man's intellect, transcending as it does the sense and the imagination of the brute, has knowledge not merely of this or that particular good, whether delectable or useful—a particular food or a particular medicine, for instance—but of good in general (universal in predication), constituting it as such, as the desirable wherever it is to be found. Since this is so, and since man's inclination is directed to the real good to be found in things, and not simply to the abstract idea of the good, it follows that he cannot find his true happiness in any finite limited good, but in the *sovereign good* alone (universal in being and causation).[6]

It is impossible for man to find in any limited good that true happiness which by his very nature he desires, for his intellect, becoming immediately aware of the limitation, conceives forthwith the idea of a higher good, and the will naturally desires it.

This fact is expressed in the profound sentence of St. Augustine's *Confessions* (Bk. I, chap. 1): "Our heart, O Lord, is restless, until it finds its rest in Thee" (*irrequietum est cor nostrum donec requiescat in Te, Domine*).

Who of us has not experienced this fact in his intimate life? In sickness we have the natural desire to recover our health as a great good. But, however happy we are in our recovery, no sooner are we cured than we realize that health

to the *bonum honestum* or moral good, superior alike to the delectable and to the useful, presupposes a supreme regulator. Or again, moral obligation, which is displayed in remorse of conscience and in the peace that comes from duty accomplished, presupposes a supreme lawgiver. Of this we will speak in the next chapter.

[6] Cf. Cajetan, *Commentary* on IaIIae, q. 2, a. 7.

alone cannot bring happiness: a man may be in perfect health and yet be overwhelmed with sadness. It is the same with the pleasures of the senses: far from being sufficient to give us happiness, let them be abused ever so little and they bring only disillusion and disgust; for our intellect, with its conception of a universal unlimited good, straightway tells us: "Now that you have obtained this sensible enjoyment which just now had such an attraction for you, you see that it is sheer emptiness incapable of filling the deep void in your heart, of satisfying your desire for happiness."

It is the same with wealth and honors, which many desire eagerly. We no sooner possess them than we realize how ephemeral and superficial is the satisfaction they give, how inadequate they, too, are to fill the void in our hearts. And intellect tells us that all these riches and honors are still but a poor finite good that is dissipated by a breath of wind.

The same must be said of power and glory. One who is lifted up on the wheel of fortune has scarcely reached the top when he begins to descend; he must give place to others, and soon he will be as a star whose light is extinguished. Even if the more fortunate retain their power and glory for a time, they never find real happiness in it; often they experience such anxiety and weariness of mind that they long to withdraw from it all.

The same applies to the knowledge of the sciences. Here it is a case of only an extremely limited good; for the true, even when complete and without admixture of error, is still the good of the intellect, not of man as a whole. Besides the intellect, the heart and will have also their profound spiritual needs, and so long as these remain unsatisfied there can be no true happiness.

Shall we find it in a most *pure and exalted form of friendship?* Such a friendship will doubtless bring us intense joy, sometimes affecting our inmost being. But we have an intellect that conceives universal and unlimited good, and here again it will not be long in perceiving that this most pure and exalted form of friendship is still but a finite good. This reminds us of those words of St. Catherine of Siena: "Would you continue long to slake your thirst with the cup of true friendship? Leave it, then, beneath the fountain of living water; otherwise it will speedily be drained and no longer satisfy your thirst." If the thirst is satisfied, it is because the person loved is made better, and in order to be made better he needs to receive a new goodness from a higher source.

Suppose we could look upon an angel and see his suprasensible, purely spiritual beauty. Once the first sense of wondering amazement had passed, our intellect, with its conception of the universal, unlimited good, would immediately remind us that even this was no more than a finite good and thereby exceedingly poor in comparison with the unlimited and perfect good itself. Two finite goods, however unequal they may be, are equally remote from the infinite; in this respect the angel is as insignificant as the grain of sand.

2) *The principle by which we ascend to God*

Can it be that this natural desire for happiness, which we all have within us, must forever remain unsatisfied? Is it possible for a natural desire to be of no effect, chimerical, without meaning or purpose?

That a desire born of a fantasy of the imagination or of an error of reason, such as the desire to have wings, may be chimerical, can well be understood. But surely it could not be so with a desire which has its immediate foundation in nature without the intervention of any conditional judgment. The *desire for happiness* is not a mere hypothetical wish; it is innate, with its immediate foundation in nature itself; and nature again is stable and constant, being found in all men, in all places, and at all times. Furthermore, this desire is of the very nature of the will, which, prior to any act, is an appetitive faculty having universal good as its object. The nature of our will can no more be the result of chance, of a fortuitous encounter, than can the nature of our intellect; because, like the intellect, the will is a principle of operation wholly simple, in no way compounded of different elements that chance might have brought together. Can this natural *desire of the will* be chimerical?

In answer to this question we say, first, that natural desire in beings inferior to ourselves is not ineffectual, as the naturalists have shown from the experimental point of view. In herbiverous animals the natural desire is for herbaceous food, and this they find; in carnivores the desire is to find flesh to eat, and they find it. Man's natural desire is for happiness, and with him true happiness is not and cannot be found in any limited good. Is this true happiness nowhere to be found? Is man's natural desire, then, to remain a deception and without finality when the natural desire of inferior beings is not in vain?

And this is not purely a naturalist's argument based on experience and the analogy of our own natural desire with that of inferior beings. It is a metaphysical argument based on the certitude of the absolute validity of the principle of finality.

If the natural desire for true happiness is chimerical, then all human activity, inspired as it is by that desire, is without finality, without a *raison d'être,* and thus contrary to the necessary and evident principle that *every agent acts for an end.* To grasp the truth of this principle, thus formulated by Aristotle, it is enough to understand the terms of the proposition. Any agent whatsoever, conscious or unconscious, has an inclination to something determinate which is appropriate to it. Now the end is precisely that determinate good to which the act of the agent or the motion of the mobile object is directed.

This principle, self-evident to one who understands the meaning of the words agent and end, may be further demonstrated by a *reductio ad absurdum;* for otherwise, says St. Thomas (Ia IIae, q. 1, a. 2), "there would be no reason why the agent should act rather than not act, no reason why it should act in this way rather than in another," why it should desire this object rather than some other.

If there were no finality in nature, if no natural agent acted for some end, there would be no reason why the eye should see and not hear or taste, no reason why the wings of the bird should be for flying and not for walking or swimming, no reason for the intellect to know rather than desire. Everything would then be for no purpose, and be unintelligible. There would be no reason why the stone should fall instead of rising, no reason why bodies should attract rather than repel one another and be dispersed, thus destroying the harmony of the universe.

The *principle of finality* has an absolute necessity and value. It is no less certain than the principle of efficient causality, that everything that happens and every contingent being demands an efficient cause, and that in the last analysis everything that happens demands an efficient cause itself uncaused, a cause that is its own activity, its own action, and is therefore its existence, since action follows being and the mode of action the mode of being.

These two *principles of efficient and final causality* are equally certain, the certitude being metaphysical and not merely physical, antecedent to a demonstration of the existence of God. Indeed, without finality, efficient causality is inconceivable: as we have just seen, it would be without a purpose and consequently unintelligible.

3) The term of this ascent

There is, then, a purpose in our natural desire for happiness; its inclination is for some good. But is this inclination for *a good that is* wholly unreal, or, though real, yet *unattainable?*

In the first place, the good to which our natural desire tends is not simply an idea in the mind, for, as Aristotle more than once pointed out, whereas truth is formally in the mind enunciating a judgment, the good is formally in things. When we desire food, it is not enough for us to have the idea: it is not the idea of bread that nourishes, but the bread itself. Hence the natural desire of the will, founded as it is in the very nature of the intellect and the will and not merely in the imagination or the vagaries of reason, tends to a real good, not merely to the idea of the good; otherwise it is no longer a desire and certainly not a natural one.

It will perhaps be said that our universal idea of good leads us to seek happiness in the simultaneous or successive enjoyment of all those finite goods that have an attraction for us, such as health and bodily pleasures, riches and honors, the delight in scientific knowledge, art and friendship. Those who in their mad career wish to enjoy every finite good, one after another, if not all at once, seem for the moment to think that herein lies true hapipness.

But experience and reason undeceive us. That empty void in the heart always remains, making itself felt in weariness of spirit; and intelligence tells us that not even the simultaneous possession of all these goods, finite and imperfect as they are, can constitute the good itself which is conceived and desired by us, any more than an innumerable multitude of idiots can equal a man of genius.

Quantity has nothing to say in the matter; it is *quality of good* that counts here. Even if the whole sum of created goods were multiplied to infinity they would not constitute that pure and perfect good which the intellect conceives and the will desires. Here is the profound reason for that weariness of spirit which the worldly experience and which they take with them wherever they go. They pursue one thing after another, yet never find any real satisfaction or true happiness.

Now if our intellect is able to conceive a universal, unlimited good, the will also, awakened as it is by the intellect, has a range and depth that is limitless. Is it possible, therefore, for its natural desire—which calls for a real good and not merely the idea of good—to be chimerical and of no effect?

This natural desire, which has its foundation not in the imagination but in our very nature, is, like that nature, some-

thing fixed and unchangeable. It can no more be ineffectual
than the desire of the herbivora or that of the carnivora; it
can no more be ineffective than is the natural ordering of the
eye for seeing, the ear for hearing, the intellect for knowing.
If therefore this natural desire for happiness cannot be ineffective, if it cannot find its satisfaction in any finite goods
or in the sum total of them, we are necessarily compelled
to affirm the existence of a pure and perfect good. That is,
the good itself or the sovereign good, which alone is capable
of responding to our aspirations. Otherwise the universal
range of our will would be a psychological absurdity, something radically unintelligible and without a purpose.

4) What does not come within the exigencies of our nature

Does it follow that this natural desire for happiness in
us demands that we attain to the intuitive vision of God, the
sovereign good?

By no means; for *the intuitive vision of the divine essence
is essentially supernatural* and therefore gratuitous, in no way
due to our nature or to the nature of angels.

This is the meaning of St. Paul's words: "Eye hath not
seen, nor ear heard; neither hath it entered into the heart
of man, what things God hath prepared for them that love
Him. But to us God hath revealed them by His Spirit. For
the Spirit searcheth all things, yea, the deep things of God"
(I Cor. 2:9).

But far inferior to the intuitive vision of the divine essence
and to Christian faith, is a natural knowledge of God as
the author of nature, which is the knowledge given us by
the proofs of His existence.

If original sin had not enfeebled our moral strength, this natural knowledge would have enabled us to attain to a naturally efficacious love for God as the author of nature, who is the sovereign good known in a natural way.

Now had man been created in a purely natural state, he would have found in this natural knowledge and naturally efficacious love for God his *true happiness*. Of course it would not have been that absolutely perfect and supernatural beatitude, which is the immediate vision of God, but a *true happiness,* nevertheless, one solid and lasting; for in the natural order, at any rate, the order embracing everything our nature demands, this natural love for God, if efficacious, does really direct our life to Him and in a true sense enables us to find our rest in Him. Such in the state of pure nature would have been the destiny of the immortal souls of the just after the probation of this life. The soul naturally desires to live forever, and a natural desire of this kind cannot be ineffective. (Cf. St. Thomas, Ia, q. 75, a. 6, c, end.)

But gratuitously we have received far more than this: we have received grace which is the seed of glory, and with it supernatural faith and a supernatural love for God, who is no longer the author merely of nature but also of grace.

And so, for us Christians, the proof we have been discussing receives strong confirmation in the happiness and peace to be found even here on earth through union with God.

In a realm far beyond any glimpse that philosophical reason might obtain, though not yet the attainment of the perfect beatitude of heaven, true happiness is ours to the extent that we love the sovereign good with a ·sincere, efficacious, generous love, and above all things, more than ourselves or any creature, and to the extent that we direct our whole life daily more and more to Him.

In spite of the occasional overwhelming sorrows of this present life, we shall have found *true happiness* and peace, at least in the summit of the soul, if we love God above all things; for peace is the tranquillity that comes with order, and here we are united to the very principle of all order and of all life.

Our proof thus receives strong confirmation from the profound experiences of the spiritual life, in which are realized the words of our Lord: "Peace I leave with you: My peace I give unto you: not as the world giveth, do I give unto you" (John 14:27). It is not in the accumulation of pleasures, riches, honors, glory, and power, but in union with God, that the Savior has given us peace. So solid and enduring is the peace He has given us that He can and actually does preserve it within us, as He predicted that He would, even in the midst of persecutions: "Blessed are the poor. . . . Blessed are they that hunger and thirst after justice. . . . Blessed are they that suffer persecution for justice' sake, for theirs is the kingdom of heaven" (Matt. 5:10). Already the kingdom of heaven is theirs in the sense that in union with God they possess through charity the beginnings of eternal life, *inchoatio vitae aeternae* (IIa IIae, q. 24, a.3 ad 2um).

Epicurus boasted that his teaching would bring happiness to his disciples even in the red-hot brazen bull of Phalaris in which men were roasted to death. Jesus alone has been able to accomplish such a thing by giving to the martyrs in the very midst of their torments peace and true happiness through union with God.

According to the degree of this union with God, the proof we have been discussing is thereby very much confirmed by reason of the profound spiritual experience; for, through the gift of wisdom, God makes Himself felt within us as the life of our life: "For the Spirit Himself giveth testimony to our spirit that we are the sons of God" (Rom. 8: 16). God makes Himself felt within us as the principle of that filial love for Him which He Himself inspires in us.

CHAPTER V

God, the Ultimate Foundation of Duty

We have been considering the proof for the existence of the sovereign good based on our natural desire for happiness. It may be summed up, we said, in this way: *A natural desire,* one that has its foundation not in the imagination or the vagaries of reason but in our very nature, which we have in common with all men, *cannot possibly be ineffective,* chimerical, deceptive; this means that it cannot be for a good that is either unreal or unattainable.

Now every man has a natural desire for happiness, and true happiness is not to be found in any finite or limited good, for our intellect, with its conception of universal, unlimited good, naturally constrains us to desire it.

There must, then, be *an unlimited good,* pure and simple, without any admixture of non-good or imperfection; without it the universal range of our will would be a psychological absurdity and without any meaning whatever.

If the herbivora find the grass they need and the carnivora the prey necessary for their sustenance, then the natural desire in man cannot be to no purpose. The natural desire for true happiness must be possible of attainment and, since it is to be found only in the knowledge and love of the sovereign good, and this is God, then God must exist.

There is another proof for God's existence, the starting-point of which is not in our desire for happiness but in moral obligation or the direction of our will to moral good. This proof leads up to the *sovereign good,* not considered as simply the supreme desirable but as possessing the right to be loved, as having a claim on our love, and as the foundation of duty.

1) The ordering of our will to moral good

This proof has its starting-point in human conscience. All men, including even those who doubt the existence of God, realize, at least vaguely, that one must *do good and avoid evil.* To recognize this truth it is enough to have a notion of "good" and to distinguish, as common sense does, between (1) sensible or purely delectable goods, (2) good that is useful in view of some end, and (3) honorable or moral good (*bonum honestum*), which is good in itself independently of the enjoyment or utility it may afford. The animal finds its complete satisfaction in delectable good of the senses; by instinct it makes use of sensible good that it finds to be useful, but without perceiving that the *raison d'être* of the useful lies in the end for which it is employed. The swallow picks up a piece of straw with which to make its nest without knowing that the straw is of use in building it. Man alone, through his reason, recognizes that the utility or *raison d'être* of the means lies in the end they subserve.

Again, he alone recognizes and can love the *honorable good;* he alone can understand this moral truth: that one must do good and avoid evil. The imagination of the brute may be trained and continually perfected in its own order, but never will it succeed in grasping this truth.

But, on the other hand, every man, however uncultured

he may be, will grasp this truth as soon as he comes to the age of reason. Everyone who has come to the full use of reason will recognize this threefold distinction in the good, even though he may not always be able to put it into words. It is obvious to anyone that a tasty fruit is a *delectable good* of the sensible order, a physical good having nothing to do with moral good, since the use it is put to may be either morally good or morally bad: the delectable is not therefore in itself moral.

Again, all are aware that a bitter medicine is not a delectable good, but one that is useful in view of some end, as a possible means of recovering their health. In this way money is useful and, from the moral point of view, the use it is put to may be either good or bad. Here is one of the most elementary principles of common sense.

Lastly, everyone who has come to the age of reason sees that transcending the delectable and the useful there is the *honorable good*, the rational or *moral good*, which is good in itself independently of any pleasure or advantage or convenience resulting from it.

In this sense *virtue is a good*, such as patience, courage, justice. That justice is a spiritual good and not a sensible one is obvious to everybody. Though it may bring joy to the person practicing it, it is good regardless of this enjoyment; it is good because it is reasonable or in conformity with right reason. We are fully aware that justice must be practiced for its own sake and not merely for the advantage to be gained, let us say, in avoiding the evil consequences of injustice. Thus, even though it should mean certain death to us, we are bound to do justice and avoid injustice, especially where the injustice is grave.

This is a perfection belonging to man as man, to man as a rational being, and not as an animal.

To know truth, to love it above all things, to act in all things in accordance with right reason, is likewise good in itself apart from the pleasure we may find in it or the advantages to be gained thereby.

Furthermore, this honorable or rational good is presented to us as the necessary end of our activity and hence as of obligation. Everyone is aware that *a rational being must behave in conformity with right reason,* even as reason itself is in conformity with the absolute principles of being or reality: "That which is, is, and cannot at the same time be and not be." The honest man who is beaten unmercifully by some scamp proves to him the superiority of the intelligible world over that of sense when he exclaims: "You may be the stronger, but that does not prove that you are right." Justice is justice.

"Do your duty, come what may," "one must do good and avoid evil." In these or equivalent formulas the idea of duty finds expression among all peoples. Pleasure and self-interest must be subordinated to duty, the delectable and the useful to the moral. Here we have an eternal truth, which has always been true and will ever be so.

What is *the proximate basis of duty* or moral obligation? As St. Thomas (Ia IIae, q. 94, a. 2) says, this basis is the principle of finality, evident to our intellect, according to which every being acts in view of some end and must tend to that end which is proportionate to it. Whence it follows that in rational beings the will must tend to the honorable or rational good, to which it has been ordered. The faculty to will and act rationally is for the rational act as the eye is for seeing, the ear for hearing, the foot for walking, the wings of the bird for flying, the cognitive faculty for knowing. A potency is for its correlative act; if it fails to tend to that act it ceases to have a *raison d'être*. It is not merely better for the faculty to tend to its act, it is its intrinsic primordial law.

Since over and above the sensible, the delectable, and the useful good, the will from its very nature is capable of desiring the honorable or rational good (and this is equivalent to saying that it is essentially ordered to that good), it cannot refuse to desire that good without ceasing to have a *raison d'être*. The will is for the purpose of loving and desiring rational good; this good must therefore be realized by it—by man, that is, who is capable of realizing this good and who exists for such purpose. This is the proximate basis of moral obligation. But is there not also a far nobler and ultimate basis?

The *voice of conscience* is peculiarly insistent at times in commanding or forbidding the performance of certain acts —in forbidding perjury or treason, for instance—or again in rebuking and condemning when a grave offense has been committed. Is not the murderer tormented by his conscience after his crime, even when the deed is perpetrated in complete secrecy? The crime is unknown to men, yet conscience never ceases to upbraid him even though he chooses to doubt God's existence.

Where does this voice of conscience come from? Is it simply the result of a logical process? Does it come simply from our own reason? No, for it makes itself heard in each and every human being; it dominates them all.

Is it the result of human legislation? No, for it is above

human legislation, above the legislation of any one nation, of every nation and of the League of Nations. It is this voice which tells us that an unjust law is not binding in conscience; those who enact unjust laws are themselves rebuked in the secrecy of their hearts by the persistent voice of right reason.

2) The ordering of our will to moral good presupposes a divine intelligent designer

Whence, then, comes this voice of conscience, so insistent at times? We take for granted that a means cannot be ordered to an end except by an intelligent designer, who alone can recognize in the end to be attained the *raison d'être* of the means, and therefore can alone determine the means to the end. We take for granted also, as was seen above (chap. 2), that the order in the physical universe presupposes a divine intelligent designer. Then with much greater reason must such an intellect be presupposed in the ordering of our will to moral good. There is no passive direction without a corresponding active direction, which in this case must be from the very Author of our nature.

Again, if from the eternal speculative truths (such as, that the same thing cannot at the same time be and not be), we pass by a necessary transition to the existence of a supreme Truth, the fountain of all other truths, why should we not ascend from the first principle of the moral law (it is necessary to do good and avoid evil) up to the eternal law?

Here we begin with the practical instead of the speculative principles; the *obligatory character* of the good merely gives a new aspect to the proof, and this characteristic, evident already in the proximate basis of moral obligation, leads us on to seek its ultimate basis.

If honorable good, to which our rational nature is ordered, *must* be desired apart from the satisfaction or advantages we derive from it; if that being which is capable of desiring it *must* do so under pain of ceasing to have a *raison d'être;* if our conscience loudly proclaims this duty and thereafter approves or condemns without our being able to stifle remorse of conscience; if, in a word, the right to be loved and practiced inherent in the good dominates the whole of our moral activity and that of every society, actual or possible, as the principle of contradition dominates all reality, actual or possible: then of necessity there must exist from all eternity some basis on which these absolute rights inherent in the good are founded.

These claims inherent in justice dominate our individual, family, social, and political lives, and dominate the international life of nations, past, present, and to come. These necessary and predominating rights cannot have their *raison d'être* in the contingent, transient realities which they dominate, nor even in those manifold and subordinate goods or duties which are imposed upon us as rational beings. Transcending as they do everything that is not the Good itself, the rights of justice can have none but that Good as their foundation, their ultimate reason.

If, then, *the proximate basis of moral obligation* lies in the essential order of things, or, to be more precise, in the rational good to which our nature and activity are essentially ordered, its *ultimate basis* is to be found in the sovereign good, our objective last end. This moral obligation could only have been established by a law of the same order as the sovereign good—by the divine wisdom, whose eternal law orders and directs all creatures to their end. Agent and end are in corresponding orders. The passive direction on the part of our will to the good presupposes an active direction on the part of Him who created it for the good. In other words, in rational beings the will must tend to the honorable or rational good, since this is the purpose for which it was created by a higher efficient cause, who Himself had in view the realization of this good.

This is why, according to common sense or natural reason, *duty is in the last resort founded on the being, intelligence, and will of God,* who has created us to know, love, and serve Him and thereby obtain eternal bliss.

And so, common sense has respect for duty, while at the same time it regards as legitimate our search after happiness. It rejects utilitarian morality on the one hand, and on the other Kantian morality, which consists in pure duty to the exclusion of all objective good. To common sense this latter is like an arid waste where the sun never shines.

Against this demonstration of God's existence, the objection is sometimes advanced that it is a begging of the question, that it involves a vicious circle. Strictly speaking, there is no moral obligation, so it is said, without a supreme lawgiver, and it is impossible to regard ourselves as subject to a categorical moral obligation unless this supreme lawgiver is first recognized. Hence the proof put forward presupposes what it seeks to prove; at the most it brings out more explicitly what is presumed to be already implicitly admitted.

To this we may reply, and rightly so, that it is sufficient first of all to show the passive direction of our will to moral good and then go on to prove the further truth that, since there can be no passive direction without an active direction, there must exist a first cause who has so given this tendency to the will. Thus we have seen that the order in the world presupposes a supreme intelligent designer, and that the eternal truths governing all contingent reality and every finite intelligence themselves require an eternal foundation.

Moreover, this passive direction of our will to moral good is not the only starting-point from which we may argue. We may also begin with moral obligation as evidenced in its effects, in the remorse felt by the murderer, for instance. Whence comes this terrible voice of remorse of conscience which the criminal never succeeds in silencing in the depths of his soul?

Right reason within us commands us to do good, that rational good to which our rational nature is directed. Nevertheless it does not command as a first and eternal cause; for in each of us reason first of all begins to command, then it slumbers, and is awakened again; it has many imperfections, many limitations. It is not the principle of all order, but is itself ordered. We must therefore ascend higher to that divine wisdom by which everything is directed to the supreme good.

There alone do we find *the ultimate basis of moral obligation or duty*. There is no vicious circle; from the feeling of remorse or from its contrary, peace of mind, we ascend to *conscience*. In the approval or disapproval of conscience lies the explanation of these feelings. We then look for the source of this voice of conscience. The ultimate source is not in our imperfect reason, for reason in its commanding had a beginning. It commands only as secondary cause, presupposing a first cause that is eternal, simple, and perfect—wisdom itself, by which everything is directed to the good.

The sovereign good is now no longer presented simply as the supreme desirable, wherein alone we may find true happiness, if we love it above all things; it is further presented as the sovereign good which must be loved above all things, which demands our love and is the foundation of duty.

From all this it is plain that, if the primary duty toward God the last end of man is denied, then every other duty is deprived of its ultimate foundation. If we deny that we are morally bound to love before all else the good as such and God the sovereign good, what proof have we that we are bound to love that far less compelling good, the general welfare of humanity, which is the main object of the League of Nations? What proof have we that we are bound to love our country and family more than our life; or that we are bound to go on living and avoid suicide, even in the most overwhelming afflictions? If the sovereign good has not an inalienable right to be loved above all things, then a fortiori inferior goods have no such right. If we are not morally bound by a last end, then no end or means whatever is morally binding. If the foundation for moral obligation is not in a supreme lawgiver, then every human law is deprived of its ultimate foundation.

Such is the proof for the existence of God as supreme lawgiver and the sovereign good, who is the foundation of duty. Such is the eminent origin of the imperious voice of conscience, that voice which torments the criminal after his crime and gives to the conscientious who have done their utmost, that peace which comes from duty accomplished.

The moral sanction

In conclusion we shall say a few words about another proof for the existence of God, a proof closely related to the preceding: that based on moral sanction.

The consideration of *heroic acts unrequited* here on earth and of *crimes that go unpunished* shows us the necessity of a sovereign judge, a rewarder and vindicator.

The existence of this sovereign judge and of an eternal sanction may be proved from the insufficiency of all other sanctions. Kant himself chose to attach some importance to this argument, but in itself it is far more convincing than he made it out to be. It may be summed up in this way:

By perseverance in virtue the just man merits happiness since he has persevered in doing good. Now the harmony prevailing between virtue and happiness, in another and better life, is accomplished by God alone. Therefore God and that other life exist.

The more exalted a man's moral life is, the firmer and livelier is his conviction resulting from this proof. In reality it presupposes the preceding proof and is a confirmation of it. If, in fact, the voice of conscience comes from the supreme lawgiver, then He must also be the sovereign judge who *rewards and vindicates*. Because He is intelligent and good, He owes it to Himself to give to every being what is necessary for it to attain the end for which He has destined it, and hence to give to the just that knowledge of truth and that beatitude which they deserve. (Cf. St. Thomas, Ia, q. 21, a. 1.) Furthermore, since the supreme lawgiver must of necessity love the good above all things, He owes it to Himself also to compel respect for its absolute rights and repress their violation (Ia IIae, q. 87, a. 1, 3).

In other words, if there is order in the physical world and if that order demands an intelligent designer, much more must there be *order in the moral world,* which is on an infinitely higher plane.

Herein is the answer to the complaints of the just who are persecuted and unjustly condemned by men. How often in this world do the wicked and indifferent triumph, while upright and high-minded souls, like Joan of Arc, are condemned? Barabbas was even preferred to Jesus; Barabbas was set free and Jesus was crucified. Injustice cannot have the last word, especially when it is so flagrant as this. There is a higher justice; its voice makes itself heard in our conscience and it will one day restore all things to the true order. Then will be clearly made manifest the two aspects of the Sovereign Good: His right to be loved above all things, which is the principle of justice, and His being essentially self-diffusive, which is the principle of mercy.

These moral proofs for the existence of God are of a nature to convince any mind that does not try to stifle the interior voice of conscience. Such a mind will have little difficulty in discovering the deeper source of this voice directing us to the good, because it comes from Him who is the good itself.

CHAPTER VI

On the Nature of God

We have seen how the classical proofs for the existence of God as presented by St. Thomas demonstrate the existence of a first mover of spiritual and corporeal beings, of a first cause of everything that comes into existence, of a necessary being on which all contingent and perishable things depend, of a supreme being, the first truth and sovereign good, and of an intelligent designer, the cause of order in the universe, to which we rightly give the name providence.

Now it is through these five attributes (first mover, first cause, etc.) that we have our conception of God. We have thus proved His existence. We must now go on to state what He is, *what formally constitutes His nature*. We cannot otherwise form a right idea of providence.

The problem

Here on earth, of course, we can have no knowledge of the divine essence as it is really in itself; for this we must have an intuitive vision of it as the blessed see it in heaven. Our knowledge of God here on earth is obtained solely through the reflection of His perfections in *the mirror of created things*. Since these are on a plane far inferior to His, they do not enable us to know Him as He is in Himself. As Plato tells us in his allegory of the cave, where God is concerned we are to some extent like men who have never seen

the sun but simply a reflection of its rays in the things it
illuminates; or like men who have never seen white light
but only the seven colors of the rainbow: violet, indigo, blue,
green, yellow, orange, and red. For such men a right conception of white light would be impossible; they could have
only a negative or relative conception of it as an inaccessible
source of light. It is the same with the divine nature: we
cannot form a proper and positive conception of it through
creatures, for the perfections which in God form an absolute
unity are in creatures multiple and divided.

Here on earth, therefore, it is impossible for us to know
the divine nature as it is in itself. If this were possible, we
should see how all the divine perfections contained in it—
such as infinite being, wisdom, love, justice, mercy—are
really identified, yet without destroying one another. As it
is, we are reduced to spelling out, as it were, and enumerating these divine perfections one after another, always with
the reservation that they are identified in one transcendent
simplicity, in the higher unity of the Deity or Divinity. But
the Deity or the very essence of God—that which makes
God to be God—we do not see, nor shall we ever be able to
do so until we reach heaven. It is as though we were gazing
at the sides of a pyramid the summit of which remains ever
invisible.

But, without knowing the divine nature as it is in itself,
can we not determine, so far as our imperfect mode of knowing permits, what it is that formally constitutes that nature?
In other words, among all the perfections we attribute to
God is there not one that is fundamental, the source as it were
of all the divine attributes and likewise the principle distinguishing God from the world?

Is there not in God some radical perfection having the same function in Him as rationality in man? Man is defined as a rational being; this, distinguishing him from inferior beings, is the principle of his distinctive human characteristics. Because man is rational, he is free, he is morally responsible for his actions, he is social and religious, he has the faculty of speech and intelligent laughter. These characteristics do not exist in the brute beast. We deduce man's characteristics as we deduce the properties of the triangle or the circle.

Is there in God some radical perfection also that allows of our defining Him, according to our imperfect mode of knowledge, in some such way as we define man, or again as we define a circle or a pyramid? In other words, is there not a certain order in the divine perfections, so that from one primary perfection all the rest may be deduced? This is the statement of the problem.

The various solutions

To the question thus stated various solutions have been given. Beginning with the least satisfactory, we shall proceed by degrees to the most profound.

1) Some (Nominalists) have held that in God there is *no fundamental perfection* from which the rest may be logically deduced. According to their view, the divine essence is merely the sum of all the perfections; there can be no question of seeking a logical order among them, since they are simply different names for the same transcendent reality.

This doctrine of Nominalism leads to the conclusion that *God is unknowable,* because His attributes cannot be deduced from one fundamental divine perfection; and, since we can give no reason why He must be wise or just or merciful, we should simply be asserting the fact without knowing why.

2) Others, inspired by Descartes, have held that *what constitutes the divine nature is liberty:* God is pre-eminently a will transcendently free. Descartes claimed that, if God so willed, He could make the circle square, mountains without valleys, or beings that at one and the same time would exist and not exist, or effects without a cause. Ockham in the Middle Ages declared that, had God so willed, He could have commanded us not to love but to hate both ourselves and Him. That is, the principle of contradiction and the distinction between moral good and evil are dependent for their truth on the free will of God. First and foremost God is said to be absolute liberty.

In the opinion of some modern philosophers (Secrétan in Switzerland, for instance), the correct definition of God is *I am what I will,* I am what I would freely be.

In reply to this view, it has been pointed out that liberty cannot be conceived as anterior to intellect. Liberty without intellect is impossible; it would be confounded with mere chance. Liberty is inconceivable without an intellect to direct it; it would be liberty without standard of any kind, without truth, without true goodness. As Leibniz remarked, to say that God, if He had wished, could have commanded us to hate Him, is to deny that He is of necessity the sovereign good; in that case, had He wished, He might well have been the Manichean principle of evil. A man would have be out of his senses to maintain such a position. To claim that God has established the distinction between good and evil by a purely arbitrary decree, to claim that He is absolute liberty without standard of any kind, is, as Leibniz again says, "to dishonor God."

Clearly, then, liberty cannot be conceived without an intellect and wisdom to direct it, and conversely intellect is conceived as anterior to the liberty it directs. The knowledge of true good, indeed, is anterior to the love of that good, which would not be so loved were it not already known.

Intellect, therefore, is prior to and the cause of liberty. Shall we say, then, that *what formally constitutes the divine nature is intellect,* the ever actual thought or eternal knowledge of the true in all its fulness? This, of course, is a divine perfection, but is it the fundamental perfection?

A number of philosophers and theologians thought so. They conceived of God as pre-eminently a pure intellectual flash subsisting eternally. During a storm at night, an immense streak of lightning may sometimes be seen, flashing from one extremity of the sky to the other; this, they would say, is a faint image of God. We also speak of "flashes of genius," as in the case of Newton's discovery of the great laws of nature. These are transitory and very confined flashes, revealing what after all is only a partial truth, like the law of universal gravitation. God, on the other hand, is a pure intellectual flash subsisting eternally, who is infinite truth and sees in one glance all actual and possible worlds, with all their laws. God is, indeed, *eternally subsistent thought itself,* truth itself ever actually known. And why is this? Because intellectual life is the highest form of life, transcending vegetative plant life and sensitive animal life; because, too, intellect is anterior to will and liberty, which it directs by pointing out the good to be desired and loved.

This is all quite true. But is subsistent thought or intellection the absolutely primary perfection in God? However lofty this way of conceiving the divine nature may be, it does not seem to be the highest.[1]

Holy Scripture provides us with a more profound conception of the divine nature. It tells us that God is being itself; He Himself has revealed His name to us as *"He who is."*

God is the eternally subsisting being

In the Book of Exodus (3:14), we are told how God, speaking to Moses from the burning bush, revealed His name. He did not say, "I am absolute liberty, I am what I will"; nor did He say, "I am intellect itself, thought eternally subsistent." He said, *"I am who am,"* that is, the eternally subsistent being

Let us call to mind this passage from Exodus: "Moses said to God: Lo, I shall go to the children of Israel, and say to them: The God of your fathers hath sent me to you. If they should say to me: What is His name? what shall I say to them? God said to Moses: I am who am. He said: Thus shalt thou say to the children of Israel: He who is hath sent me to you." He who is: in Hebrew, Yahweh, from which the word

---

[1] In favor of this view it is said that since sanctifying grace is a participation in the divine nature ordered essentially to the beatific vision, it is a participation in that nature in so far as it is intellectual life. It would seem, then, that the divine nature is fundamentally the supreme intellectual life, eternally subsistent thought, rather than being itself.

To this we reply that *sanctifying grace is a participation in the divine nature* as it is in itself and not simply as our imperfect mode of knowledge conceives it. It is a participation in the Deity, whose formal signification transcends even that of being and intellection. Conceived simply as subsistent being, God contains only implicitly, *actu implicite,* the rest of the divine perfections deducible from it; whereas the Deity as it is in itself and as contemplated by the blessed in heaven contains all the divine attributes explicitly, *actu explicite.* The blessed behold them immediately in the Deity and have no need to deduce them.

Jehovah has been formed. "This is my name forever, and this is my memorial unto all generations" (*ibid.*, 15).

Again, in the last book of the New Testament (Apocalypse, 1:8), we read: "I am Alpha and Omega, the beginning and the end, saith the Lord God, who is and who was and who is to come, the Almighty." (Cf. 1:4.)

Under this title God has frequently revealed Himself to His saints, to St. Catherine of Siena, for instance: "I am He who is, thou art that which is not."

God, then, is not only pure spirit, *He is being itself* subsisting immaterial at the summit of all things and transcending any limits imposed by either space or matter or a finite spiritual essence.

In our imperfect mode of knowledge, must we not say that subsistent being is the formal constituent of the divine nature?

It would not seem a difficult matter to establish the truth of this. In fact, what formally constitutes the divine nature is that which in God we conceive to be the fundamental perfection distinguishing Him from creatures and the source from which His attributes are deduced.

Now, because *God is the self-subsisting being,* the infinite ocean of spiritual being, unlimited, unmaterialized, He is distinguished from every material or spiritual creature. The divine essence alone is existence itself, it alone of necessity exists. No creature is self-existent; none can say: I am being, truth, life, etc. Jesus alone among men said, "I am the truth and the life," which was equivalent to saying, "I am God."

Upon this culminating point, namely, the self-subsisting being, converge the five proofs for the existence of God, as developed by St. Thomas: the first mover, the first cause, the necessary being, the supreme being, the intelligent designer of order in the universe. All these attributes must be predicated of the self-subsisting and immaterial being who is at the summit of all things. Again, from this culminating point are deduced all the divine attributes, as the characteristics of man are deduced from his rationality.

As will be seen more clearly in what follows, the self-subsisting and immaterial being who is at the summit of all things must be absolutely one and simple, must be truth itself ever actually known, the good itself ever actually loved. By reason of His perfect and unique immateriality He must be intelligence itself, thought itself eternally subsistent, wisdom itself; subsistent will and love; hence justice and mercy.

Conversely, we see that justice and mercy presuppose the love of the good; that love presupposes an intellect which enlightens it; that intellect presupposes an intelligent being and at the same time an intelligible being which it contemplates.

It remains true, therefore, that of all the names of God, the primary and most distinctive is *"He who is,"* Yahweh. It is pre-eminently His name, says St. Thomas (Ia, q. 13, a. 11), and that for three reasons:

1) Because it expresses not one form of being or one particular essence, but *being itself;* and God alone is being itself, He alone is self-existent.

2) It is *the most universal name,* embracing being in all its fulness, with all its perfections—the boundless, shoreless, ocean, as it were, of omnipotent, omniscient, spiritual substance.

3) This name, "He who is," signifies not only being, but the *ever-present being,* for whom there is neither past nor future.

Here, then, is what formally constitutes the divine nature according to our imperfect manner of understanding, which consists in deducing from this formal constituent the divine attributes, enumerating them one after another: unity, wisdom, love, justice, mercy and the rest, yet without ever perceiving how they are fused together and identified in the intimate life of God, which is the Deity.

The Deity

In this life we can have no knowledge of the Deity, of the divine nature, such as it really is; for this we should need to have an intuitive vision of it as the blessed have in heaven, without the intervention of any created image. Only in heaven shall we see how wisdom is identical with God's utterly free good pleasure; how, for all its freedom, this good pleasure is by no means a caprice, since it is penetrated through and through by wisdom. Then only shall we see how infinite justice and mercy are identified in the love of the sovereign good, which has the right to be loved above all else and which tends to communicate itself to us for our happiness.

The Deity, as it really is, remains for us a secret, a profound mystery. Indeed, the mystics have called it the Great Darkness, a light-transcending darkness; it is the "light inaccessible" spoken of in Scripture.

Although we cannot have knowledge of the Deity as it really is, we are permitted to participate in it through sanctifying grace, which is in very truth a participation in the divine nature as it really is,[2] preparing us in this present life to see and love God some day as He sees and loves Himself.

[2] See preceding note.

From this we see the value of sanctifying grace, which far surpasses the natural life of the intellect, whether in us or even in the angels. This truth leads St. Thomas to remark that the least degree of sanctifying grace in the soul of a little child just baptized is of more value than all corporeal and spiritual natures taken together: "The good of grace in one is greater than the good of nature in the whole universe" (Ia IIae, q. 113, a. 9 ad 2um).

Pascal expresses this well in one of the finest pages of his *Pensées:* "The least of minds is greater than all material objects, the firmament, the stars, the earth and its kingdoms; for the mind has knowledge of all these things and of itself; whereas things material have no knowledge at all. Bodies and minds, all these taken together and the effects produced by them, do not equal the least act of charity. This latter is of an infinitely higher order. From the sum total of material things there could not possibly issue one little thought, because thought is of another order. From bodies and minds we cannot possibly have an act of true charity, for the latter, too, is of another order, pertaining to the supernatural. The saints have their realm, their glory, their luster, and have no need of temporal or spiritual aggrandizement, which in no way affects them, neither increasing nor decreasing their greatness. The saints are seen by God and the angels, not by bodies or by curious minds. God suffices for them." [3] This sums up the value of the hidden life.

In the present life this holiness reveals most clearly, though in the obscurity of faith, what constitutes the intimate life of God, the Deity. This it does because holiness, which is

---

[3] Pascal, *Pensées* (Havet ed.), art. 18.

the life of grace in its perfection, is a real, living participation in this same intimate life of God, preparing us to behold it some future day. Hence those words of the psalmist (Ps. 67: 36): "God is wonderful in His saints."

PART II

THE PERFECTIONS OF GOD WHICH HIS PROVIDENCE
PRESUPPOSES

CHAPTER VII

THE DIVINE SIMPLICITY

We have seen that the formal constituent of the divine nature according to our imperfect mode of knowledge is subsistent being, for this distinguishes Him from every other being and is the source from which all His attributes may be deduced, as man's characteristics are deduced from the fact that he is a rational being. And now, in order to have a right idea of providence, we must consider those divine perfections which it presupposes. A full consideration of these perfections helps us to a true notion of providence and gradually leads us to a more exact understanding of it.

We distinguish between the attributes relative to God's being (His simplicity, infinity, eternity, incomprehensibility) and those relating to the divine operations (in the intellect, wisdom and providence; in the will, love with its two great virtues, mercy and justice; and finally omnipotence).

All these attributes are absolute perfections, implying no imperfection, and they may be deduced from what we conceive to be the formal constituent of the divine nature.[1]

Our Lord said: "Be ye perfect as your heavenly Father is perfect." Perfect, not merely like the angels, but as our heavenly Father is perfect; because we have received sanctifying

---

[1] It must be noted, however, that the act of creation, being a free act, cannot be deduced from the divine nature; neither can the exercise of mercy and justice with respect to creatures.

grace, which should be constantly increasing in us and which is a participation, not in the angelic nature, but in the divine nature itself. Since, then, every passing day ought to see in our lives a gradually increasing participation in these infinite perfections of God, we should frequently make them the subject of contemplation in our prayer, by slowly meditating, for instance, on the Our Father.

We shall speak first of God's simplicity, which is so marked a feature in the ways of divine providence.

The divine simplicity and its reflections

What is simplicity in general? As unity is the non-division of being, so simplicity is the opposite of composition, complexity, and complication. *The simple is opposed to what is compounded* of different parts, opposed therefore to what is complicated, pretentious, or tainted with affectation. From the moral point of view simplicity or integrity is opposed to duplicity.

We speak of a child's outlook as simple because it goes straight to the point; it has no concealed motives; its inclination is not in several directions at once. When a child says a thing, it is not thinking of something else; when it says "yes," it does not mean "no"; it is not two-faced or deceitful. Our Lord tells us: "If thy eye be single [simple], thy whole body will be lightsome." That is, if our intention is straightforward and simple, then there will be a unity, truth, and transparency in our whole life, instead of its being divided as it is with those who seek to serve two masters, God and wealth. And when we consider the complexity of motive, the insincerity we find in the world and the complications arising from lying and deceit, we cannot help feeling that the moral virtue of simplicity, of candor and uprightness, is the reflection of a divine perfection. As St. Thomas says, "Simplicity makes the intention right by excluding duplicity" (IIa IIae, q. 109, a. 2 ad 4um).

But *what is divine simplicity?* It is the absence of all compounding of different parts, the absence of all division.

1) There cannot be in God a distinction of quantitative parts as in matter. Every material thing has extended parts that are contiguous, whether these parts are similar as in the diamond, or different, like the members and the organs of a living being: the eyes, ears, and the rest.

The simplicity of God, on the contrary, is *the simplicity of pure spirit,* incomparably superior to that of the purest diamond, or to the unity of the most perfect organism. In God we do not find a distinction of two parts as soul and body, the one giving life to the other: the latter would be less perfect; it would not be life itself, but would merely participate in life; it would not be the principle of all order, but would itself be ordered. No imperfection or composition of any kind exists in God. Every compound requires a cause uniting the elements composing it, whereas God is the supreme cause uncaused. His simplicity therefore is absolute.

2) *The simplicity of God far surpasses that of the angels.* Of course an angel is pure spirit, but his essence is not self-existent: it is merely susceptible or capable of existence; it is not existence itself. An angel is a compound of finite essence and limited existence, whereas, as we have seen, God is self-subsisting, purely immaterial being.

An angel can acquire knowledge only by means of an intellectual faculty; he can desire only through another faculty, the will. These two faculties with their successive acts of thought and desire are accidents distinct from the angel's substance; his substance remains always the same while his thoughts succeed one another. In God, on the other hand, there can be no question of composition of substance and accidents, because the divine substance is the fulness of being, the fulness also of truth ever apprehended and of goodness ever loved. In Him no succession of thoughts takes place: there is but *one unchanging, subsistent thought,* embracing all truth. In Him no successive acts of will occur; there is but *one subsistent, unchanging act of will,* which is directed to all that He wills.

Therefore divine simplicity or divine unity, is the absence of all composition and division in being, thought, and volition.

3) *The simplicity of God's intellect* is that of the intuitive glance, excluding all error and ignorance, and directed from above and unchangingly upon all knowable truth.

The simplicity of His will or intention is that of a transcendently pure intention, disposing all things admirably and permitting evil only in view of a greater good.

But the most beautiful feature of God's simplicity is that it unites within itself perfections that are apparently at opposite extremes: absolute immutability and absolute liberty, infinite wisdom and a good pleasure so free as to seem at times to be arbitrariness; or again, infinite justice inexorable toward unrepented sin, and infinite mercy. All these infinite perfections are fused together and identified in God's simplicity, yet without destroying one another. In this especially consists the transcendence and splendor of this divine attribute.

We have a reflection of this exalted simplicity in a child's simplicity of outlook, and to a greater degree in that of the saints, rising above the frequently deceitful entanglements of the world and all sorts of duplicity.

Let us now come down once more to creatures. We find a vast difference between the simplicity of God, with the holiness it reflects, and the seeming simplicity which consists in giving vent to everything that comes into our heart and mind at the risk of contradicting ourselves from one day to the next when impressions have altered and people with whom we live have ceased to please us. This seeming simplicity is sheer fickleness and contradiction, a complication therefore and a more or less conscious lie. *God's simplicity,* on the other hand, *is an unalterable unity,* the simplicity of unchanging supreme wisdom and of the purest and strongest love of the good, remaining ever the same and infinitely surpassing our susceptibility and unstable opinions.

We have a glimpse of this divine simplicity when we consider the soul that has acquired a simple outlook, so that it is now able to judge of all things wisely in the light of God and to desire nothing but for His sake. The complex soul, on the other hand, is one that bases all its judgments on the varying impressions caused by the emotions and that desires things from motives of self-interest with its changing caprices, now clinging to them obstinately, now changing with every mood or with time and circumstances. And whereas the complex soul is agitated by mere trifles, the soul that has acquired simplicity of purpose, by reason of its wisdom and unselfish love, is always at rest. The gift of wisdom brings peace, that tranquillity which comes from order, together with that unity and harmony which characterize the simplified life united with God.

The souls of such men as St. Joseph, St. John, St. Francis, St. Dominic, the Curé of Ars give us some idea of this simplicity of God; but still more the soul of Mary, and especially the holy soul of Jesus, who said: "If thy eye be single, thy whole body shall be lightsome." That is, if your soul is simple in its outlook, it will be in all things enlightened, steadfast, loyal, sincere, and free from all duplicity. "Be ye wise as serpents [so as not to be seduced by the world], and simple as doves," so as to remain always in God's truth. "I confess to Thee, O Father, . . . because Thou hast hid these things from the wise and prudent, and hast revealed them to little ones." "Let your speech be yea, yea: no, no" (Matt. 10: 16; 11: 25; 5: 37).

In the Old Testament we read: "Seek the Lord in simplicity of heart" (Wis. 1: 1); "Better is the poor man that walketh in his simplicity, than a rich man that is perverse in his lips and unwise" (Prov. 19: 1). "Let us all die in our innocency," cried the Machabees amid the injustices that oppressed them (I Mach. 2: 37). "Obey . . . in simplicity of heart," said St. Paul (Col. 3: 22); and he admonishes the Corinthians not to lose "the simplicity. that is in Christ" (II Cor. 11: 3).

This simplicity, says Bossuet, enables an introverted soul to comprehend even the heights of God, the ways of Providence, the unfathomable mysteries which to a complex soul are a scandal, the mysteries of infinite justice and mercy, and the supreme liberty of the divine good pleasure. All these mysteries, in spite of their transcendence and obscurity, are simple for those of simple vision.

The reason is that, in divine matters, the simplest things, such as the Our Father, are also the most profound. On the other hand, in the things of this world, containing both good and evil closely intermingled and thereby exceedingly complex, anybody who is simple is lacking in penetration and will remain naïve, unsuspecting, and shallow. In the things of God simplicity is combined with depth and loftiness; for the sublimest of divine things as also the deepest things of our heart, are simplicity itself.

The perfect image of God's simplicity

The purest and most exalted image that has been given us of the divine simplicity is *the holiness of Jesus,* which embraces, as it were fused together, virtues to all appearances at opposite extremes. Let us call to mind the simplicity He displayed in His relations with His adversaries, with His heavenly Father, and with souls.

To the Pharisees, wishing to put Him to death, He says without fear of contradiction: "Which of you shall convince me of sin?" (John 8: 46.) Their duplicity aroused His holy indignation: "Woe to you scribes and Pharisees, hypocrites; because you shut the kingdom of heaven against men, for you yourselves do not enter in; and those that are going in, you suffer not to enter. . . . Woe to you, blind guides . . . you are like to whited sepulchers, which outwardly appear to men beautiful, but within are full of dead men's bones, and of all filthiness" (Matt. 23: 13, 25, 27).

Referring to His heavenly Father, He says: "My meat is

to do the will of Him that sent me. . . . I do always the
things that please Him. . . . I honor my Father. . . . I seek
not my own glory" (John 4: 34; 8: 29, 49, 50). "My Father,
if it be possible, let this chalice pass from me. Nevertheless
not as I will, but as Thou wilt." "Father, into Thy hands I
commend My spirit." "It is consummated" (Matt. 26: 39;
Luke 23: 46; John 19: 30).

And lastly, with regard to the faithful, He says: "Learn of
Me, because I am meek, and humble of heart; and you shall
find rest to your souls" (Matt. 11: 29). Such is this simplicity
of His that He alone can speak of His own humility without
losing it.

He is the good shepherd of souls, who prefers the company
of the poor and the weak, the afflicted and little children, and
of sinners too, in order to win them back. He is the good
shepherd, who in all simplicity gives His life for His sheep,
praying for His executioners and saying to the good thief:
"This day thou shalt be with Me in paradise" (Luke 23: 43).

But the most astonishing feature of our Lord's simplicity
is that it unites in itself virtues that to all appearances are
at opposite extremes, and each virtue carried to its highest
degree of perfection.

In Him are reconciled in a simple unity that holy severity
of justice He metes out to the hypocritical Pharisees and the
abounding mercy He displays toward all those souls whose
shepherd He is; and the rigor of His justice is always subordinate to the love of the good from which it proceeds.

In Him are reconciled in the greatest simplicity the most
profound humility and the loftiest dignity, magnanimity or
grandeur of soul. He lived for thirty years the hidden life of
a poor artisan, saying that He came not to be ministered

unto but to minister. He fled to the mountain when they would have made Him king, washed the feet of His disciples on Holy Thursday, and for our sake accepted the final humiliations of the passion. On the other hand, during the same passion with lofty dignity He proclaimed the universality of His kingdom. "Pilate said to Him: Art Thou the king of the Jews? . . . What hast Thou done? . . . Jesus answered: Thou sayest that I am a king. For this was I born, and for this came I into the world; that I should give testimony to the truth. Everyone that is of the truth, heareth My voice" (John 18: 33 ff.). With simplicity and noble majesty He answered Caiphas, who adjured Him to declare whether He was the son of God: "Thou hast said it. Nevertheless I say to you, hereafter you shall see the Son of man sitting on the right hand of the power of God, and coming in the clouds of heaven" (Matt. 26: 64).

This profound humility and lofty dignity are found reconciled in Jesus' simplicity. Yet He, the humblest of men, was condemned for an alleged crime of blasphemy and pride.

In Him likewise are reconciled the most perfect gentleness, which constrained Him to pray for His executioners, and the most heroic fortitude in martyrdom, abandoned as He was by His own people and by all but a few of His disciples in the saddest hours of the passion and crucifixion. This simplicity of His had such nobility about it that the centurion, witnessing His death, could not help but glorify God, saying that "indeed this was a just man" (Luke 23: 47).

Great and wondrously sublime is simplicity when it thus reconciles in itself these apparently opposite virtues. It is the highest expression of the beautiful. For *the beautiful is har-*

mony, the splendor arising out of unity and diversity; and the greater the diversity, the more profound is the unity, the more extraordinary is the beauty. It then is rightly called sublime. In very truth it is the image of that divine simplicity which reconciles within itself infinite wisdom and the freest good pleasure, infinite justice, inexorable at times, and infinite mercy, all the energy of love combined with all its tenderness.

For this reason God alone can produce in the soul this surpassing simplicity, which is the image of His own. In us temperament is determined in one particular direction, inclining us either to indulgence or to severity, to a broad and comprehensive view of things, or to practical details, but not both ways at once. If, then, a soul with perfect simplicity practices at one and the same time virtues that are apparently extreme opposites, it is because almighty God is very intimately present in the soul, impressing His likeness upon it.

Bossuet (*discours sur l'histoire universelle,* Part II, chap. 19) expresses this thought beautifully when he says: "Who would not admire the condescension with which Jesus tempers His doctrine? It is milk for babes and, taken as a whole, is bread also for the strong. We see Him abounding in the secrets of God, yet He is not astonished thereby, as other mortals are with whom God holds communion. He speaks of these things as one born to these secrets and to this glory. And what He possesses without measure (John 3:34), He dispenses with moderation so as to adapt it to our infirmities."

Pascal in his *Pensées* gives similar expression to our Lord's simplicity, the purest image of the simplicity of God:

Jesus Christ, without wealth or fortune or display of scientific knowledge, is in an order of holiness all His own. He was neither an inventor nor a monarch; but He was humble, patient, holy, holy to God, free from all sin. To those loving eyes that perceive the wisdom in Him, with what stupendous magnificence He came! . . . Never had man such repute, never did man incur greater ignominy. . . . From whom did the Evangelists learn the qualities of a supremely heroic soul, that they picture it so perfectly in Jesus Christ? Why did they make Him weak in His agony? Did they not know how to picture a death borne with constancy? Yes indeed, for the same St. Luke pictures the death of St. Stephen as more bravely born than that of Jesus Christ. They make Him susceptible of fear before the necessity of dying arose, but full of fortitude thereafter. When therefore they portray Him as being so sorrowful, it is because in that hour His sorrow is self-inflicted (desiring to experience the crushing burden of anguish in order to suffer even that for us); but, when He is afflicted by men, it is then His fortitude is supreme, with that strength which is their salvation.

This simplicity of Jesus, purest image of God's simplicity, is apparent in every detail of His life. Père Grou remarks: "It is impossible to speak of things so exalted, so divine, in a simpler way. The prophets appear to be struck with amazement at the great truths they proclaim. . . . Jesus is self-possessed in all that He says, because He is drawing on His own resources . . . the treasury of His knowledge is within Him and in communicating it He does not exhaust it" (*L'intérieur de Jésus,* chap. 29).

Thus we are able to form some faint idea of the simplicity of God, the simplicity of His being, thought, and love. It is a simplicity uniting in its transcendence such apparently opposite attributes as justice and mercy, uniting without destroying them, but, on the other hand, containing them in their pure state without any imperfection or diminution. It will be granted us to behold this simplicity in eternal life, if gradually each day we draw nigh to it in simplicity of heart, without which there can be no contemplation of God and no true love.

CHAPTER VIII

The Infinity of God

We have seen how the simplicity of God, the simplicity of pure spirit, of being itself, unites within itself, to the exclusion of all real distinction, such apparently opposite perfections as justice and mercy. We have seen, too, how this divine simplicity is reflected in the outlook of a child, in that of the saints. But it is seen especially in the exalted simplicity of our Lord's holy soul, which, like the divine simplicity, unites within itself such seemingly opposite virtues as the most profound humility and the most grandiose magnanimity, the most compassionate gentleness and the most heroic fortitude, a rigorous justice and a most tender mercy.

We must now consider another attribute of the divine Being, His infinity: without it we can have no conception of divine wisdom or providence.

This attribute at first sight appears to be opposed to the preceding; for our intellect, always more or less a slave to the imagination, represents the divine simplicity as a point like the apex of a pyramid. Now a point is indivisible and without extension, and hence is not infinite. How can God be both supremely simple and infinite?

The reason is that the divine simplicity is not that of a point in space; it is a spiritual simplicity, far transcending space and the point. Again, *the infinity of God is an infinity of perfection,* far transcending what might be the material infinity of a world that would have no limits.

Many errors about the divine infinity are the result of confusing the *quantitative infinity* of unlimited extension or of time without beginning, with the *qualitative infinity* of, say, infinite wisdom and infinite love. But the difference between them is enormous; it is the same as the difference between corporeal beings and the infinitely perfect pure Spirit.

Nor must we confuse this *infinity of perfection,* in the highest degree determinate and so complete as to admit of no increase, with the *indetermination of matter,* which is capable of receiving forms of every kind. These are at opposite poles: on the one hand, we have the absolutely imperfect indetermination of matter, and on the other, the supremely perfect infinity of the pure Spirit, who is being itself.

The a priori proof of the divine infinity

How do we prove the divine infinity thus conceived as an infinity of perfection?

A beautiful proof is given us by St. Thomas (Ia, q. 7, a. 1). It is a proof that will appeal to the artist. St. Thomas notes that the artistic ideal, the ideal form as conceived by the artist—the form, for instance, of the statue of Moses in the mind of Michelangelo—possesses a certain infinity of perfection before it is materialized or limited to a particular portion of matter and localized in space. For in the mind of Michelangelo this ideal form of the Moses is independent of any material limitation, and may be produced indefinitely in marble, clay, or bronze. The same applies to any ideal form whatever, even the specific form of things in nature: the specific form of a lily, for instance, or of a rose, a lion, or an eagle.

Before being materialized or limited to a particular portion of matter and localized in space, these specific forms have a certain formal infinity or *infinity of perfection,* which consists in their being independent of all material limitation. Thus the idea of a lily transcends all particular lilies, the idea of an eagle transcends all those eagles whose essence it expresses. It is a principle that *"every form, before being received into matter, possesses a certain infinity of perfection."*

Now, as St. Thomas notes, it is a simple matter to apply this principle to God; for of all formal perfections the most perfect is not that of a lily or an eagle or the ideal man, but that of being or existence, which is the ultimate actuality of all things. Every *perfection* in the universe is something *susceptible of existence,* but none is existence itself; it can receive existence as matter receives the form of a lily or a rose.

If, therefore, God is self-existent, St. Thomas concludes, if He is being, existence itself, *He is also infinite,* not in quantity but *in quality or perfection.* If the ideal lily is independent of every individual material limitation, the self-subsisting being will transcend every limitation whatsoever, not only of space and matter but of essence also. Even the most perfect angel has no more than a finite existence conditioned by the limitations of his spiritual essence; whereas in God existence is not received into an essence susceptible of existence: He is the unreceived and eternally subsistent existence.

God is thus in the highest degree determinate, perfect, complete: He is absolutely incapable of receiving additions. He is at the same time infinite with an unlimited perfection, and incomprehensible, "the infinite ocean of being," says St. John Damascene, but a spiritual ocean, boundless, shoreless, far transcending space and the point and infinitely surpassing a material world supposedly infinite or limitless in quantity.

It is at once the infinity of being, of pure spirit, of wisdom, goodness, love and power; for infinity is a mode of all the attributes.

Such is the a priori proof as given by St. Thomas. It proceeds from the principle that every form, like that of a lily, before being received into matter, possesses a certain infinity of perfection. Now the most formal element, the ultimate actuality in all things is existence. Therefore God, who is being, existence itself, is *infinite with an infinity of perfection* transcending every limitation, whether of space or of matter or even of essence. He thus infinitely surpasses every material thing and every created pure spirit.

The a posteriori proof of the divine infinity

There is another, an a posteriori proof of the divine infinity, which shows that the production of finite things *ex nihilo,* their creation from nothing, presupposes an infinitely active power which can belong only to an infinitely perfect cause. (Cf. St. Thomas, Ia, q. 45, a. 5.)

In fact the only way a finite cause can produce its effect is by transforming an already existing object capable of such transformation. Thus a sculptor, in order to carve his statue, requires a material; so also a teacher gradually forms the intelligence of his pupil, but he did not give him intelligence.

The greater the poverty of the object to be transformed, the greater must be the wealth and fecundity of the transforming active power. The poorer the soil, the more it must be cultivated, good seed sown in it and fertilized. But what if the soil is so poor as to be altogether worthless? It would then require an *active power,* not only exceedingly rich and fruitful, but *infinitely perfect;* and this is *creative power.*

Created agents are transformative, not creative. To produce the entire being of any finite thing whatever, no matter how minute—to produce the total entity of a grain of sand, for instance, to produce it from nothing—an infinite power is required, a power that can belong only to infinitely perfect Being. It follows, therefore, that the first cause of everything that comes into existence must be infinitely perfect.

Not only was it impossible for even the most exalted angel to create the physical universe, but he cannot create so much as a speck of dust; and it will ever be so. To create anything out of nothing—that is, without any pre-existing subject whatever—an infinite power is required.

Against this traditional and revealed teaching, pantheism urges a somewhat trivial objection. *To the infinite,* it says, *nothing can be added;* if therefore the universe is added to the being of God, as a new reality, the being of God is not infinite.

It is easy to answer this. There can be no addition made to the infinite in the same order: that is, no addition can be made to its being, its wisdom, its goodness, its power. But there is no repugnance whatever in something being added in a lower order, as an effect is added to the transcendent cause producing it. To deny this would be to refuse to the infinite Being the power of producing an effect distinct from Himself; He would then no longer be infinite.

But if this is so, the pantheist insists, more being and perfection will exist after the production of created things than before, which is equivalent to saying that the greater comes from the less.

The traditional answer given in theology is, that after creation many beings exist, but there is not more being or more perfection than before. Similarly, when a great teacher like St. Thomas has trained several pupils, there are many that are learned, but there is no more learning than before unless the pupils excel their master in knowledge. This being so, we can with even greater truth say that after creation the world has many beings but not more being, many living beings but not more life, many intellects but not more wisdom. He who is infinite being, infinite life, infinite wisdom, already existed before creation, containing in Himself in an eminent degree the limited perfections of created beings.

Such is the infinity of God, *an infinity of perfection which is the plenitude* not of quantity or extension, but *of being, life, wisdom, holiness, and love.*

We are made for the Infinite

In this mystery of the divine infinity we find the practical and important lesson that we are made for the Infinite; to know infinite truth and to love the infinite good, which is God.

The proof of this truth lies in the fact that the two higher faculties in us, intellect and will, have an infinite range.

Whereas our senses apprehend only a sensible mode of being, whereas the eye apprehends only color and our ear perceives only sound, the intellect grasps the being or reality of things, their existence. It perceives that being, subject to varying degrees of limitation, in the stone, the plant, the brute, and in man, does not of itself involve limitations. And so our intellect, far surpassing sense and imagination, aspires to a knowledge of finite beings and also of the infinite being, so far, at any rate, as such a knowledge is possible for us. Our intellect aspires to a knowledge not merely of the multiple and restricted truths of physics, mathematics, or psychology, but of the supreme and infinite truth, the transcendent source of all other truths. What we tell children in the catechism is this: "Why did God make you? God made me to know Him." And we add: "To love Him, and to serve Him in this world, and to be happy with Him forever in the next."

As our intellect has an unlimited range, and is able to have knowledge of being in all its universality and hence of the supreme Being, so also *our will has an unlimited range.* The will is directed by the intellect, which conceives not merely a particular sensible good that is delectable or useful, such as a fruit or a tool, but it conceives good as such, moral good, virtues such as justice and courage. It even reaches out beyond some special moral good, such as the object of justice or temperance, and apprehends universal good, good of whatever kind, everything in fact that is capable of perfecting us. Lastly, our intellect, far superior to the senses, ascends to a knowledge of the supreme and infinite good, in which every other good has its source; then the will, illumined by the intellect, desires this supreme and infinite good. The will has a range and unlimited capacity, which can be satisfied in God alone, as we explained at some length in Part I, chapter 4, where we spoke of the sovereign good and the natural desire for happiness.

Nevertheless our intellect and will are not destined naturally to know and love God in His intimate life. In that God is the author of nature, they can attain to Him in the natural order only because His perfections are reflected in created things.

In baptism a supernatural life and inclination were given to us, far surpassing our natural faculties of intellect and will. We received sanctifying grace, which is a participation in the divine nature and the intimate life of God; and with grace we received faith, hope, and charity, which give a vaster and more exalted range to our higher faculties.

We now gradually obtain a better grasp of the meaning and import of those words of the catechism: "Why did God make you? God made me to know Him, to love Him, and to serve Him in this world, and to be happy with Him forever in the next."

The purpose of our existence, therefore, is to acquire not a merely natural knowledge and love of the infinite God as the author of nature, but a supernatural knowledge and love, the beginning of that eternal life in which we shall see and love God even as He sees and loves Himself.

We shall then have an intuitive vision of that spiritual infinite, which is God, a light infinitely strong and soft. Its brightness we shall be able to bear because our intellect will be elevated and fortified by the light of glory. We shall have an intuitive vision of that God who is infinite goodness, combining all the strength of justice with all the tenderness of mercy. And this supernatural elevation to the immediate vision and love of infinite truth and goodness will be ours forever; it will be a continuous vision and love that nothing henceforth will interrupt or diminish.

Yet in one sense *the infinite will still surpass us;* because our vision of the divine essence will never be the same as the vision God has of Himself, which is completely comprehensive. In heaven each one of the blessed has this intuitive vision of God, but with a power of penetration in proportion to their merits and the intensity of their charity. Similarly here on earth we all have direct vision of a landscape stretching out before us, but we see it better if our sight is keener. In heaven our vision of the infinite God will be immediate, but proportionate to the intensity of our charity and the light of glory. Great saints like the Apostles will see Him better, and their vision will be more penetrating than ours; but they, too, will be surpassed by St. Joseph, and St. Joseph by the Blessed Virgin; and surpassing her, the holy soul of Christ united to the person of the Word. It is pleasant to think that the Blessed Virgin, whose intellect is naturally inferior to that of the angels, has nevertheless a better vision of the divine essence than even the most exalted of them. Since her charity surpasses theirs, she has received the light of glory in a higher degree, inferior only to that of the human intellect of Jesus.

Such is the spiritual lesson we receive in this mystery of the divine infinity. *We are made for the Infinite:* to know God in His intimate life and to love Him above all things. That is why nothing in this world can really satisfy us and why we are free to respond or not to the attraction offered by finite good. Each time we experience within ourselves the limitations and the poverty of these perishable things, we should give thanks to God; for it gives us the opportunity, amounting sometimes to an urgent necessity, of pondering on the infinite riches, the infinite fulness of truth and goodness that are in Him.

CHAPTER IX

THE IMMENSITY OF GOD

God, we have said, is infinite: not in quantity, as though He were an unlimited material body, but in quality or perfection, the only kind of infinity possible with Him who is purest spirit, who is being itself subsisting in His immateriality at the summit of all things. This infinity is a mode of all His attributes, and thus we speak of His infinite wisdom, His infinite goodness, His infinite power.

And now, if we are to have a right idea of providence and its universal scope including every age and every place, we must consider the divine immensity and eternity in their relation to space and time, which are on an infinitely lower plane.

If we consider the perfect being of God as related to space, we attribute to Him immensity and ubiquity. When we say He is *immense,* we mean that He is *immeasurable and able to be in every place.* In attributing *ubiquity* to Him, we affirm that He is *actually present everywhere.* Before creation God was immense, but He was not actually present in all things, since things as yet did not exist.

It would be a gross error to picture the divine immensity as unlimited space, and it is equally false to conceive the divine eternity as unlimited time, as we shall see later on.

God is pure spirit: there cannot be parts in Him as there are in what is extended; we cannot distinguish in Him the three spatial dimensions, length, breadth, and height or depth. When we apply these terms occasionally to the divine intellect, we do so purely by way of metaphor. In reality, God infinitely transcends space, even unlimited space, as the divine eternity infinitely transcends time, even unlimited time.

It was in attributing this *spatial immensity* to God that Spinoza erred. Were it so, God would no longer be pure spirit but would have a body, and thus one part of Him would be less perfect than another; He would not be perfection itself. Hence the divine immensity is not something material, but spiritual, and in an order infinitely transcending space.

If we would have some idea of the majesty of this divine perfection, three quite distinct *modes of divine presence* must be considered:

1) The general presence of God in all things *by His immensity*.

2) The special presence of God *in the souls of the just*.

3) The unique presence of the Word *in the humanity of our Savior,* and the reflection of this presence in the Church and in the vicar of Christ.

The general presence of God by His immensity

God is everywhere. What meaning are we to give to this phrase which so often occurs in Holy Scripture? First, God is everywhere *by His power,* to which all things are subjected, through which also He sets every being in motion, and directs it to action. Secondly, God is everywhere *by His presence,* in that all things are known to Him. All things are laid bare to His sight, even to the minutest detail, to the most profound secrets of our hearts and the innermost recesses of conscience. Lastly, God is present *by His essence,* in that by His preservative action, which is identical with His very being, He maintains every creature in existence.

Moreover, as in creation God's action is immediate without any creature or instrument intervening, so too *His preservative action,* which is the continuation of His creative act, is exercized immediately in every creature and upon what is most intimate in them, their very being. He is thus present even to those far distant nebulae which our telescopes barely succeed in bringing to view.

Therefore God, though not corporeal, is everywhere, not as a material body is in place, but *by a simple virtual contact of His creative and preservative power,* wherever in fact there are bodies to be maintained in existence. Besides this, in a sphere of being transcending space, He is present to every spirit, whom He maintains in being as He does the rest of creatures.

And so God as pure spirit is in every being, in every soul, of which He is the transcendent center as the apex of the pyramid contains in a transcendent manner all its sides. God is that spiritual force which maintains everything in existence. As the liturgy has it:

Rerum Deus tenax vigor
Immotus in te permanens.
(God powerful sustainer of all things
Thou who dost remain permanently unmoved.)

The special presence of God in the just

There is another presence of God, which is peculiar to the soul in the state of grace whether on earth, in purgatory, or in heaven. God is no longer present simply as conserving cause—as such He is within even inanimate bodies—but *He dwells in the souls of the just* as in a temple, the object of a quasi-experimental knowledge and love.

Our Lord said: "If any man love me, he will keep my word. And my Father will love him: and we will come to him and will make our abode with him" (John 14: 23). What is meant by "We will come"? Who will come? Is it simply created grace? No, in the souls of the just the three divine Persons come to take up their abode: the Father and the Son, and with them the Holy Ghost, whom the Son has promised.

This is what the Apostle St. John understood it to mean when he said: "God is charity: and he that abideth in charity, abideth in God, and God in him" (I John 4: 16).

However great the earthly distance separating souls that are in the state of grace, be it from Rome to Japan, it is the same God who dwells in them all, enlightening, strengthening, and drawing them to Himself.

The same is brought out by St. Paul (I Cor. 3: 16): "Know you not that you are the temple of God and that the Spirit of God dwelleth in you?" "Know you not that your members are the temple of the Holy Ghost, who is in you, whom you have from God: and you are not your own? For you are bought with a great price. Glorify and bear God in your body" (*ibid.*, 6: 19–20), that is, by comporting yourselves in a manner worthy of Him. And St. Paul says to the Romans

(5: 5): "The charity of God is poured forth in our hearts by the Holy Ghost, who is given to us."

This sublime doctrine was a commonplace in the early Church: the martyrs proclaimed it openly before their judges. Thus St. Lucy of Syracuse answers the judge Paschasius: "Words can never be wanting to those who bear within them the Holy Ghost." "Is the Holy Ghost within thee, then?" "Yes, all who lead a chaste and upright life are the temples of the Holy Ghost."

The creeds and councils of the Church, the Council of Trent, for instance, affirm that the Blessed Trinity dwells in the souls of the just as in a temple and from time to time makes its presence felt by a more luminous inspiration, a more profound peace, like that which the disciples experienced as they conversed with our Lord on the way to Emmaus (Luke 24: 42): "Was not our heart burning within us, whilst He spoke in the way, and opened to us the Scripture?" In fine, as St. Paul says to the Romans (8: 16), "the Spirit Himself giveth testimony to our spirit that we are the sons of God."

God makes this special presence of His felt in us by that filial love for Him with which He himself inspires us and which, like the peace it brings us, can come only from Him. (Cf. St. Thomas, *Comment. in Ep. ad Rom.*, 8: 16.)

The unique presence of God in the humanity of Jesus

Surpassing the general presence of God in all things, even His special presence in the souls of the just, is that unique and quite exceptional *presence of the Word in the humanity of Jesus.*

This presence of the Word in the sacred humanity of Jesus

is not, as in the saints, a purely accidental union of knowledge and love. It is *a union that is substantial* in the sense that
the Word assumed and made His own forever the humanity
of Jesus which consisted of His holy soul and His body
virginally conceived. There is thus in Jesus Christ but one
Person, possessing both the divine nature and a human nature
without mutual confusion, in some such way as each one of
us possesses his soul and body unconfused.

Obviously this substantial union of Christ's humanity with
the Word of God immeasurably surpasses both the general
presence of God in all things by immensity and even that
special presence of His in the souls of the just on earth, in
purgatory, or in heaven.

Moreover, in the sacred humanity of Jesus there is a wonderful *participation in the divine immensity,* since by Eucharistic consecration His body is made present throughout
the world *on every altar* where the consecrated host is reserved. His body is present there not as localized in space,
but after the manner of substance. Substance is not of itself
extended; in certain respects it transcends extension and
space; and this helps us to understand how the selfsame
body of Christ remaining present in heaven can, without
being multiplied, become really present throughout the world
in every tabernacle where there are consecrated hosts. We
have here a remote likeness to that presence by which God
Himself is in every material being, maintaining it in existence;
it is a reflection of the divine immensity.

A further reflection of this divine perfection is seen in that
universal sway exerted by the Church simultaneously in every
quarter of the globe. In a certain sense we can say that *the*

Church is everywhere present upon the face of the earth, for the soul of the Church includes all who are in the state of grace. Moreover, the Church, being both one and catholic, exercises the same supernatural influence wherever the Gospel is preached.

In spite of the diversity of nations, races, manners, customs, and institutions, the Church, wheresoever her influence extends, effects a unity of faith and hierarchical obedience; unity of worship, especially in the Mass; one common nourishment in communion; unity of life, since all must find their nourishment in Jesus Christ; unity of Christian dispositions, of hope and charity. Since grace here on earth and glory hereafter are the principle of life for all, they have in the merits of Christ the same resources and a common inheritance in eternal life.

Now the Church thus present among the nations for nearly two thousand years would not be able to exercise this influence of hers without *the supreme pastor* appointed by our lord to be His vicar. The exercise of papal and episcopal jurisdiction preserves intact the doctrines of the Gospel in the bosom of the Church through an infallible teaching office, and safeguards Christian morality and Christian perfection by maintaining the divine law and imposing ecclesiastical laws, and safeguards Christian worship also through the various forms of the liturgy.

Christ Jesus promised to St. Peter and his successors and conferred on them the primacy of jurisdiction over the universal Church (Matt. 16: 16; John 21: 15). He also said to them: "I am with you all days, even to the consummation of the world."

To sum up, then: God, pure spirit, is immense and everywhere present inasmuch as through His creative power He maintains in existence and sets in motion every creature, corporeal and spiritual, and all things are laid bare to His sight, even the most intimate secrets of the heart, secrets that not even the angels can discern by their natural knowledge.

Besides this universal presence in every creature, there is that special presence of God in the souls of the just, who are in the state of grace. He is within them as in a temple, to be known and loved by them, and He makes His presence felt there from time to time in that filial love for Him which He alone can inspire.

In a manner still more distinctive the Word of God is present in the humanity of Christ, with which He is united not merely in an accidental way through knowledge and love, but substantially, forming with it but one Person, one being, yet without confusion of the two natures.

As a wonderful reflection of the divine immensity, our Savior's sacred humanity is really and substantially present throughout the world in every tabernacle where the consecrated host is reserved. Everywhere it is the same body of the Savior, unmultiplied yet really present, after the manner of substance—a remote resemblance to that presence by which God is within all creatures as pure spirit and unmultiplied, maintaining them in existence.

And lastly, there is that other reflection of the divine immensity in the vicar of Christ. As visible head of the Church, through the influence of his teaching and jurisdiction he is present to the entire Church. In a certain sense he reaches out to each one of the faithful in every clime and nation, preserving them all in the unity of faith, obedience, and worship, of hope and charity, and as supreme shepherd leading them on to the eternal pastures.

As in God this space-transcending immensity is united with an eternity that transcends time, so is it with the power of the pastoral office in the Church. It extends to all the faithful in space, and also extends to them all as they succeed one another in time, from the foundation of the Church until the end of the world.

The majesty of the Church is most clearly seen when viewed in the higher light of the divine perfections reflected in her: the divine immensity in her catholicity, the divine eternity in her indefectibility, the divine unity and holiness in her own unity and holiness.

Dominating the various dioceses and religious orders, the majesty of the Church is already a participation in the majesty of Christ and of God Himself. In spite of human shortcomings, which creep in wherever men are to be found, this supernatural beauty of the Church is clearly the beauty of God's own kingdom.

We should rid ourselves of the habit of viewing things horizontally and superficially, as if all had the same value and importance. This is a materialist point of view, a leveling conception that blots out all elevation and depth. We should accustom ourselves rather to look down upon things vertically, so to speak, or in their depth. Above all is God, pure spirit, unchangeable, eternal, immense, conserving and giving life to all things. Then comes the humanity of our Savior, the channel through which every grace is transmitted to us and which is present in all the tabernacles of the world. Lower still is our Lady, the mediatrix and coredemptrix; and after her the saints; then come the supreme pastor of the Church and the bishops. After them the faithful who are in the state of grace and those Christians also who, though not in the state of grace, yet as Catholics, keep the faith as revealed by God. And last of all are those souls who are seeking for the truth and those, too, who are still wandering astray, who yet at certain moments receive from God and our Lord graces of illumination and inspiration.

This way of looking at things as it were perpendicularly or, if you will, in their height and depth rather than superficially, is precisely that contemplation which proceeds from faith illumined by the gifts of understanding and wisdom. It should normally be accompanied by a prayer that is catholic, or universal—a prayer ascending to the eternity and immensity of God through the Sacred Heart of Jesus and the intercession of Mary. Such a prayer begs God to pour out the abundance of His mercy upon the supreme pastor of the Church, upon the bishops and generals of orders, and upon all the faithful, that they may be loyal to the vocation to which they have been called, responding to whatever God demands of them, and so walk in the path of holiness that leads to Him.

CHAPTER X

THE ETERNITY OF GOD

Having discussed the divine immensity in its relation to space, we must now consider God's eternity in relation to time. Without it we can have no conception of Providence, whose decrees are eternal.

Let us examine the wrong notion people sometimes have of this divine eternity, and then we shall better understand the true definition of it, which is likewise a very beautiful one.

What is eternity?

There is a partially erroneous conception of the divine eternity current among those who are content to define it as a duration without beginning and without end, thinking of it vaguely as time without limit either in the past or in the future.

Such a notion of eternity is inadequate: because a time that had no beginning, no first day, would always be, nevertheless, a succession of days and years and centuries, *a succession embracing a past, a present, and a future.* That *is not eternity* at all. We might go back in the past and number the centuries without ever coming to an end, just as in thinking of the time to come we picture to ourselves the future acts of immortal souls as an endless series. Even if time had no beginning, there would still have been a succession of varying moments.

The present instant, which constitutes the reality of time, is an instant fleeting between the past and the future (*"nunc fluens,"* says St. Thomas), an instant fleeting like the waters of a river, or like the apparent movement of the sun by which we count the days and the hours. What, then, is time? As Aristotle says, it is the measure of motion, more especially of the sun's motion, or rather that of the earth around the sun, the rotation of the earth on its axis constituting one day as its revolution around the sun constitutes one year. If the earth and the sun had been created by God from all eternity and the regular motion of the earth around the sun had been without beginning, there would not have been a first day or a first year, but there would always have been a succession of years and centuries. Such a succession would then have been a duration without either beginning or end, but a duration, nevertheless, infinitely inferior to eternity; for there would always have been the distinction between past, present, and future. In other words, multiply the centuries by thousands and thousands, and it will always be time; however long drawn out, it will never be eternity.

If, then, to define the divine eternity as a duration without either beginning or end is inadequate, what is it? The answer of theology is that it is a duration without either beginning or end, but with this very distinctive characteristic, that in it there is *no succession either past or future, but an everlasting present.* It is not a fleeting instant, like the passing of time, but *an immobile instant* which never passes, an unchanging instant. It is "the now that stands, not that flows away," says St. Thomas (Ia, q. 10, a. 2, obj. 1a), like a perpetual morning that had no dawn and will know no evening.

How are we to conceive this unique instant of an unchanging eternity? Whereas time, this succession of days and years, is the measure of the apparent motion of the sun or the real motion of the earth, eternity is the measure or duration of the being, thought, and love of God. Now these are absolutely immutable, without either change or variation or vicissitude. Since God is of necessity the infinite fulness of being, there is nothing for Him to gain or to lose. God can never increase or diminish in perfection; He is perfection itself unchangeable.

This absolute fixity of the divine being necessarily extends to His wisdom and His will; any change or progress in the divine knowledge and love would argue imperfection.

The unchangeableness, however, is not *the unchangeableness* of inertia or death; it is that *of supreme life,* possessing once and for all everything it is possible and right that it should possess, neither having to acquire it nor being able to lose it.

Thus we come to the true definition of eternity: an exceedingly profound and beautiful definition, one full of spiritual instruction for us.

Boethius, in his *Consolations of Philosophy,* formulated what has continued to be the classical definition: *Aeternitas est interminabilis vitae tota simul et perfecta possessio* ("eternity is the simultaneous possession in all its prefection of endless life"). It is the uniformity of changeless life, without either beginning or end, and possessed wholly at once. The principal phrase in the definition is *tota simul* ("wholly at once"). The unique distinction of the divine eternity is not that it is without beginning or end, but that it is without change, so that God possesses His infinite life wholly at once.

Plato says that time is the mobile image of an immobile eternity, so far, at any rate, as it is possible for a passing instant to be the image of an instant that does not pass.

Time, too, with its succession of moments has often been compared to the foot of a lofty mountain the summit of which represents the unique instant of eternity. From the summit of this eternity of His, God sees in a single glance the whole series of generations succeeding one another in time, as a man from the top of a mountain can see in one glance all who pass on their way in the valley below. Thus the unique, unvarying instant of eternity corresponds to each successive moment of time, the moments of our birth and death included. Time is thus, as it were, the small change in the currency of eternity.

What characterizes time is change or motion, which is measured by time. The distinctive characteristic of *eternity* is *that unchangeable instant* in which God possesses His infinite, endless life wholly at once.[1]

Here on earth we have not, when born, the fulness of life. In childhood we have not yet the vigor of youth or the experience that comes with age; and then, when we reach maturity, we no longer possess the freshness of childhood or the readiness of youth. Not only is this true of our life as a whole, but we do not possess one year of it *all at once*. The year has its changing seasons, so that what summer brings, winter denies. The same must be said of the weeks and the

[1] Although our happiness in heaven will have a beginning, it will be rightly called eternal life, for it will have as its measure a participated eternity. The beatific vision, in fact, is an ever-unchanging act, far transcending the continuous time of our earthly life, and that discrete time marking the thought succession of the angel. This is the element of truth in Plato's allegory of the cave.

days. Our life is distributed: hours of prayer are distinct from
hours of work, and these again from hours of rest and recrea-
tion. Just as we do not hear the whole of a melody at once,
so it is with our life: its events happen in succession.

On the other hand, it is said of Mozart that he was eventually able to hear a melody not as something continuous, in
the way other listeners do, but *all at once,* in the law that
gave it birth. In composing the opening bars of a melody, he
foresaw and in some way heard its finale. To hear a melody
all at once is a faint image of that divine eternity in which
God possesses His infinite life of thought and love simultaneously and without any succession. In the life and thought
of God it is impossible for Him to distinguish between a
before and an after, a past and a future, a childhood, youth,
and maturer age.

We have another faint image of the divine eternity in a
great scholar who spends long years in studying successively
all the branches of a particular science, and eventually is
able to view them all in the general principles governing the
science, in the master idea from which the other ideas are
successive developments. Thus Newton must have seen the
various laws of physics as consequences of one supreme law;
and at the end of his life St. Thomas saw somewhat at a
glance the whole of theology as contained in a few general
principles.

Another and closer image of the divine eternity is to
be found in the soul of a saint who has reached a life of
almost continuous union with God; he has now risen beyond
the vicissitudes and flight of time. The saint, too, has his hours
of work as well as of prayer, but even his work is a prayer;
and because in the summit of his soul he remains in almost

continuous union with God, he possesses his life in a manner "all at once"; instead of dividing and dissipating his life, he unifies it.

The eternity of God, then, is the duration of a life that not only had no beginning and will have no end, but that is absolutely unchangeable and consequently wholly present to itself in *an instant that never passes*. In one absolute unfleeting "now" it condenses in a transcendent manner all the varying moments that succeed one another in time.

With men, captivated as they are by sense, an unchangeable eternity has the appearance of death; for their idea of immobility is that of inertia and nothing more; it does not extend to that immobility which comes from a fulness of life so perfect that any progress in it is unthinkable.

It follows that the divine thought, since its measure is eternity, embraces in a single glance all time, every succeeding generation, every age. In a single glance it sees the centuries preparing for the coming of Christ and thereafter reaping the benefits of that coming. In that same unique glance, the divine thought sees where our souls will be in a hundred, two hundred, a thousand years to come, and forever. If only this truth were kept in mind, many objections against providence would vanish. The true notion of providence is, as it were, the resultant of the contemplation of those divine perfections which it presupposes.

As the thought of God is unchangeable, so also is His love. With no shadow of change in itself, it summons souls into existence at the moment it has fixed from all eternity. From all eternity love pronounces a free fiat to be freely realized in time. At the appointed time the soul is created, justified in baptism or by conversion, receives a multitude of graces and in the end, if no resistance is offered, that grace of a happy death by which it is saved. The created effect is new, not so the divine act producing it: *Est novitas effectus absque novitate actionis,* says St. Thomas. The divine action is eternal, but produces its effect in time and when it wills.

On the heights of eternity God remains unchanging; but beneath Him all is change, save only those souls who cleave unalterably to Him and so share in His eternity.

Eternity and the value of time

What is the spiritual lesson for us in this divine perfection of eternity? The great lesson to be learnt is that union with God on earth brings us near to eternity. It also makes clearer to us the full value of the time allotted us for our journey: a bare sixty or eighty years, an exceedingly short span on which depends an eternity, the briefest of prefaces to an endless volume.

The thought of eternity brings home to us especially the high value we should place on *the grace of the present moment.* For the proper performance of our duty at any given instant we require a particular grace, the grace we ask for in the Hail Mary: "Holy Mary, Mother of God, pray for us sinners now and at the hour of our death. Amen." Pray for us sinners now. Here we beg for those special graces, varying with each moment, which enable us to cope with our duties in the course of the day and reveal to us the importance of all those trivial things that bear some relation to eternity. Although, as we utter the word "now," we are often full of distractions, Mary as she listens is all attention. She receives our prayer gladly, and forthwith the grace we need at the moment to persevere in our prayer, in suffering, in whatever we are doing, comes down to us, even as the air we breathe enters our breast. As the present minute is passing, let us remember that the body and its sensibilities, alternating between joy and sadness, are not the only realities; there is also our spiritual soul, with the influence Christ has upon it, and the indwelling of the three Persons of the Blessed Trinity. Whereas the superficial and lightminded have a horizontal view of things, seeing material things and the life of the soul from the same plane of every fleeting time, the saints have unceasingly a perpendicular view of things; they see them from above and penetrate their depths, contemplating God at the summit of them all. The thought of eternity is the standard by which they estimate the value of time, past, present, and to come, and thus their judgments are gradually brought to the true focus.

Following their example, let us abandon to infinite mercy the whole of our life, both past and future. In a very practical way, inspired by faith, let us live the life of the present moment. In this fleeting now, be it dull or joyful or fraught with pain, let us see a faint image of the unique instant of changeless eternity; and because of the actual grace it brings us, let us see in it also a living proof of the fatherly kindness of God.

In this spirit let us go forward in the power of our Lord who in the sacrifice of the mass never ceases to offer Himself for us by an ever-living interior oblation in His heart, an oblation that transcends time as does the vision that hallows His holy soul.

Walking thus, we draw close to that eternity which we are some day to enter. In what will this entry into glory consist? We shall receive eternal life, which will consist in seeing God as He sees Himself. It will be an *intuitive vision,* never interrupted by either slumber or distraction, an unchanging vision of the self-same infinite object, which will be of inexhaustible profundity for us. This vision will be succeeded by a love for God equally changeless, which nothing can ever destroy or diminish. This vision and love will no longer be measured by time, but by a participated eternity. Although they are to have a beginning, they will henceforth be without end, without change of any kind, without before or after; the instant which is to be the measure of our beatific vision will be the unique instant of changeless eternity.

We are given an inkling of what this means, when, in the contemplation of some lofty truth or at prayer, we are so absorbed at times that we no longer take account of the passing hours. If such is our occasional experience, what will it be in the future life, which is not only future but is rightly called eternal, since it will no longer be measured by time but by eternity, which is the measure of the simultaneous being and life of God? Then we, too, shall possess *all our love at once* instead of seeing it languish, wavering between lukewarmness and a passing fervor, *all our knowledge at once* and no longer piecemeal.

Let us end with this thought from St. Augustine: "Unite thy heart to God's eternity and thou, too, shalt be eternal; be thou united to God's eternity and there await with Him the things that pass beneath thee" (*Comm. in Psalm.* 91).

It is only to us that eternity is obscure; in itself it is far more luminous than fleeting time, for it is the unchangeableness of the supremely luminous knowledge and love of God.

CHAPTER XI

THE DIVINE INCOMPREHENSIBILITY

The light and shade in the mysteries of God's life

As we have seen, the attributes of God relative to His being are simplicity, infinity, immensity, and eternity. Before passing on to treat of those which, like wisdom and providence, relate to His operations, it will be well to say something of the divine incomprehensibility, which is so marked a feature of the divine governance in certain of its ways.

Therein will be found an important lesson for our own spiritual life. The point we shall particularly stress is that, although from certain angles God is presented to us in the clearest *light,* in other respects He remains in the deepest *shadow.* As in paintings we have light and shade, so also in the teachings of revelation we find lights and shadows, which are incomparably more beautiful than those we admire in the great masters. And the same lights and shadows in which God is represented to us will be found reproduced to some extent in our own spiritual life; for grace is a participation in the divine nature, or in the intimate life of God.

The high lights in the Divinity

Let us speak first of God's features that are quite clear to us. By the natural exercise of our reason, apart even from faith, we are able here on earth to demonstrate the existence of God, the first mover of spiritual and corporeal beings, the first cause of everything that exists, the necessary being, the sovereign good, and the source of order in the world.

In the mirror of created things we discover a reflection of God's absolute perfections and thus acquire a positive knowledge of whatever is similar or analogically common in God and His works: His reality, His actuality, His goodness, wisdom, and power.

When we wish to point out His distinctive characteristics, we do so by way of negation or by relating Him to the object of our experience. Thus we speak of God as the infinite or non-finite Being, as unchangeable, or again as the supreme good.

These rational convictions, already of themselves firmly established, receive further confirmation from divine revelation accepted through faith. These convictions are adamantine and unassailable. To us it is quite clear that God cannot exist without being infinitely perfect, that He can neither be deceived Himself nor deceive us, that He cannot will what is evil or be in any way the cause of sin. Indeed we are incomparably more certain of the rectitude of God's intentions than we are of even the best of our own. From this angle God stands out before our minds in a light almost dazzlingly clear. Again, it is quite evident to us that on the one hand God is the author of all good, including also the good contained in our meritorious consent, and that on the other hand He never demands the impossible. Nothing can prevail against these supremely evident truths, which have the force of conviction for every right mind that is open to truth. Obviously God cannot exist without being at once supremely just and supremely merciful, supremely wise and at the same time supremely free.

And yet, with all this dazzling clarity, there is in God that which for us is very obscure. What is the cause of this?

The light-transcending darkness in God

The obscurity confronting us in God is owing to the fact that He is far *too luminous* for the feeble sight of our intellect, which is unable to endure His infinite splendor.

To us God is invisible and incomprehensible for the reason that, as Scripture says, "He inhabiteth light inaccessible" (I Tim. 6:16), which has for us the same effect as darkness. To the owl, in the order of sense perception, darkness appears to begin at sunrise, because its feeble sight can perceive only the faint glimmer that comes with the twilight or just before the dawn, and is dazzled by the excessive brilliance of the sun. Where God, the Sun of the spirit world, is concerned, our intellect is in much the same condition. Its intellectuality is of the lowest degree, being inferior to that of the angel; it sees intelligible truths only dimly and in a half-light, as it were, as reflected in a mirror of a lower order, the things of sense.[1]

As St. Thomas notes (Ia, q. 76, a. 5), our intellect requires to be united with the senses so as to be presented with its proper object. This lowest degree of intellectuality attains first of all in cognition its proper object, the being of sensible things, which is the lowest degree of the intelligible; and in that object it acquires a very imperfect knowledge of God's existence, and sees the reflection of His divine perfections.

[1] This is the element of truth in Plato's allegory of the cave.

Whereas, then, many things are invisible through not being sufficiently luminous or not sufficiently illuminating, *God is invisible because for us He is far too luminous.*[2]

That God, who is pure spirit, cannot be seen by bodily eyes, is quite evident, since these perceive only what is sensible. But neither can He be seen by a created intellect when this is left to its purely natural resources. Not even the highest among the angels can directly see God through the purely natural power of their intellect; for them, too, *God is a light overpowering* in its intensity, a naturally inaccessible light. For the angels, the sole natural means of knowing God is in the mirror of spiritual creatures which are their proper object, this mirror being their own essence or that of other angels. They have a natural knowledge of God as the author of their nature, but they cannot have a natural knowledge of Him in His intimate life or see Him face to face.

To see God, the angels, like human souls, must have received the light of glory, that supernatural light to which their nature has no claim whatever, but which is infused in order to fortify their intellects and enable them to endure

---

[2] Scripture more often speaks of that lower darkness in which the soul perishes; but it also speaks of the higher obscurity of faith, corresponding to the "light inaccessible" where God abides. Of the lower darkness it is said: The wicked man "shall not depart out of darkness" (Job 15: 30). The nations before the coming of Christ "sat in darkness and in the shadow of death" (Ps. 106: 10). It was in the midst of this darkness that the Light of salvation descended from on high: "To the righteous a light is risen up in darkness" (Ps. 111: 4); "The people that walked in darkness have seen a great light" (Is. 9: 2; Matt. 4: 16); "For you were heretofore darkness, but now light in the Lord" (Eph. 5: 8); "God is light, and in Him there is no darkness" (I John 1: 5).

But sometimes, relatively to us, God is spoken of as a divine darkness: "Clouds and darkness are round about Him. . . . His lightnings have shone forth in the world" (Ps. 96: 2, 4); "And the glory of the Lord dwelt upon Sinai, covering it with a cloud six days: and the seventh day He called him out of the midst of the cloud" (Ex. 24: 16; cf. Ex. 19: 9; 20: 21).

the brightness of Him who is light itself.[3] God Himself cannot give us a created idea capable of representing His divine essence as it is in itself. Such an idea must always be imperfect, intelligible only by participation, and hence wholly inadequate to represent, as it really is, that eternally subsistent, purely intellectual flash, the essence of God with its infinite truth.

If God wishes to reveal Himself as He really is, this can be only by direct vision with no created idea intervening, unfolding to our gaze the divine essence in all its splendor, and at the same time sustaining and fortifying our intellect, which when left to itself is too feeble to behold it.[4]

It is in this way the blessed in heaven see God. We, too, desire to attain to this same vision, in which our everlasting happiness will consist.[5]

God is therefore invisible to our mental as well as to our bodily sight because of the exceeding intensity of His radiance.

But how is it that in this invisible God there is so much that is *transparently clear* to us and at the same time so much that is *profoundly obscure?* What is the source of this fascinating, mysterious light and shade?

Evidently God cannot exist without being supremely wise, supremely good, and supremely just; He is the author of all good and never commands what is impossible. Then how is it that side by side with this dazzling radiance there is so much obscurity?

It is due to the fact that our knowledge of the divine per-

[3] Cf. St. Thomas, Ia, q. 12, a. 4; q. 56, a. 3.
[4] Cf. St. Thomas, Ia, q. 12, a. 2.
[5] Cf. St. Thomas, Ia, q. 12, a. 1.

fections is obtained solely from their reflection in creatures. Although we can enumerate them one after another, we are unable naturally to perceive how they are united in the intimate life of God, in the eminence of the Deity. This intimate mode of their union is entirely hidden from us; its radiance is too overpowering, it is too exalted to be reflected in any created mirror. As we said above, where the Deity is concerned, we are like men who have never seen white light but only the seven colors of the rainbow in the clear waters of a lake.

Doubtless in the divine rainbow we see its various colors: that God, for example, is *infinitely wise and supremely free.* But we cannot see how infinite wisdom is intimately reconciled with a good pleasure so free as to appear to us at certain times sheer caprice. And yet, however surprising it may seem, this good pleasure is still supremely wise. We accept it in the obscurity of faith, but only in heaven will it be clearly seen.

Again, we are certain that God is *infinitely merciful,* that He is also *infinitely just,* and that He exercises both His mercy and His justice with a sovereign freedom in which wisdom is never wanting. If, says St. Augustine, to the good thief was granted the grace of a happy death, it was through mercy; if it was denied to the other, it was through justice. Here we have a mystery: we cannot see how infinite mercy, infinite justice, and a sovereign liberty are intimately reconciled. For this we must have a direct intuition of the divine essence, of the Deity, in the eminence of which these perfections are reconciled, and that far more profoundly, more perfectly, than the seven colors are contained in white light.

In God truths that relate to each attribute considered apart are quite clear. But so soon as we consider their intimate reconciliation, there descends a darkness that transcends the light.

Once again, we see quite distinctly that in His exceeding goodness and power *God cannot permit evil unless for some greater good,* as He permits persecution for the glory of the martyrs. But for us this greater good is often very obscure, to be seen clearly only in heaven. This truth is eloquently brought out in the Book of Job.[6] There is enough light for our Lord to have said: "He that followeth me walketh not in darkness." [7] Thus, however obscure in itself our cross may be, we are able to bear it, all being made clear to us when we reflect that it is ordained for the good of our souls and the glory of God.

Our life is frequently cast in this mysterious light and shade, which appears in our very existence when this is viewed in its relations with Him who, without fully revealing Himself as yet, is ever drawing us to Him.

Hence arises that ardent desire to see God, that supernatural, efficacious desire proceeding from infused hope and charity. Hence, too, in every man arises a natural and inefficacious desire, a natural velleity, to behold God face to face, if only to solve the enigma how attributes so apparently opposed as infinite justice and infinite mercy are reconciled in Him.[8]

From this it follows that what is obscure and incomprehensible for us in God transcends what is clearly seen. Here,

[6] Cf. *Comment. S. Thomae in Job,* chaps. 4, 6, 8.
[7] John 8: 12.
[8] Cf. St. Thomas, Ia, q. 12, a. 1.

in fact, *the darkness is light-transcending*. What the mystics call the great darkness is the Deity, the intimate life of God, the "light inaccessible" mentioned by St. Paul (I Tim. 6:6).

We now understand what St. Teresa means when she says: "The more obscure the mysteries of God, the greater is my devotion to them." She indeed realized that this obscurity is not that of absurdity or incoherence, but the obscurity of a light that is too intense for our feeble vision.

In this divine light and shade, then, the shadows transcend the light. Faith tells us that this impenetrable obscurity is the sovereign good in its more intimate characteristics, so that it is to this absolutely eminent Goodness, though still a mystery incomprehensible to the intellect, that our charity cleaves; the food of love in this life is mystery, which it adores. Here on earth *love is superior to the intellect*. As St. Thomas says, so long as we have not attained to the beatific vision of the divine essence, our intellect, with its very imperfect conception of God, brings Him down in some sort to our level, imposing upon Him as it were the limitations of our own restricted ideas; whereas love does not bring God down to our level, but uplifts us and unites us to Him (Ia, q. 82, a. 3; IIa IIae, q. 23, a. 5; q. 27, a. 4).

Therefore in this divine light and shade the shadows transcend the light and, for the saints here on earth, this light-transcending darkness exerts such an attraction on the love uniting them to God. "The just man lives by faith" (Rom. 1:17) and finds his support not only in its light but also in the divine darkness which corresponds to all that is most intimate in God. It is upon the incomprehensibility of the divine life that the contemplative is reared; he grasps the full meaning of that phrase of St. Thomas: "Faith is of things unseen" (IIa IIae, q. 1, a. 4, 5).

Finally, even for the blessed in heaven God remains in a certain sense incomprehensible, although they see Him face to face. No creature, no idea intervenes between Him and them in their vision of Him, and yet that vision can never be comprehensive like the vision God alone naturally has of Himself. Why is this?

St. Thomas provides a simple explanation: *To comprehend a thing in the true sense of the word, is to know it as far as it can be known.* A person can know a proposition of geometry without comprehending it, as is the case with anyone who accepts it on the word of the learned; he knows all the elements in the proposition (subject, verb, predicate) but he does not grasp the proof, and hence does not know it as far as it can be known (cf. Ia, q. 12, a. 7). Thus the pupil who knows his master's teaching in all its parts does not penetrate so deeply as his master, for he has only a confused grasp of the radical connection of each part with the fundamental principles. Or again, a shortsighted person will see the whole of a landscape, but not so distinctly as one whose eyesight is good.

So also in heaven each one of the blessed sees the whole of the divine essence, for it is indivisible. But, since it is the infinite truth, infinitely knowable, they cannot penetrate it so deeply as God. The degree of penetration is according to the intensity of the light of glory they have received, and this again is in proportion to their merits and their love for God acquired here on earth. Consequently they cannot take in at a glance, as God does, the countless possible beings His divine essence virtually contains, and which He could create if He chose.

The divine light and shade of which we have just been speaking contain much that will enlighten our own spiritual life. Our Lord thus expresses it: "He that followeth me walketh not in darkness, but shall have the light of life" (John 8:12).

Since the life of grace within us is a participation in the intimate life of God, it, too, will be for us a mysterious light and shade, which we must be careful not to distort or confuse. Grace brings us enlightenment, consolation, and peace, that tranquillity which comes from order. These are the high lights; we are no longer in the "shadow of death." On the other hand, it is on a plane so exalted that it is beyond the reach of reason; we can never have absolute certitude that we are in the state of grace, though we may have sufficient indications of its presence to permit our approaching the holy table.

Moreover, along the path we have to pursue through life are lights and shadows of another sort. The precepts of God and His Church, the orders of superiors, the advice of spiritual directors—these are rays of light. But we find shadows, too, lurking in the depths of conscience. Not always can we easily distinguish true humility from false, dignity from pride, confidence from presumption, fortitude from temerity. Lastly— and it is here especially that the interior drama lies—in this obscurity characteristic of our life there is *the darkness* descending *from above,* the obscurity of grace with its overpowering radiance, and that other *darkness from below,* arising from the lower elements in our disordered nature.

Let us often ask the good God to enlighten us through the gifts of the Holy Spirit, that we may walk aright amid this interior light and shadow. To deny the light because of the shadows and thus substitute the absurd for the mystery, would result in error and discouragement. Let us leave the mystery its rightful place. Let us ask of God the grace to distinguish between the light-transcending darkness from above and that lower darkness which is the darkness of death. And, that we may the more surely obtain this grace, let us often repeat this prayer: "Grant me, O Lord, to know the obstacles that I am more or less conscious of placing in the way of grace and its working in me, and give me the strength to remove them, no matter what it may cost me." In this way we shall discover the true light, and if darkness persists it will be the darkness from on high, that which enables the just man to live; for to our poor intellect it is but an aspect of the light of life and of the sovereign good. This is what is meant by these words: "He that followeth me walketh not in darkness, but shall have the light of life." [9] He who follows me walks neither in the darkness of religious ignorance nor in the darkness of sin and condemnation, but in the light, for "I am the way, the truth, and the life"; therefore "he shall have the light of life," which shall never be extinguished.

[9] Cf. John 8: 12.

CHAPTER XII

The Wisdom of God

Hitherto we have been considering the attributes relative to God's being itself: such as His simplicity, eternity, incomprehensibility. We must now treat of those relating to the divine operations.

God, the self-subsisting Being, is by definition immaterial and therefore intelligent. The two great attributes of His intellect are wisdom and providence.

On the other hand, free will is an absolute perfection resulting from intellect. The act of the divine will is love, and its two great virtues are justice and mercy. As for the external works of God, they have their source in omnipotence.

And so by degrees what may be called the spiritual features of God stand out more clearly. Just as with us, wisdom and prudence are found in the intellect, and in the will are found justice and the other virtues regarding our neighbor, so also in God's intellect are wisdom and providence, and in His will are justice and mercy. These are the divine virtues, as it were, but with this difference, that obviously in God there can be no virtue regarding one who is superior to Him.

First of all we shall speak of the divine wisdom. All that revelation and theology tell us about it, illumines their teaching on providence.

What are we to understand by wisdom?

Before we can attribute wisdom to God, we must know the meaning of the word, or what people usually understand by it. This will help us further to distinguish between two very different kinds of wisdom: the wisdom of the world and the wisdom of God. That they know what wisdom is, is the boastful claim of all, even the skeptic, who would have it consist in universal doubt.

That *wisdom is a comprehensive view embracing all things,* everyone is agreed. But after that, what divergences there are! We may view things from above, believing that they all proceed from a holy love, or at least are permitted by it, and that all things converge upon one supreme good. Or we may view things from below, considering them the result of a material, blind fatality without any ultimate purpose. Another divergence is that there is a wisdom characterized by a false optimism, shutting its eyes to the existence of evil, and there is a pessimistic, depressing wisdom that sees no good in anything.

St. Paul often speaks of *the wisdom of this world,* which, he says, is stupidity or foolishness in the eyes of God (I Cor. 3: 19). Its peculiarity is that it *views all things from below,* estimating the whole of human life by the earthly pleasures it brings, or by the material interests to be safeguarded, or again by the satisfaction our ambition and pride may derive from it.

To adopt this attitude in our estimation of things, is to make of self the center of all things, unwittingly to adore self. Practically it amounts to a denial of God and a looking upon others as, so to speak, non-existent.

If the worldling feels himself incapable of playing such a part, he takes as his standard of judgment the opinion of the world, and sometimes becomes its very slave that he may obtain its favors. In the opinion of the world wisdom in the conduct of life usually consists not in the golden mean between two extreme vices, but in an easy-going mediocrity lying midway between the true good and an excessive crudeness or perversity in evildoing. In the eyes of the world Christian perfection is as much an excess in one direction as downright wickedness is in the other. We must avoid extremes in everything, we are told. And so the mediocre comes to be called good, whereas it is nothing but an unstable, confused state lying between the good and the bad. People forget the meaning of the school marks given to children on their reports: very good, good, fair, mediocre, bad, very bad. The difference between the mediocre and the good is lost sight of, the one is confused with the other; instead of rising higher, a man will remain permanently halfway. Hence the word charity is sometimes applied to a reprehensible toleration of the worst evils. Calling itself tolerance and prudent moderation, this "wisdom of the flesh" is equally indulgent to vice and indifferent to virtue.

It is particularly severe toward anything of a higher standard and thus seems to rebuke it. Sometimes it even hates heroic virtue, which is holiness. We have an instance of this in the age of persecutions, which continued even under Marcus Aurelius. This emperor, though wise according to this world's standards, was never able to perceive the sublimity of Christianity, in spite of the blood of so many martyrs.

As St. Paul says, this self-complacent wisdom is simply "foolishness with God" (I Cor. 3:19). Because of its self-complacency it goes so far as to base all its estimations concerning even the most sublime things, even salvation, upon what is sheer mediocrity and emptiness. It completely overturns the scales of values and well deserves to be called stupidity.

It is clear, therefore, that true wisdom views things from a higher standpoint, considering them as dependent on God their supreme cause and directed to God their last end; whereas stupidity, the opposite of wisdom, is the outlook of the fool, who considers all things from the lowest standpoint, reducing them to the basest possible level, a material, blind fatality or the transitory pleasures of this present life. It was this that made our Lord say: "What doth it profit a man, if he gain the whole world and suffer the loss of his own soul?" And St. Paul says: "If any man among you seem to be wise in this world, let him become a fool, that he may be wise. For the wisdom of this world is foolishness with God. For it is written: I will catch the wise in their own craftiness. And again: The Lord knoweth the thoughts of the wise, that they are vain. Let no man therefore glory in men" (I Cor. 3: 18–21).

In contrast to this let us see what the wisdom of God is, considering it first in itself and then in relation to ourselves.

The divine wisdom in itself

In itself the divine wisdom is *the knowledge God has of Himself and of all things,* in so far as He is their supreme cause and last end: the divine knowledge of all things through their highest causes.

In other words, it is an uncreated *luminous knowledge,* penetrating God's entire being and from these heights extending eternally in all its purity and without contamination of any kind to everything possible as well as to everything that is or has been or will be, however lowly, however evil, and all this *in a single glance* and from the loftiest standpoint conceivable.

Let us pause to consider each of these terms and so obtain a glimpse of the wonders they seek to express.

a) Divine wisdom is *an uncreated luminous knowledge.* The Book of Wisdom tells us: "She is more meautiful than the sun . . . being compared with the light, she is found before it. For after this cometh night, but no evil can overcome wisdom. . . . She is a certain pure emanation of the glory of the almighty God: and therefore no defiled thing cometh into her. For she is the brightness of eternal light" (Wis. 7: 25, 26, 29).

b) This uncreated luminous knowledge *penetrates God's entire being.* To His intelligence there is nothing in Him that is hidden, obscure, mysterious. We, on the other hand, are a mystery to ourselves, by reason of the thousand and one more or less unconscious movements of our sensibility influencing our judgments and our will; by reason, too, of the mysterious graces offered us and often perhaps indirectly rejected. Not even the most introverted souls can boast of a complete knowledge of self. "Neither do I judge my own self," says St. Paul. "For I am not conscious to myself of anything. Yet am I not hereby justified: but He that judgeth me, is the Lord" (I Cor. 4: 3, 4).

God's self-knowledge is absolutely *complete,* extending to all that is knowable in Him. Our knowledge of God is through creatures, as He is reflected in them; the knowledge God has of Himself is *immediate.*

The blessed in heaven see Him face to face, but this does not thereby exhaust the infinite fulness of His being and truth. God's vision of Himself is both immediate and comprehensive. His infinite knowledge exhausts the infinite depths of truth in Him.

What is more, so completely does this luminous thought of His penetrate His wholly immaterial being, that it is absolutely identified with it. There is no slumber here to interrupt the spiritual life, no progress from an imperfect to a more perfect knowledge. He is essentially and from all eternity perfection itself, a pure intellectual flash subsisting eternally, the uncreated spiritual light transcending all things. (Cf. St. Thomas, Ia, q. 14, a. 1–4.)

c) From these heights God's knowledge extends instantaneously, in the unique instant of eternity, to every possible mode of existence, as well as to everything that exists now or has existed or will exist, however lowly, however evil.

In what way does God know *every possible mode of existence,* the innumerable, infinite multitude of beings that might exist? Through the exhaustive knowledge He has of His own omnipotence, which is able to produce them. He is like the artist who delights in contemplating the exquisite works of art he has conceived and might execute, though they will never see the light of day.

And how does God know from His high abode the things that exist now, and all that has been or will be? Whence does He get this knowledge? Does He acquire it as we do from the things themselves as one after another they come into existence? We ourselves thus learn from events as they happen, and our knowledge, imperfect to begin with, becomes more perfect. But can God have anything to learn from facts as they occur? Obviously not; for His knowledge cannot pass from a less to a more perfect state: He is perfection itself. What then, must our answer be?

We must say, St. Thomas remarks (Ia, q. 14, a. 8), that whereas with us knowledge is gauged by the objects on which it depends, *the wisdom of God is the cause of things;* wisdom is their measure, they are not the measure of wisdom. Divine wisdom is the cause of things as the art of the sculptor is the cause of the statue, as Beethoven's art produced his immortal symphonies, as Dante's art produced the *Divine Comedy.*

But the sculptor's work is no more than a lifeless statue; the great musician or the great poet can only weave a harmony of sounds or words to express his thought. God, however, through His wisdom can create beings that are living, conscious, intelligent: human souls and myriads of angels. "God's knowledge in conjunction with His will is the cause of things as the artist's art is the cause of the work of art" (Ia, q. 14, a. 8).

God, in fact, can no more go a begging to created things for His wisdom than Beethoven could learn anything new from his own score: that is quite clear. God can have nothing to learn from events as they occur; on the contrary, it is from the fecundity of His knowledge that He confers existence upon them. The reason is that His knowledge extends not only to all that He is Himself, but also to all that He can do, to all that He actually realizes, whether by His own power exclusively as when He created in the beginning, or with and through our co-operation as when He directs us to the free performance of our everyday actions. In the unique instant of eternity, God already knows all that will come to pass—all the prayers, for instance, that under His direction we shall freely offer Him later on in order to obtain the graces we need. We will return to this point when we come to speak of providence.

Obviously, then, God's knowledge, far from being caused by things as it is with us, is itself their cause; they are the works of the divine art, of God's genius.

But are these created things known to God only in a general, vague way, or distinctly and to the last detail? Revelation tells us that "all the ways of men are open to His eyes" (Prov. 16:2), that the very hairs of our head are all numbered, that even the least of our actions are known to Him.

Why is this? Because in the production of every least thing God concurs, as to whatever reality and goodness are in it. Only one thing God cannot produce, and that is sin; for sin as such is a disorder, and disorder has no being but is simply the absence of what ought to be. Since, then, the divine causality *embraces all things,* down to the least detail, so also must the divine knowledge; for obviously God knows all that He does Himself and all that He concurs in producing. *As for sin, He merely permits it,* tolerates it in view of some greater good. It is through this permission that He has knowledge of it; and He sees it in its final overthrow, which in its own way will once more contribute to the manifestation of the good. We shall see this truth more clearly when we come to speak of God's providence.

Therefore, God's knowledge of whatever reality and goodness there is in the universe is from Himself; the source upon which He draws for that knowledge is Himself.

*The divine wisdom compared with the highest
human wisdom*

With us, the knowledge of spiritual and divine things is obtained from below, in the mirror of sensible things. God, on the other hand, views all things from on high, in Himself and His own eminent causality.

Do what we may, we here on earth see the spiritual and the divine only through their reflection in material things. It is owing to this that we attach immense importance to material happenings, such as the loss of an eye, whereas events of the spiritual world, with consequences that are incalculable, are allowed to pass almost unnoticed, such as an act of charity in the order of goodness, or in the sphere of evil a mortal sin. In other words, we see the spiritual and the divine as in the twilight, in the shadow of the sensible; to use the expression of St. Augustine, ours is an evening vision.

With God it is quite the contrary. In the light of an eternal morning His knowledge is first of all directed to Himself, and in His own very pure essence He sees from above all possible creatures, and those that now exist or have existed or will exist. It is from on high and *in spiritual things* that *He sees the material.* To hear a symphony, He has no need of senses as we have; His knowledge of it is from a higher source, in the musical law that gave it birth, and thus it far surpasses the knowledge of the genius who composed it.

It is not through the body that God views the soul of the just; it is rather through the soul that He views the body as a sort of radiation of the soul. Hence His sight is not dazzled by outward show, by wealth and its trappings; what counts with God is charity. A beggar in rags but with the heart of a saint, is of incomparably greater worth in the sight of God than a Caesar in all the splendor of his human glory. Again, to Him there is an immense difference between a little child before it is baptized and the same child after baptism.

Looked at in the light of this world our Savior's passion appears to us enshrouded in gloom, but how radiant it must be when seen from on high, as the culminating point of history, that point to which everything in the Old Testament led up and from which everything in the New descends!

God does not see created things immediately in themselves, in the dim glimmer of their created illumination, as though descending to their level and made dependent on them; *He sees them in Himself and His own radiant light.* God cannot see created things except from above: any other mode of knowledge would argue imperfection and would cease to be divine contemplation. Whatever reality and goodness there is in creatures is seen by the divine wisdom as a radiation of the glory of "Him who is."

Whereas we can hardly conceive of eternity except by relating it to the particular time period in which we live, God sees the whole succession of time periods in the light of an unchanging eternity. As a man standing on the summit of a mountain takes in at a single glance all who follow one another in the plain below, so also in one eternal instant God sees the entire succession of time periods; our birth simultaneously with our death, our trials with the glory they merit, the sufferings of the just with the endless spiritual profit resulting from them. He sees the effects in their causes, and the means in the ends they subserve.

The lives of the saints are very beautiful even in their external aspect as history records them; but they are incomparably more beautiful in the mind of God, who sees everything in its true inwardness and from above, who sees directly the grace in the souls of the just with their actual degree of charity and the degree they will have reached at the end of their journey. He sees our lives in the light of the divine idea directing them, an idea that will be fully realized only in heaven. Between God's wisdom and ours there is all the difference we observe between a stained-glass window as seen from within the church and as seen from without.

This infinite wisdom of God has been revealed to us in the person of our Lord the incarnate Word, in His life and preaching, His death, resurrection, and ascension. Our Lord has bestowed upon us a participation in this selfsame divine wisdom through living faith illumined by the gifts of the Holy Ghost, the gifts of wisdom and understanding, enabling us to penetrate and experience the sweetness of the mysteries of salvation. Let our practical conclusion be to accustom ourselves by degrees to see all things from God's higher point of view, considering them not as something that may give us pleasure or satisfy our self-love and pride, but in their relation to God the first cause and last end. In the spirit of faith and by the dim light it sheds let us accustom ourselves gradually *to see all things in God*. Let us see in the pleasant events of our life the tokens of God's goodness, and also in the painful and unexpected afflictions a call to a higher life, as being so many graces sent for our purification, and therefore often more to be prized than consolations. St. Peter crucified was nearer to God than on Thabor.

By thus accustoming ourselves to live by faith and the

gift of wisdom we shall become every day better fitted to enter into that knowledge which is to be ours at the end of our journey through life. We shall then see God face to face, and in Him all that emanates from Him, especially those things we have loved on earth with a supernatural love. St. Francis and St. Dominic thus behold in God the destinies of their orders, and a Christian mother on entering heaven sees in Him the spiritual needs of the son she has left on earth and the prayers she must offer for him.

This wisdom corresponds to the beatitude promised to peacemakers. In heaven, of course, it will be the source of unchanging peace as well as perfect joy; here on earth, even when the joy is absent, it brings us peace, that tranquillity which comes from order through union with God.

CHAPTER XIII

The Will and Holy Love of God

Now that we have spoken of God's intellect and wisdom, a right conception of providence requires further that we consider the nature of His holy will and the love He has both for Himself and for us. Providence in God, like prudence in us, presupposes the love of the supreme good, to which it directs all things.

No word is so much profaned as love. There is a carnal wisdom which St. Paul calls stupidity and foolishness, and there is also a baser sort of love which is simply the grossest egoism and which often through jealousy is instantly transformed into a raging hatred. But however low a soul may sink, it can never quite forget that in true love we have a perfection so exalted and so pure that we should look in vain for any trace of imperfection in it.

If we were asked whether God can be sad, we at once see that this cannot be. If we were asked whether He can be angry, we promptly understand that the term can be attributed to Him only by way of metaphor to express His justice. If we were asked whether love is to be found formally in Him, without the least hesitation we say that He loves us in the strict and fullest sense of the term.

Let us see, then, (1) in what way love is in God, in what way He loves Himself, and (2) the nature of His love for us.

We will follow St. Thomas throughout (Ia, q. 19, 20), and while we are speaking of God's love for us we shall see with him what is meant by the will of expression in God and the will of His good pleasure. This distinction is of the first importance for a right understanding of what self-abandonment to Providence must be.

The love of God for Himself

Love as it is in God *cannot consist in a sensible passion or emotion,* however well regulated. There can be no sensibility in God, because He is pure spirit.

But there can be no divine intellect, with its knowledge of the good, unless there is a divine will to will that good. This will cannot be a simple faculty of willing. It would be imperfect, were it not of itself always in act. The first act of the will is love for the good, a love entirely spiritual as is the intellect which directs it. The other acts of the will (desiring, willing, consenting, choosing, utilizing, and even hating) all proceed from love, that is the very awakening of the will in its contact with the good which is its object (Ia, q. 20, a. 1).

In God, then, a wholly spiritual and eternal act of love for the good necessarily exists, and this good loved from all eternity is God Himself, His infinite perfection, which is the fulness of being. *God loves Himself* as much as He is capable of being loved, that is, *infinitely.* This necessary act is not inferior to liberty but transcends it. Indeed this love is identified with the sovereign good, the supreme object of love. From its ardor it is rightly termed a zealous love; it is like an eternally subsisting burning flame, *ignis ardens.* As the Scripture says, "God is a consuming fire" (Deut. 4:24).

We do well to contemplate this burning love for the good which exists from all eternity in God, especially when we consider the amount of injustice and jealousy that is in the world and feel in our hearts how feeble at times is our own love for the good, how lacking in constancy and perseverance.

We read in the Gospel: "Blessed are they that hunger and thirst after justice: for they shall have their fill" (Matt. 5:6). This is that burning love for the good which is mightier than all contradictions, than all weariness and temptations to discouragement we may meet with, a love mighty as death, even mightier than death, as seen in our Lord and the martyrs. Yet this mighty, ardent love for the good, which must eventually dominate everything in our hearts, is but a spark springing from that spiritual furnace in God, *the uncreated love for the sovereign good.*

The characteristics of this love

In the first place, it is *supremely holy,* or rather it is holiness itself; that is to say, it is absolutely pure, and in its purity unchangeable. Absolutely pure, for obviously it cannot in any way be sullied or debased by sin or imperfection, since sin consists in turning one's back on God and His commands, and imperfection is a refusal to follow His counsels.

And in its purity *it is unchangeable.* God can never cease to be the sovereign good. He can never cease to know and hence to love Himself. He necessarily loves Himself, and His love not only cleaves unalterably to the sovereign good, but is identified with it, loving it above all things. (Cf. St. Thomas, Ia, q. 19, a. 3, 7.)

Certain philosophers, such as Kant, have gone so far astray as to see in this love of God preferring Himself to all else, not the absolute holiness it is, but the very height of egoism. They have also maintained that God cannot love Himself above all things, that He could not have created us for His own glory, but for ourselves alone, and that consequently it is not He but our own personal dignity that should hold the supreme place in our love.

On the plea of absolving God of egoism, this novel aberration places egoism before us as the ideal we should aim at. It confounds the two extremes, holiness and egoism, because it neglects to define what egoism is.

Egoism is an inordinate self-love in which self is preferred to God the sovereign good, or to one's family or country. But how can God prefer Himself to the sovereign good, since He is identified with it?

Hence *God in preferring Himself to all things is preferring the sovereign good.* For Him to do otherwise would be an intolerable disorder; He would be like the miser who prefers his gold to his own personal dignity. For God to prefer any creature to Himself would amount to a mortal sin in Him, and that is the final absurdity.

When God creates, therefore, it is not out of egoism at all; on the contrary, it is to manifest His goodness externally. In subordinating everything to Himself He is subordinating us to the sovereign good, and this He does for our greater happiness. Our beatitude is incomparably greater in the possession and love of God through praise than if it were a mere complacency in our own personal dignity. The more we give glory to God, the greater will be our own glory. "Not to us, O Lord, not to us: but to Thy name give glory" (Ps. 113: 1). Our greatest glory, O Lord, is to give glory to Thee.

God's love for Himself has no taint of egoism; rather it

is holiness itself. And not only is it absolutely pure and incapable of sin, but it has as its inevitable sequel *a holy hatred of everything that is evil*. In fact, no true love of the good can exist without a detestation of evil; we cannot love the sovereign good above all things without a sovereign detestation of sin. God cannot have that holy zeal for His own glory, which is the manifestation of His goodness, without an equally ardent detestation of sin. This is quite evident. With Him there can be no bargaining or compromising with evil. This, in the divine light and shade, stands out in clear relief. Nevertheless—and here is the shadow—sin does occur. Where sin is wilfully persisted in, the love of God, which is gentleness itself, becomes a thing of terror. "Love is as strong as death, jealousy as hard as hell" (Cant. 8:6). God detests sin with a burning hatred, which is simply the obverse of His ardent love for the good.

God's love for Himself is at once an alluring holiness and a thing of dread, gentle yet terrible, like the house of God which Jacob speaks of (Gen. 28:17).

This holiness implies all perfections, even those so apparently opposed as infinite justice and infinite mercy, the two great virtues of divine love.

In this holy love of God for Himself is contained a twofold lesson. In the first place, since God is infinitely better than we are, *we must love Him more than ourselves,* at least in preference to ourselves with a love based on a right estimation of values, with a love, too, that is efficacious and orients our whole life to Him. Secondly, as God loves Himself with a holy love, so ought we *to love with a holy love our own soul and its destiny,* for it has been created to give glory to God eternally. Let us love ourselves with this holy

love, in God and for His sake; this is the way to overcome
that inordinate love of self in which egoism consists. With
the egoist, self-love is in one sense excessive, since he devotes
too much love to the lower element in him; but in another
sense it falls short of what it should be: he does not love
sufficiently the spiritual element in his soul, that element
which was created to hymn the glories of God. (Cf.
St. Thomas, Ia IIae, q. 29, a. 4; IIa IIae, q. 25, a. 7.)

God's love for us

Such being the love God has for Himself, how can it be
directed to anything else besides? Some unbelievers, as also
the deists, hold that God cannot possibly love us in the true
sense of the term: the use of the word "love" in this connection is purely metaphorical. To love some other being,
they say, is to be attracted by it. But God, the plenitude of all
good, can find nothing in us to attract Him; He cannot be
passive to an attraction exerted by so paltry a good as we
are.

The answer to this deist objection is that in the love God
has for us there is no passivity whatever; it is essentially active, creative, life-giving: it is sheer generosity and is supremely free. It is true love in the strictest and highest sense
of the word.

No passivity is possible in the love God has for us. Obviously He cannot be attracted by a created good, or be passive
under the attraction of a good so paltry, or be captivated by
it. He loves us, not because He found us worthy of love; on
the contrary, *in His sight we are made worthy of His love
because He has first loved us.* "What hast thou that thou
hast not received?" says St. Paul (I Cor. 4: 7); and St. Thomas

says: "The love of God is the cause infusing and creating goodness in things" (Ia, q. 20, a. 2).

Any good in us, whether natural or supernatural, can come only from God, the source of all good, can come only from His creative, life-giving love. This love of His does not presuppose anything worthy of love in us, but is the very source of that worthiness, creating, conserving, increasing it in us, yet without violence to our liberty.

For what reason, then, has God loved us with this creative love? Why has He given us existence, life, intellect, and will? Out of sheer generosity. Is it not characteristic of goodness to be diffusive of itself and to give itself in generous abundance? Since goodness tends naturally to communicate itself, it is essentially diffusive of itself. In the physical order the sun gives out light and genial heat; plants and animals, upon reaching maturity, tend to reproduce themselves. In the moral and spiritual order a person who, like the saints, has a passion for goodness will know no rest until he has aroused in others the same aspirations, the same love. Since God is the sovereign good and the fulness of all being, the eternal love of the good having all the zeal and ardor of love, it is most fitting that He should give of the riches that are in Him, even as a singer delights in re-echoing abroad the rich melodies of his song. It is in the highest degree fitting, therefore, that God should love us with this creative love by giving us existence and life.

But does it follow that creation is not a free act; that, unless He created, God would be neither good nor wise? By no means. Scripture tells us that "God worketh all things according to the counsel of His will" (Ephes. 1: 11), and the Church proclaims the absolute liberty of creative love. It is indeed highly appropriate that God should create, but also that He should be altogether free in creating, so that there would have been nothing derogatory to Him in not creating: in His own intimate life God would have none the less been infinitely good and infinitely wise. As Bossuet says, God is no greater for having created the universe. The fact of His conferring existence on us cannot bring the smallest increase to His infinite perfection. Creation is an absolutely free act of love. In this sense even the natural gifts we have received are gratuitous.

But in God there is a still greater and freer act of love, by which He has bestowed on us the even more gratuitous gift of grace, that participation in His intimate life, a gift to which our nature has no claim whatever. By this life-giving love He has made us worthy to be loved in His sight, and that not merely as creatures but as His children, thus fitting us to behold Him and love Him for eternity.

We are loved by God far more than we think. To realize the extent of His love for us, we should have to know fully the value of grace when it has reached its final development in the glory of heaven; we would have to see God, if only for an instant.

In the incarnation, the redemption, and the Eucharist, God's love for us reaches its consummation. To realize how intense is this love, we should have to appreciate to the full the infinite value of the redemptive part of the incarnation and the merits our Lord gained for us, and hence the value of all the spiritual graces that flow from them. In giving birth to Mary, St. Anne was far more loved by God than she knew, for she could not have foreseen that the child God had given her would be the mother of the Savior and of all mankind. So, too, is it with us, though with due reserves: God loves us far more than we think, especially in times of trial when He appears to desert us; for it is then He bestows upon us His most precious, most profound, most life-giving graces. At such times as these, let us say with St. Teresa: "Lord, Thou knowest all things, canst do all things, and Thou dost love me."

Such in essence is the love God has for us, a creative and life-giving love; supremely generous and supremely free.

The characteristics of this love

They are principally four: It is universal; yet it has its free preferences; and these are wholly actuated by wisdom; and it is invincible.

It is universal, extending to the very least of creatures. God loves them as a farm owner loves his fields, his house, and the animals that serve his needs. But first and foremost this love is directed to the souls of human beings: to the soul of a sinner that it may be converted, to the soul of a just man that it may persevere, to the soul tried by temptation that it may not faint, and to the soul in its last hour on earth before it comes before God's judgment seat (Ia, q. 20, a. 2, 3).

Nevertheless, for all its universality, this love has *its free preferences.* If to every soul it gives the graces sufficient and necessary for salvation, upon some—St. Joseph, for instance, St. Peter, St. John, St. Paul, the founders of religious orders— it confers graces of predilection. And every one of these saints will confess with St. Paul (I Cor. 4:7), "What hast thou that thou hast not received?" and again, "It is God who worketh in us both to will and to accomplish, according to

His good will" (Phil. 2: 13). As the singer imparts at will a greater resonance to certain notes, so also God in the bestowal of His graces shows His predilection for some over others. The divine seed that God casts into souls depends for its degree of beauty entirely upon His good pleasure.

Yet this supreme liberty in His preferences preserves always that admirable *order which wisdom and charity demand.* "It is always the best that God prefers," says St. Thomas, "for, since He is the source of all goodness, one thing would not be better than another, did He not love it with a greater love" (Ia, q. 20, a. 3).

God prefers spiritual to corporeal beings, the latter being created for the former. The Mother of the incarnate Word is preferred before every other created being; and God's only Son is preferred before His Virgin Mother. Christ was delivered up on our behalf, not because He was loved less by God than we are, but that by saving us He might emerge gloriously triumphant over the devil, sin, and death (Ia, q. 20, a. 4 ad 1um).

In the love of God everything is subordinated to the *manifestation of His goodness.* This is the constant refrain of the psalm: "Praise the Lord for He is good; for His mercy endureth forever" (Ps. 135).

One last perfection of divine love: in its strength *it is invincible,* in the sense that without its divine permission nothing can resist it and that by its power everything is made to conspire to the eventual fulfilment of the good. In this sense the love of God is mightier than death: mightier than physical death, since it raised up Christ Jesus and will raise us up at the last day; mightier than spiritual death, for it is able to convert the most hardened sinner, raising to life again the soul that is dead, and that not once, but many times, in the course of its earthly existence.

The will of expression and the will of good pleasure in God

That our will should be made to conform to the divine will and its holy love is of course obvious; for, as St. Thomas says,[1] any goodness in our voluntary acts and in the will itself depends on the end to which they are directed. Now the ultimate end of the human will is the sovereign good, which is also the primary object of the divine will, that object in view of which all other things are willed by it.

Here, however, we must distinguish with the whole of tradition between the divine will of good pleasure and the divine will of expression.[2] By *the divine will of expression* we mean all those external signs that reveal God's will—commands, prohibitions, the spirit underlying the counsels, and everything that happens by His will or permission. The divine will thus expressed, especially in commands, comes within the domain of obedience, and, as St. Thomas remarks,[3] is what we refer to when we say in the Our Father, "Thy will be done."

The divine will of good pleasure is the interior act of God's will, which often is not yet revealed or expressed externally. Upon it depends our still uncertain future—future events, future joys and trials, whether of long or short duration, the hour and circumstances of our death, and so on. As St. Fran-

[1] Cf. St. Thomas, IaIIae, q. 19, a.9.
[2] Cf. St. Thomas, Ia, q. 19, a. 11, 12.
[3] Cf. St. Thomas, Ia, q. 19, a. 11.

cis of Sales remarks [4] and Bossuet after him,[5] whereas the expressed will of God is the domain of obedience, the will of His good pleasure is the domain of trusting surrender. As we will explain at some length later on, in making our will conform daily to the divine will as expressed, we must for the rest abandon ourselves in all confidence to the divine will of good pleasure, for we are certain beforehand that it wills nothing, permits nothing, unless for the spiritual and eternal welfare of those who love God and persevere in that love.

Such is God's holy will and His love for us. It is this love that has been revealed to us in our Lord, whose heart is a glowing furnace of charity.

Christ's love for us, like that of His heavenly Father, is absolutely holy and inspired by sheer generosity: He has not been drawn to us, but we to Him: "You have not chosen me," He says, "but I have chosen you" (John 15:16). Again, the love of Jesus for His Father and for us has ever been invincible: it constrained Him to submit to death, and by His death he raises up souls to a new life, once again directing upon them the stream of the divine mercies.

As a practical conclusion, we must allow ourselves to be loved by this exceedingly holy, purifying, life-giving love, and submit to its purifications, however painful they may be at times. And it should be met with *a generous response,* according to these words of St. John: "Let us love God: because He hath first loved us" (I John 4:10). We must love the Lord for His own sake, with a purity of intention rising above the promptings of vainglory and pride and that self-seeking which is induced by jealousy and the desire for the esteem of men.

[4] *Treatise on the Love of God,* Bk. VIII, chap. 3; Bk. IX, chap. 6.
[5] *Etats d'oraison,* Bk. VIII, 9.

The beginning in us of a pure love for God will then be some participation in that love which God has for Himself, a spark from that divine furnace of His own self-love. And as our love grows purer daily, it will increase in holiness, generosity, and strength. Indeed it will make us invincible, according to the phrase of St. Paul (Rom. 8: 1), "If God be with us, who is against us?" And finally, our love thus gradually purified will enable us to triumph over death itself and will open the gates of paradise to us. When we enter into glory, we shall be established forever in a supernatural love for God that can nevermore be lost or lessened.

PART III

PROVIDENCE ACCORDING TO REVELATION

CHAPTER XIV

The Notion of Providence

Having spoken of those divine perfections which the notion of providence presupposes, we must go on to consider in what this providence consists. What revelation has told us about God's wisdom and His love will give us a clearer insight into its teaching concerning the divine governance. This teaching far surpasses that of the philosophers, many of whom maintain that providence does not extend beyond the general laws governing the universe; that it does not reach down to individuals and the details of their existence, to future free actions and the secrets of the heart. On the other hand, certain heretics have held that since providence extends infallibly to the least of our actions, there can be no such thing as liberty. The revealed teaching is the golden mean lying between these two extreme positions and transcending them.

Providence, as we shall see, is a sort of extension of God's wisdom, which "reacheth from end to end mightily and ordereth all things sweetly" (Wis. 8: 1; 14: 3). "Since," says St. Thomas, "God is the cause of all things by His intellect (in conjunction with His will), it is necessary that the type of the order of things toward their end should pre-exist in the divine mind; and the type of things ordered toward an end is, properly speaking, providence" (Ia, q. 22,

a. 1).[1] As for the divine governance, though the expression is generally used as synonymous with providence, it is, strictly speaking, the execution of the providential plan (*ibid.,* ad 2um).

St. Thomas *(ibid.)* also points out that providence in God corresponds to the virtue of prudence in us, which regulates the means with a view to the attainment of some end, which exercises foresight in anticipation of the future. We have, besides a purely personal prudence, that higher prudence which a father must exercise to provide for his family's needs, and higher still, the prudence demanded in the head of the state that should be found in our lawmakers and other government officials for the promotion of the common interests of the nation. Likewise in God there is a providence *directing all things to the good of the universe,* the manifestation of the divine goodness in every order, from the inanimate creation even to the angels and saints in heaven.

And so by a comparison with the virtue of prudence is formed the analogical notion of providence, a notion accessible to commonsense reason and abundantly confirmed by revelation. A prudent person will first desire the end and then, having decided on the means to be employed, will begin using them; thus the end, which held first place in his desire, is the last in actual attainment. So we look upon God as intending from all eternity first the end and purpose of the universe and then the means necessary for the realization or attainment of that end. This commonsense view is expressed by the philosophers when they say that the end is first in the order of intention but last in order of execution.

[1] See Part I, chap. 2: "On the order in the world."

This point is of paramount importance when we are considering the end and purpose of the universe of material and spiritual beings.

From this general notion of providence we deduce its characteristics. We will briefly indicate them here before looking for a more vivid and detailed account of them in Scripture.

1) *The absolute universality of providence* is deduced from the absolute universality of divine causality, which in this case is the causality of an intellectual agent. "The causality of God," says St. Thomas, "extends to all beings, not only as to the constituent principles of species, but also as to the individualizing principles (for these also belong to the realm of being); it extends not only to things incorruptible but also to those corruptible. Hence all things that exist in whatsoever manner are necessarily directed by God toward some end" (Ia, q. 22, a. 2). This is demanded by the principle of finality, which states that every agent acts for some end and the supreme agent for the supreme end known to Him, to which He subordinates all else. That end, as we saw when speaking of the love of God, is the manifestation of His goodness, His infinite perfection, and His various attributes.

As we shall see, it is constantly asserted in the Old and New Testaments that the plan of providence has been fixed immediately by God Himself down to the last detail. His practical knowledge would be imperfect, were it not as far-reaching as His causality, and without that causality nothing comes into existence. Obviously, therefore, as was stated above, any reality or goodness in creatures and their actions is caused by God. This means that with the exception of evil (that privation and disorder in which sin consists), all things have God as their first if not exclusive cause.[2] As for physical evil and suffering, God wills them only in an accidental way, in view of a higher good.[3] From the absolute universality of providence we deduce a second characteristic.

2) This universal and immediate sway exerted by providence, does not destroy, but *safeguards the freedom of our actions*. Not only does it safeguard liberty, but actuates it,[4] for the precise reason that providence extends even to the free mode of our actions, which it produces in us with our co-operation; for this free mode in our choice, this indifference dominating our desire, is still within the realm of being, and nothing exists unless it be from God.[5] The slightest idiosyncrasy of temperament and character, the consequences of heredity, the influence exerted on our actions by the emotions —all are known to providence; it penetrates into the innermost recesses of conscience, and has at its disposal every sort of grace to enlighten, attract, and strengthen us. There is

[2] Cf. St. Thomas, Ia, q.79, a.1, 2.

[3] Physical evils, sickness, for instance, are not willed by God directly, but only in an accidental way, insomuch as He wills a higher good of which physical evil is the necessary condition. Thus the lion depends for its existence on the killing of the gazelle, patience in sickness presupposes pain, the heroism of the saints presupposes the sufferings they endure. (Cf. St. Thomas, Ia, q. 19, a. 9; q. 22, a. 2 ad 2um.)

[4] Cf. St. Thomas, Ia, q.83, a.1 ad 3um: "God, by moving voluntary causes, does not deprive their actions of being voluntary, but rather is He the cause of this very thing in them." Cf. also, Ia, q.103, a.5–8; q.105, a.4, 5; q.106, a.2; IaIIae, q.10, a.4 ad 1um et ad 3um; q.109, a.1, etc.

[5] The free mode in our choice consists in the indifference that dominates our will in its actual process of tending to a particular object presented as good under one aspect and not good under another, and consequently as unable to exert an invincible attraction upon it (IaIIae, q.10, a.2). This free mode in our choice is still within the sphere of being, of reality, and as such comes under the adequate object of the divine omnipotence. On the contrary, this cannot be so with the disorder of sin. God, in His causation infallible, can no more be the cause of sin than the eye can perceive sound (IaIIae, q.79, a.1, 2).

thus a gentleness in its control that yields nothing to strength. *Suaviter et fortiter* it produces and preserves the divine seed in the heart and watches over its development (Ia, q. 22, a. 4).

3) Although providence, as the divine ordinance, extends immediately to all reality and goodness, to the last and least fiber of every being, nevertheless in the execution of the plan of providence, *God governs the lower creation through the higher,* to which He thus communicates the dignity of causality (Ia, q. 22, a. 3).

These various characteristics of providence we will now consider as they are presented to us in the Old and New Testaments. No better way can be found to make our knowledge of them not merely abstract and theoretical, but living and spiritually fruitful.

CHAPTER XV

THE CHARACTERISTICS OF PROVIDENCE ACCORDING TO THE OLD TESTAMENT

In many passages of the Old Testament (e. g., Wis. 6: 8; 8: 1; 11: 21; 12: 13; 17: 2), the doctrine about providence is expressed in terms that are formal and explicit, and implicitly it is indicated in a multitude of other texts. Indeed the Book of Job is devoted entirely to the consideration of providence in relation to the trials the just endure; and wherever we find mention of prayer, we have an equivalent affirmation of providence, for prayer presupposes it.

The Old Testament teaching on this subject may be summed up in these two fundamental points:

1) A universal and infallible providence directs all things to a good purpose.

2) For us providence is an evident fact, sometimes even a startling fact, though in certain of its ways it remains absolutely unfathomable.

We have chosen an abundant array of Scriptural texts, and grouped them in such a way that they explain one another. The words of the texts are more beautiful than any commentary can make them.

A universal and infallible providence directs all things to a good purpose

1) *The universality of providence,* reaching down to the minutest things, is clearly taught in the Old Testament. The

Book of Wisdom declares it repeatedly: "God made the little and the great, and He hath equally care of all" (6:8); "Wisdom reacheth from end to end mightily and ordereth all things sweetly" (8:1); "Thou hast ordered all things in number, measure, and weight" (11:21); "There is no other God but Thou, who hast care of all, that Thou shouldst show that Thou dost not give judgment unjustly" (12:13). The author then gives this striking example:

Again, another, designing to sail, and beginning to make his voyage through the raging waves. . . . The wood that carrieth him the desire of gain devised, and the workman built it by his skill. But Thy providence, O Father, governeth it: for Thou hast made a way even in the sea, and a most sure path even among the waves, showing that Thou art able to save out of all things. . . . Therefore men also trust their lives even to a little wood, and passing over the sea by ship are saved (14:1–5).

This simple description of the confidence shown by those who sail the seas on a "little wood" proclaims more clearly than all the writings of Plato and Aristotle the existence of a providence extending to the minutest things. We find the same explicit declarations in certain beautiful prayers of the Old Testament: for instance, in Judith's prayer before she set out for the camp of Holofernes:

Assist, I beseech Thee, O Lord God, me a widow. For Thou hast done the things of old, and hast devised one thing after another: and what Thou hast designed hath been done. For all Thy ways are prepared, and in Thy providence Thou hast placed Thy judgments. Look upon the camp of the Assyrians now, as Thou wast pleased to look upon the camp of the Egyptians . . . and the waters overwhelmed them. So may it be with these also, O Lord, who trust in their multitude, and in their chariots, and in their pikes, and in their shields, and in their arrows, and glory in their spears: and know not that Thou art our God, who destroyest wars from the beginning. And the Lord is Thy name. . . . The prayer of the humble and the meek have always pleased Thee. O God of the heavens, Creator of the waters, and Lord of the whole creation, hear me a poor wretch, making supplication to Thee, and presuming of Thy mercy (Judith 9: 3–17).

Here, besides the existence of an all-embracing providence and the rectitude of its ways, there is also brought out the freedom of the divine election regarding the nation from which the Savior was to be born.

But what is the manner of this divine ordinance?

2) *The infallibility of providence* touching everything that happens, including even our present and future free actions, is stressed in the Old Testament no less clearly than its universal extent. In this connection we must cite especially the prayer of Mardochai (Esther 13: 9–17), in which he implores God's help against Aman and the enemies of the chosen people:

O Lord, Lord almighty King, for all things are in Thy power, and there is none that can resist Thy will, if Thou determine to save Israel. Thou hast made heaven and earth, and all things that are under the cope of heaven. Thou art the Lord of all, and there is none that can resist Thy majesty. Thou knowest all things, and Thou knowest that it was not out of pride and contempt or any desire of glory that I refused to worship the proud Aman. . . . But I feared lest I should transfer the honor of my God to a man. . . . And now, O Lord, O King, O God of Abraham, have mercy on Thy people, because our enemies resolve to destroy us. . . . Hear my supplication. . . . And turn our mourning into joy, that we may live and praise Thy name.

Not less touching is Queen Esther's prayer in those same circumstances (14: 12–19), bringing out even more clearly the infallibility of providence regarding even the free acts of men; for she asks that the heart of King Assuerus be changed, and her prayer is answered: "Remember, O Lord, and show Thyself to us in the time of our tribulation, and give me boldness, O Lord, King of gods, and of all power. Give me a well ordered speech in my mouth in the presence of the lion: and turn his heart to the hatred of our enemy; that both he himself may perish, and the rest that consent to him. But deliver us by Thy hand: and help me who hath no helper, but Thee, O Lord, who hast the knowledge of all things. And Thou knowest that I hate the glory of the wicked. . . . Deliver us from the hand of the wicked. And deliver me from my fear." In fact, as we read a little later on (15: 11), "God changed the king's spirit into mildness; and all in haste and in fear [seeing Esther faint before him], he leaped from his throne and held her in his arms till she came to herself." Thereupon, after speedily assuring himself of Aman's treachery, he sent him to his punishment, and leant all the weight of his power to the Jews in defending themselves against their enemies.[1]

From this it is plain that divine providence extends infallibly not only to the least external happening but also to the most intimate secrets of the heart and every free action; for, in answer to the prayer of the just, it brings about a change in the interior dispositions of the will of kings. Socrates and Plato never rose to such lofty conceptions, to such firm convictions on this matter of the divine governance.

Many other texts in the Bible to the same effect are repeat-

---

[1] Cf. also Daniel 13: 42: The prayer of Susanna.

edly insisted upon by both St. Augustine and St. Thomas.

In Proverbs, for instance, we read (21: 1): "As the division of the waters, so the heart of the king is in the hand of the Lord: whithersoever He will He shall turn it. Every way of man seemeth right to himself: but the Lord weigheth the hearts." Again, in Ecclesiasticus (33: 13) we read: "As the potter's clay is in his hand, to fashion and order it: all his ways are according to his ordering. So man is in the hand of Him who made Him: and He will render to him according to His judgment." Again, Isaias in his prophecies against the heathen (14: 24) says: "The Lord of hosts hath sworn, saying: Surely as I have thought, so shall it be. And as I have purposed, so shall it fall out: that I will destroy the Assyrian in My land . . . and his yoke shall be taken away from them." "This is the hand," the prophet adds, "that is stretched out upon all nations. For the Lord of hosts hath decreed, and who can disannul it? And His hand is stretched out, and who shall turn it away?" Always there is the same insistence on the liberty of the divine election, on a universal and infallible providence reaching down to the minutest detail and to the free actions of men.

3) For what end has this universal and infallible providence directed all things? Though the psalms do not bring that full light to bear which comes with the Gospel, they frequently answer this question when they declare that *God directs all things* to good, *for the manifestation of His goodness, His mercy, and His justice,* and that He is in no way the cause of sin, but permits it in view of a greater good. Providence is thus presented as a divine virtue inseparably united with mercy and justice, just as true prudence in the

man of virtue can never be at variance with the moral virtues of justice, fortitude, and moderation which are intimately connected with it. Only in God, however, can this connection of the virtues reach its supreme perfection.

Again and again we find in the psalms such expressions as these: "All the ways of the Lord are mercy and truth" (24: 10); "All His works are done with faithfulness. He loveth mercy and judgment [Heb., justice and right]; the earth is full of the mercy of the Lord" (32: 4–5); "Show, O Lord, Thy ways to me, and teach me Thy paths. Direct me in Thy truth, and teach me; for Thou art God my Savior, and on Thee I have waited all the day long. Remember, O Lord, Thy bowels of compassion; and Thy mercies that are from the beginning of the world. The sins of my youth and my ignorances do not remember. According to Thy mercy remember me: for Thy goodness' sake, O Lord" (24: 4–7). "The Lord ruleth me: and I shall want nothing. He hath set me in a place of pasture. He hath brought me up on the water of refreshment: He hath converted my soul. He hath led me on the paths of justice, for His name's sake. For though I should walk in the midst of the shadow of death, I will fear no evils, for Thou art with me. Thy rod and Thy staff: they have comforted me" (22: 1–5). "In Thee, O Lord, have I hoped, let me never be confounded. . . . My lots are in Thy hands. Deliver me out of the hands of my enemies, and from them that persecute me. Make Thy face to shine on Thy servant: save me in Thy mercy. . . . O how great is the multitude of Thy sweetness, O Lord, which Thou has hidden from them that fear Thee! Which Thou has wrought for them that hope in Thee, in the sight of the sons of men. Thou shalt hide them in the secret of Thy face from the disturbance of men. Thou shalt protect them in Thy tabernacle from the contradiction of tongues" (30: 1, 16, 17, 20).

Here we have the twofold foundation of our hope and trust in God: His providence, with its individual care for each one of the just, and His omnipotence. All these passages in the psalms may be summed up in St. Teresa's words already quoted: "Lord, Thou knowest all things, canst do all things, and Thou lovest me."

Since providence is of such absolute universality, extending to the minutest details, and since at the same time it is infallible and directs all things to good, surely it ought to be quite evident to those who are willing to see it. How, then, in its ways is it so often impenetrable even to the just? The Old Testament more than once touches on this great problem.

Providence is for us an evident fact, yet in certain of its ways it remains absolutely unfathomable

According to the Bible, *the evidence that providence in general exists,* is obtained either from the order apparent in the world or from the history of the chosen people or again from the main features of the lives of the just and of the wicked.

The order apparent in the world, declare the psalms, proclaims the existence of an intelligent designer: "The heavens show forth the glory of God: and the firmament declareth the work of His hands" (18: 2); "Sing ye to the Lord with praise: sing to our God upon the harp; who covereth the heavens with clouds, and prepareth rain for the earth; who maketh grass to grow on the mountains, and herbs for the service of men, who giveth to beasts their food, and to the young ravens that call upon Him" (146: 7; cf. Job 38: 41); "All men are vain, in whom there is not the knowledge of God: and who by these good things that are seen could not understand Him that He is. Neither by attending to the works have acknowledged who was the workman. . . . They are not to be pardoned. For if they were able to know so much as to make a judgment of the world, how did not they more easily find out the Lord thereof?" (Wis. 13: 1, 4, 8.)

Providence is no less clearly seen in *the history of the chosen people,* as the psalms again remind us, especially Ps. 113, *In exitu Israel de Aegypto:*

When Israel went out of Egypt . . . the sea saw and fled: Jordan was turned back. . . . What ailed thee, O thou sea, that thou didst flee? and thou, O Jordan, that thou wast turned back? Ye mountains that skipped like rams, and ye hills like lambs of the flock? At the presence of the God of Jacob: who turned the rock into pools of water, and the stony hill into fountains of waters. Not to us, O Lord, not to us: but to Thy name give glory. For Thy mercy and for Thy truth's sake. . . . The Lord hath been mindful of us and hath blessed us. He hath blessed the house of Israel. . . . He hath blessed all that fear the Lord, both little and great. . . . But we that live bless the Lord: from this time now and forever.

Lastly, providence is clearly shown in *the general life of the just,* in the often perceptible happiness with which it rewards them. As we read in psalm 111:

Blessed is the man that feareth the Lord: he shall delight exceedingly in His commandments. His seed shall be mighty on the earth: the generation of the righteous shall be blessed. Glory and wealth shall be in his house: and his justice remaineth forever and ever. To the righteous a light hath risen up in darkness: He is merciful, compasisonate and just. . . . His heart is ready to hope in the Lord, his heart is strengthened: he shall not be moved until he look over his enemies. He hath given to the poor: His justice remaineth forever and ever.

The providence of God is especially to be seen in the case of *those in tribulation,* "raising up the needy from the earth and lifting up the poor out of the dunghill. That He may place him with the princes of His people" (Ps. 112:7).

On the other hand, *the malice of the wicked* receives its chastisement even in this world, often in a most striking way, another sign of the divine governance: "Be not delighted in the paths of the wicked. . . . Flee from it, pass not by it. . . . They eat the bread of wickedness. . . . But the path of the just, as a shining light, goeth forward and increaseth even to a perfect day. The way of the wicked is darksome: they know not where they fall" (Prov., chap. 4).[2] God withdraws His blessing from the wicked and delivers them up to their own blindness; but to His servants He lends His aid, sometimes in marvelous ways, as when He said to Elias (III Kings 17:3): "Get thee hence and go towards the east and hide thyself by the torrent Carith. . . . I have commanded the ravens to feed thee there." In obedience to the word of the Lord he departed and took up his abode by the

[2] Ps. 36: 10–15: "Yet a little while, and the wicked shall not be: and thou shalt seek his place, and shalt not find it. But the meek shall inherit the land: and shall delight in abundance of peace. The sinner shall watch the just man: and shall gnash upon him his teeth. But the Lord shall laugh at him: for He foreseeth that His day shall come. The wicked have drawn out the sword: they have bent their bow. To cast down the poor and needy, to kill the upright of heart. Let their sword enter into their own hearts: and let their bow be broken." Ps. 33: 22: "The death of the wicked is very evil: and they that hate the just shall be guilty."

torrent of Carith; and the ravens brought him bread and meat in the morning and eventide, and he drank water from the torrent.

Although providence is thus evident in the life of the just taken as a whole, nevertheless in some of its ways *it remains inscrutable*. Especially is this so in its more advanced stages, where the obscurity is due solely to an overpowering radiance dazzling our feeble sight. An outstanding example is that passage from Isaias which predicts the sufferings of the Servant of Yahweh, or the Savior.

Again in psalm 33: 20, we read: "Many are the tribulations of the just; but out of them all will the Lord deliver them." Judith says:

Our fathers were tempted that they might be proved, whether they worshiped their God truly. . . . Abraham was tempted and, being proved by many tribulations, was made the friend of God. So Isaac, so Jacob, so Moses, and all that have pleased God, have passed through many tribulations, remaining faithful. . . . Let us not revenge ourselves for these things which we suffer. But esteeming these very punishments to be less than our sins deserve, let us believe that these scourges of the Lord, with which like servants we are chastised, have happened for our amendment, and not for our destruction (Judith 8: 21–27).

The prophets often spoke of the mysterious character of certain ways of providence, especially when, like Jeremias, they realized the comparative futility of their efforts. Isaias (55: 6) writes:

Seek ye the Lord while He may be found: call upon Him while He is near. Let the wicked forsake his way and the unjust man his thoughts, and let him return to the Lord; and He will have mercy on him: and to our God; for He is bountiful to forgive. For my thoughts are not your thoughts: nor your ways my ways, saith the Lord. For as the heavens are exalted above the earth, so are my ways exalted above your ways, and my thoughts above your thoughts.

We find the same expressed in psalm 35: 7: "Thy justice, O Lord, is as the mountains of God: Thy judgments are a great deep."

Nevertheless, in this higher darkness, so different from the lower darkness of sin and death, the just man discovers which way his true path lies: he learns to distinguish more and more clearly these two kinds of darkness, which are at opposite extremes.[3] Let us say with the just Tobias (13: 1) after the trials he had endured:

Thou art great, O Lord, forever, and Thy kingdom is unto all ages. For Thou scourgest and Thou savest: Thou leadest down to hell, and bringest up again: and there is none that can escape Thy hand. Give glory to the Lord, ye children of Israel: and praise Him in the sight of the Gentiles. Because He has therefore scattered you among the Gentiles, who know not Him, that you may declare His wonderful works: and make them know that there is no other almighty God besides Him. He hath chastised us for our iniquities: and He will save us for His own mercy.[4] Be converted, therefore, ye sinners: and do justice before God, believing that He will show His mercy to you.

---

[3] In certain difficult problems presented by the spiritual life in a concrete case—to decide, for example, whether one who at times is in close union with God but is gravely ill, is being inspired by God in certain courses—the outcome of the enquiry will be obscure, but whether the obscurity is from above or from below will depend upon the method pursued.

[4] One of the councils of the Church says the same with St. Prosper: "That some are saved is the gift of Him who saves; that some perish is the fault of them that perish" (Council of Chiersy, Denzinger, n.318).

These, then, are the principal statements in the Old Testament concerning providence. It is *universal,* extending to the minutest detail, to the secrets of the heart. It is *infallible,* regarding everything that happens, even our free actions. *It directs all things to good,* and at the prayer of the just will change the heart of the sinner. For those who will but see, it is an evident fact, yet in certain of its ways it remains inscrutable. This teaching shows us what confidence we should have in God and with what wholehearted abandonment we should surrender ourselves to Him in times of trial by perfect conformity to His divine will; then will He direct all things to our sanctification and salvation. And so the Gospel proclaims: "Seek ye first the kingdom of God and His justice: and all these things shall be added unto you" (Luke 12: 31).

CHAPTER XVI

The Hidden Ways of Providence and the Book of Job

We cannot speak of the Old Testament witness to providence without pausing to consider the Book of Job. It will be well to pass in review the general ideas it contains, with particular stress on the meaning and significance of the conclusion to which they lead.

The book treats of *the mystery of suffering* or the distribution of happiness and misfortune in this present life. Why is it that here on earth even the just must at times endure so many evils? What is the purpose of this in the plan of divine providence? We shall see that the general answer to this question is made more precise in numerous other passages of the Bible which point out that these trials of God's servants are ordained for a greater good.

There is now practically unanimous agreement with the Church Fathers that Job was a real person. The conversation between Job and his friends must have been substantially that attributed to them by the inspired writer, who then gave to the book the form of a didactic poem, its main purpose being to instruct. From the literary point of view it is unusually rich in style. Its purpose is to give the reason for the ills of this present life. Let us see first of all how the problem is presented, and then what solution is given to it.[1]

---

[1] Cf. *Dictionnaire de la Bible,* art. "Job." The brief summaries given of the long discourses of Job and his friends are taken from Crampon's translation.

A review of the more important of these texts will be of particular profit to those souls who find themselves unable to look upon the question of pure love as just a theoretical problem, but who view it as a question in which they are deeply and passionately interested. God's love is concerned more with their griefs than with their words or their writings; it is because, as with Job, their words are the fruit of their griefs that they are the source at times of so much good.

Let us obtain light on this point by consulting St. Thomas' commentary on the Book of Job, which anticipates some of the most sublime pages of St. John of the Cross in *The Dark Night of the Soul,* concerning the passive purifications that distinigush the night of the spirit.[2]

Is it always on account of sin that misfortune befalls us in this life?

Is even the innocent man struck down, and if so, why? This is the question Job asks himself, afflicted as he is by the loathsome disease. The very beginning of the book (1:1) says of him that he was "simple and upright, and fearing God, and avoiding evil," that he had great possessions, and that he frequently reminded his sons of their duties toward God, offering holocausts for each one of them.

The Most High God Himself declares of him: "There is none like him in the earth, a simple and upright man, and fearing God, and avoiding evil" (1:8); to which Satan replies: "Doth Job fear God in vain? . . . His possession hath increased on the earth. . . . But stretch forth Thy hand a

---

[2] Cf. the *Commentary of St. Thomas on the Book of Job,* chaps. 4, 6, 8, 9 (lesson in its entirety), 19, 28. Again St. Thomas, IaIIae, q. 87, a. 7, 8; *De Malo,* q. 5, a. 4; and the *Commentary on St. John,* 9: 2.

little, and touch all that he hath: and see if he blesseth Thee not to Thy face" (1:9-11).

"Then the Lord said to Satan: Behold, all that he hath is in thy hand. . . . And Satan went forth from the presence of the Lord." These words recall those our Lord addressed to St. Peter before His passion: "Simon, Simon, behold Satan hath desired to have you, that he may sift you as wheat. But I have prayed for thee, that thy faith fail not" (Luke 22:31).

The best always are the ones who must undergo this winnowing. This first and most important chapter of the whole book throws light on all that follows, the conclusion especially. But Job is not himself aware of what the Lord has said to Satan or of what he has permitted him to do. Such are, indeed, the hidden ways of providence, whose secret is here revealed to us in the opening chapter of the book, while for the one afflicted they remain a profound mystery.

In point of fact, Job is deprived of all his possessions, and his sons and daughters meet their death in a tempest. Yet the patriarch is resigned to God's will, saying: *The Lord gave, and the Lord hath taken away. . . . Blessed be the name of the Lord"* (1:21). Then Satan obtains leave from God to afflict the holy man "with a very grievous ulcer, from the sole of the foot even to the top of the head" (2:7). But still, in spite of the insults of his wife, who bids him "bless God and die," Job continues faithful to God.

At this point three of his friends arrive to console him: the aged Eliphaz, the middle-aged Baldad, and a young man named Sophar. They remain for a long time weeping, unable to utter a word at the sight of the intense affliction of their unfortunate friend.

After the coming of his friends, for seven days and nights

of suffering, Job himself remains silent. Then, having reached the limit of endurance, he opens his lips and says: "Let the day perish wherein I was born. Why is light given to him that is in misery, and life to them that are in bitterness of soul? . . . That look for death, and it cometh not, as they that dig for a treasure. . . . I am not at ease, neither am I quiet, neither have I rest" [3] (3: 3, 20, 21, 26).

Thereupon Job's friends address him thus: "Behold thou hast taught many. . . . Thy words have confirmed many that were staggering. . . . But now the scourge is come upon thee, and thou faintest" (4: 1-5). Eliphaz, the eldest, anxious to preserve his reputation for wisdom, is astonished that Job should let himself be so deeply discouraged: the innocent, he says, cannot perish: it is only the wicked who are consumed by the divine wrath. Then he relates how it was revealed to him one night that no man is just in the sight of God. Job, therefore, must cease complaining so bitterly unless he wishes to share the fate of the wicked; let him confess his guilt and implore God's mercy, for God chastises as a father, and the wounds He inflicts He will also heal (chaps. 4, 5).

Job replies that his complaints fall far short of the sufferings he endures: death itself would be more welcome. He hoped to receive some consolation from his friends, but he was deceived in his expectations; and yet, all that his friends can reproach him with is, that he spoke somewhat hastily (6: 24-30). Then, turning to God, he lays before Him his misfortune, imploring Him to put an end to it by death

---

[3] The author has followed Crampon's translation of the discourses of Job and his friends. The reading of Job 3: 26 is that of the Revised Version. The Douay Version, following the Vulgate, has: "Have I not dissembled? Have I not kept silence? Have I not been quiet?" [Tr.]

(7: 1–21). "I have had empty months, and have numbered to myself wearisome nights. . . . So that my soul rather chooseth hanging, and my bones death. . . . How long wilt Thou not spare me? . . . I have sinned. What shall I do to Thee, O Keeper of men? Why dost Thou not remove my sin?"

It is Baldad, middle-aged, opulent, self-confident, who, instead of consoling his friend, replies by insisting that God is not unjust; such misfortunes as these He inflicts only on those who have sinned grievously. He then exhorts Job to return to God (chap. 8). Job acknowledges that God is wise and just; but, he adds, "if any man is innocent, surely it is I." And he continues to give free vent to his complaining (chaps. 9, 10).

Sophar, the third and youngest of his friends, a passionate, hot-headed youth, takes the theme from the other two: in his opinion Job's wickedness far outweighs the severity of his chastisement, and he, too, exhorts him to return to God.

In chapters 12, 13, and 14, Job acknowledges once again the infinite wisdom of God, His justice, and His power, sounding the praises of the divine perfections even more loudly than his friends. Then, in chapter 13, he continues: "Although He should kill me, I will trust in Him. But yet I will prove my ways in His sight: and He shall be my savior. . . . I shall be found just. How many are my iniquities and sins? Make me know my crimes and offenses." Finally he becomes less vehement, excuses himself, and implores His judge to have pity on him.

But he does not succeed in convincing his friends. In the harshest terms Eliphaz continues to maintain that Job does wrong to complain, seeing that before God all men are guilty (chap. 15).

Job answers (chap. 16): "I have often heard such things as these: you are all troublesome comforters. . . . I also could speak like you: and would God your soul were for my soul." Once again he testifies to his innocence, calling upon God Himself to judge between him and his friends. "Behold my witness is in heaven: and He that knoweth my conscience is on high. My friends are full of words: my eye poureth out tears to God."

As St. Thomas says in his commentary, Job's friends have no thought for the future life; they believe that the just must be rewarded and the wicked punished even in this world.

Baldad repeats what he has already said, that here on earth misfortune is always the lot of the wicked. But this time he adds neither consolation nor promise: to him Job is now a hardened sinner, and he treats him accordingly. We see, therefore, that of all the trials Job had to endure, one of the severest comes from his own friends. Losing sight of the future life, they repeat insistently that all accounts must be settled here on earth, and thus they oppress him with their arguments.

It is then that Job, who is a figure of the Christ to come, is uplifted by an inspiration from on high to that mystery of the after-life which was hinted at in the prologue. He answers (chap. 19):

Behold these ten times you confound me, and are not ashamed to oppress me. For I have been ignorant, my ignorance shall be with me. But you set yourselves up against me, and reprove me with my reproaches. At least now understand that God hath not afflicted me with an equal judgment. . . . He hath hedged in my path round about, and I cannot pass: and in my way He hath set darkness. . . . He hath taken away my hope, as from a tree that is plucked up. . . . He hath counted me as His enemy. . . . He hath put my brethren far from me: and my acquaintance like strangers have departed from me. . . . Even fools despised me. . . . Have pity on me, have pity on me, at least you my friends, because the hand of the Lord hath touched me. . . . Who will grant that my words may be written . . . graven with an instrument in flint stone? For I know that my Redeemer liveth, and in the last day I shall rise out of the earth. And I shall be clothed again with my skin: and in my flesh I shall see God. Whom I myself shall see, and my eyes behold: and not another. This my hope is laid up in my bosom. Why then do you say now: Let us persecute him. Know ye that there is judgment.

In spite of this sublime cry of hope, the young Sophar returns to his original theme, insisting that the misfortunes of this present life can be explained only as a chastisement of sin.

Job, on the contrary, proves from experience that this is a false principle (chap. 21). Doubtless, in many cases the wicked do receive signal punishment, but there are cases also in which outwardly they are successful up to the very moment of their death, whereas occasionally the just have much to suffer.

Eliphaz comes back persistently to his point; he even goes so far as to give a long list of the sins Job must have committed: "Thou hast withdrawn bread from the hungry. . . . Thou hast sent widows away empty" (chap. 22).

In chapters 28-31 Job maintains that misfortune in this world is not always a chastisement for a sinful life. He does not know, he confesses, why he should suffer, but this God knows in His great wisdom, which to man is unfathomable. Chapter 31 concludes the first part of the book, and with it the colloquies of Job, "who ends by reducing his opponents to silence, but without himself discovering the clue to the enigma." [4]

With the second part there enters a young man, Eliu by name, who gives proof of some degree of intelligence, "but apparently is not altogether free from over-confidence." [5] He maintains that Job is being punished not for any serious crime, but for not having been sufficiently humble before God; the bitter complaints to which he gave way are themselves an indication of his interior feelings. Let him repent, therefore, and God will reinstate him in his former happiness (chaps. 32–37). To this Job has no answer, for what Eliu has said is quite possible and is to a great extent true. Thus every aspect of the problem of suffering has now been presented; yet still there is something lacking.

The meaning and significance of the Lord's reply

Finally, in the third part, the Lord Himself intervenes in response to Job's petition to plead his cause before Him (13:22).

It is contrary to God's dignity to enter into discussion with men. He answers by unrolling before the eyes of Job a magnificent panorama of the wonders of creation, from the stars in the heavens to the wondrous effects of animal instinct (chaps. 38, 39).

Shalt thou be able to join the shining stars, the Pleiades, or canst thou stop the turning about of Arcturus? Can'st thou bring forth the day star in its time? . . . Dost thou know the order of heaven? And canst thou set down the reason thereof on the earth? . . .

[4] *Dictionnaire de la Bible*, art. "Job," col. 1560.
[5] Le Hir,

Wilt thou take the prey for the lioness, and satisfy the appetite of her whelps? . . . Wilt thou give strength to the horse? . . . Will the eagle mount up at thy command, and make her nest in high places?

All these works reveal a wisdom, a providence, a perfect adaptation of means to ends that bear witness to the absolute goodness of their author, and they should teach men to accept humbly and without murmuring whatever the Almighty may direct or permit. As we read these words uttered by "Him who is," we realize intuitively almost that He is the author and conserver of our being, that He has knit together, as it were, our essence and existence, which He continues to conserve, and that He is the cause of all that is real and good in creation. It has been said that this divine answer does not touch the philosophical aspect of the question under discussion. As a matter of fact, it shows that God does nothing but for a good purpose, and that if already in the things of sense there is this wonderful order, much more sublime must be the order in the spiritual world, even though it must at times be obscure to us on account of its transcendence. Later on we shall see our Lord making use of a more striking similitude: "Behold the birds of the air, for they neither sow, nor do they reap . . . and your heavenly Father feedeth them. Are not you of much more value than they?" (Matt. 6: 26.) And so the divine answer arouses in the heart of Job sentiments of humility and resignation.

In conclusion, God ironically invites Job to take over the government of the world and maintain there the reign of order and of justice (41: 1-9). Would he be able to do so, powerless and unarmed as he was, in face of the two monsters

He names? Yet these are no more than a plaything in the hands of God.[6] In His description (chap. 40) of the mighty strength with which He has endowed Behemoth and Leviathan (the hippopotamus and the crocodile), the Lord suggests the parallel that if, like these monsters, the devil has sometimes extraordinary power in afflicting men, nevertheless he cannot exercise that power without the permission of God, who can make its very fury subserve His own good purpose.[7]

And so in the end (chap. 42) *Job makes his humble confession:* "I know that Thou canst do all things. . . . I have spoken unwisely, and things that above measure exceed my knowledge." He thus acknowledges that his complaining was excessive and his words sometimes unconsidered. Nevertheless the Lord tells Eliphaz: "My wrath is kindled against thee, and against thy two friends, because you have not spoken the thing that is right before Me, as My servant Job hath. . . . Offer for yourselves a holocaust. And My servant Job shall pray for you. His face I will accept, that folly may not be imputed to you." And the Lord blessed the latter days of Job with even greater blessings than before, and he died in peace very advanced in years.

The clue to the whole book is to be found in the first chapter, where we are told how the Lord permitted the devil

[6] Cf. *Dictionnaire de la Bible,* art. "Job," col. 1574.

[7] Some of the expressions God uses here to describe the strength with which He has endowed these monsters recall what theology has to say about the nature of the devil. As nature, as reality and goodness, he is still loved by God, for he is still His work. We are reminded, too, that, as St. Thomas says, the devils continue of their nature to love existence as such (as prescinding from their unhappy condition), and life as such; and therefore they continue of their very nature to love the author of their life, Him whom as their judge they hate. Nevertheless; rather than exist in their miserable state they would prefer not to exist at all. (Cf. St. Thomas, Ia, q.60, a.5, ad 5um.)

to try His servant Job. The conclusion, then, is obvious: If men are visited by God with tribulation, He does so not exclusively as a chastisement for their sins, but to prove them as gold is proved in the furnace and make them advance in virtue. It is the purification of love, as the great Christian mystics call it. In the prologue Satan asked (1:9): "Doth Job fear God in vain? . . . His possessions have increased on the earth." Now we see how even in the greatest adversity Job still remained faithful to God. That this is the meaning of the trials sent upon the just is shown in many other passages of the Old Testament.

The trials of the just serve a higher purpose

This teaching receives its confirmation in the two great trials recorded in Genesis: Abraham preparing, at God's command, to sacrifice his son Isaac (Gen., chap. 22) and Joseph sold in captivity by his brethren (Gen., chap. 37).

God tried Abraham by commanding him to offer as a holocaust his son Isaac, the son of promise. As St. Paul tells the Hebrews (11:17): "By faith Abraham, when he was tried, offered Isaac: and he that had received the promises offered up his only begotten son (to whom it was said: In Isaac shall thy seed be called), accounting that God is able to raise up even from the dead. Whereupon also He received him for a parable." The angel of the Lord stayed the hand of the patriarch, who heard a voice from heaven saying: "Because thou hast done this thing, and hast not spared thy only begotten son for My sake: I will bless thee, and I will multiply thy seed as the stars of heaven. . . . And in thy seed shall all the nations of the earth be blessed: because thou hast obeyed My voice" (Gen. 22:16).

Jospeh was tried when, through envy of him, and his dreams and inspirations, his brethren sold him into captivity. Calumniated by his master's wife, the innocent Joseph was cast into prison, subsequently to be raised to the first rank by Pharaoh, who recognized in him the spirit of the Lord (Gen. 41:38). Later still, when under the stress of famine his brethren came seeking corn in Egypt, he said to them:

I am Joseph. Is my father yet living? . . . I am Joseph, your brother, whom you sold into Egypt. Be not afraid, and let it not seem to you a hard case that you sold me into these countries: for God sent me before you into Egypt for your preservation. . . . Not by your counsel was I sent hither, but by the will of God: who hath made me . . . lord of his [Pharaoh's] whole house, and governor in all the land of Egypt. . . . And falling upon the neck of his brother Benjamin, he embraced him and wept" (Gen. 45:3-14).

What more eloquent declaration than this of providence, of the divine governance, which turns to good account the trials of the just, sometimes even to the welfare of their persecutors, when their eyes at last are opened?

The same is repeatedly brought out by the psalms, notably 90:11-16, from which the gradual and tract for the first Sunday in Lent are taken:

He hath given His angels charge over thee to keep thee in all thy ways.[8] In their hands they shall bear thee up, lest thou dash thy foot against a stone. Thou shalt walk upon the asp and the basilisk: and thou shalt tramp under foot the lion and the dragon. . . . He that dwelleth in the aid of the most High shall abide under the protection of heaven. He shall say to the Lord: Thou art my protector

---

[8] We are reminded of Moses rescued from the waters and the constant assistance given to him by the Lord.

and my refuge: my God in whom I trust. For He hath delivered me from the snare of the hunters: and from the sharp word. He will overshadow thee with his shoulders: and under his wings thou shalt trust. His truth shall compass thee with a shield: thou shalt not be afraid of the terror of the night, of the arrow·that flieth in the day. . . . A thousand shall fall at thy side, and ten thousand at thy right hand: but it shall not come nigh thee. . . . For He [the Lord] hath given His angels charge over Thee, to keep Thee in all Thy ways. . . . [He will say]: Because he hoped in me I will deliver him: I will protect him because he hath known my name. He shall cry to me and I will hear him: I am with him in tribulation, I will deliver him, and I will glorify him. I will fill him with length of days: and I will show him my salvation.

In these admirable verses, full of a sublime poetry and a forceful spiritual realism, we are given *a glimpse of the future life.*

It is true, doubtless, that the Old Testament rarely mentions this future life except in a veiled way and usually in symbols. Yet *Isaias* (60: 19), describing the glories of the New Jerusalem, wrote: "The Lord shall be unto thee for an everlasting light, and thy God for thy glory. The sun shall go down no more. . . . For the Lord shall be unto thee for an everlasting light: and the days of thy mourning shall be ended." And again (65: 19): "I will rejoice in Jerusalem and joy in My people, saith the Lord, and the voice of weeping shall no more be heard in her, nor the voice of crying."

Still more clearly in the Book of Wisdom (3: 1) we read:

The souls of the just are in the hands of God: and the torment of death shall not touch them. In the sight of the unwise they seemed to die: and their departure was taken for misery, and their going away from us, for utter destruction: but they are in peace. . . .

Their hope is full of immortality.[9] Afflicted in few things, in many they shall be rewarded: because God hath tried them, and found them worthy of Himself. As gold is tried in the furnace He hath proved them, and as a victim of a holocaust He hath received them: and in time there shall be respect had to them. The just shall shine, and shall run to and fro like sparks among the reeds. They shall judge nations, and rule over people: and their Lord shall reign forever . . . for grace and peace is to His elect. . . . Then shall the just stand with great constancy against those that have afflicted them and taken away their labors. . . . [These shall say] within themselves: . . . These are they whom we had some time in derision and for a parable of reproach. We fools esteemed their lives madness and their end without honor. Behold how they are numbered among the children of God, and their lot is among the saints. Therefore we have erred from the way of truth. . . . What hath pride profited us? But the just shall live for evermore: and their reward is with the Lord, and the care of them with the Most High. Therefore they shall receive a kingdom of glory and a crown of beauty, at the hand of the Lord: for with His right hand He will cover them (5: 1).

These words, "But the just shall live for evermore: and their reward is with the Lord," can refer only to eternal life. The psalmist had already declared: "But as for me, I will appear before Thy sight in justice: I shall be satisfied when Thy glory shall appear" (Ps. 16: 15). Daniel declares (12: 13): "They that are learned [in the things of God, and keep His law] shall shine as the stars for all eternity." Finally, in his martyrdom, one of the seven Machabees thus addresses his executioner: "Thou indeed, O most wicked man, destroyest us out of this present life: but the King of the world will

[9] After the death of the just of the Old Testament, they had to await in limbo the coming of the Redeemer who was to open to them the gates of paradise.

raise us up, who die for His laws, in the resurrection of eternal life" (II Mach. 7:9). Tobias had declared: "Thou art great, O Lord, forever, and Thy kingdom is unto all ages. For Thou scourgest, and Thou savest: Thou leadest down to hell, and bringest up again. . . . He hath chastised us for our iniquities: and He will save us for His own mercy" (Tob. 13:1-2, 5).

Many other texts of the Old Testament give us an insight into the meaning of the trials sent by God and hint clearly at the higher purpose He has in view. Judith exhorts the ancients of Israel to wait patiently for help from the Lord:

They must remember how our father Abraham was tempted, and being proved by many tribulations, was made the friend of God. So Isaac, so Jacob, so Moses, and all that have pleased God, passed through many tribulations, remaining faithful. . . . As for us . . . let us believe that these scourges of the Lord, with which like servants we are chastised, have happened for our amendment, and not for our destruction (Judith 8:22-23, 26-27).

The *advantages to be gained by suffering* are thus declared by Ecclesiasticus (2:1-10):

Son, when thou comest to the service of God . . . prepare thy soul for temptation. Humble thy heart, and endure: incline thy ear, and receive the words of understanding: and make not haste in the time of clouds. Wait on God with patience: join thyself to God and endure, that thy life may be increased in the latter end. Take all that shall be brought upon thee: and in thy sorrow endure, and in thy humiliation keep patience. For gold and silver are tried in the fire, but acceptable men in the furnace of tribulation. Believe God, and He will recover thee and direct thy way. . . . Ye that fear the Lord, hope in Him: and mercy shall come to you for your delight.

The Book of Wisdom (chaps. 15–17) contrasts the trials of the good with those of the wicked, and shows their gradation. The Egyptians are scourged with extraordinary plagues, but the Israelites by looking upon the brazen serpent are healed of the serpents' bite; they are fed with manna from heaven, are led forward by the pillar of fire, and find a passage through the Red Sea, in which the Egyptians are swallowed up. And in Isaias we read: "I have blotted out thy iniquities as a cloud and thy sins as a mist: return to Me, for I have redeemed thee" (45:22; cf. 46:2–6).

Micheas foretells how God will have mercy on His people (7:14–20): "He will send His fury in no more, because He delighteth in mercy. He will turn again and have mercy on us: He will put away our iniquities and He will cast all our sins into the bottom of the sea. Thou wilt perform . . . the mercy to Abraham: which Thou hast sworn to our fathers from the days of old."

All these Old Testament texts setting forth the reason why trials are sent upon the just throw light on the final conclusion of the Book of Job. But it is the Gospel that brings full light to bear upon the last things; only Christianity can provide the final solution. That solution, however, is foreshadowed in the Book of Wisdom (245–250 B.C.). What the Book of Job declares is that the justice of God, which, as Job himself recognizes, must some day have effect, is infinitely beyond our restricted view, and again that in this world virtue, instead of having as its inseparable accompaniment what men commonly call happiness, is often seen to be subjected to the severest trials.

With the Christian saints, in fact, the love of the cross is seen to increase as they grow in the love of God and likeness to Christ crucified, of whom holy Job was a figure.

When misfortune overtakes us, whether the affliction is a trial or a chastisement, this remains obscure for each of us. Usually it is both, but then what is the measure of each? Only God knows. *St. Paul,* writing to the Hebrews, gives the solution when he speaks of perseverance in the midst of trial after the example of Christ (chap. 12):

Let us run by patience to the fight proposed to us: looking on Jesus, the author and finisher of faith, who, having joy set before Him, endured the cross, despising the shame, and now sitteth on the right hand of the throne of God. For think diligently upon Him that endured such opposition from sinners against Himself: that you be not wearied, fainting in your minds. For you have not resisted unto blood, striving against sin. . . . Whom the Lord loveth, He chastiseth: and He scourgeth every son whom He receiveth. . . . For what son is there, whom the father doth not correct? . . . [God chastises us] for our profit, that we might receive His sanctification.

It remains true, therefore, that, as Job says (chap. 7), "the life of man upon earth is a warfare and his days are like the days of a hireling." But upon His servants the Lord bestows His grace; although, as St. Paul says (Rom. 8: 38), "to them that love God all things work together unto good," to the very end. All things—graces, natural qualities, contradictions, sickness, and, as St. Augustine says, even sin. For God permits sin in the lives of His servants, as He permitted Peter's denial, that He may lead them to a deeper humility and thereby to a purer love.

CHAPTER XVII

PROVIDENCE ACCORDING TO THE GOSPEL

The existence of providence, its absolute universality extending to the smallest detail, and its infallibility regarding everything that comes to pass, not excepting our future free actions—all this the New Testament again brings out, even more clearly than the Old. Much more explicit, too, than in the Old Testament is the conception given us here of that higher good to which all things have been directed by providence, though in certain of its more advanced ways it still remains unfathomable. These fundamental points we shall examine one by one, giving prominence to the Gospel texts that most clearly express them.

The higher good to which all things are directed by providence

Our Lord in the Gospels raises our minds to the contemplation of the divine governance by directing our attention to the admirable order prevailing in the things of sense, and giving us some idea of how much more so this order of providence is to be found in spiritual things, an order more sublime, more bountiful, more salutary, and imperishable. We have seen that a similar order is to be found, though less clearly, in God's answer at the end of the Book of Job; if there are such extraordinary marvels to be met with in the world of sense, what wonderful order ought we not to expect in the spiritual world.

In the Gospel of St. Matthew we read (6: 25–34):

Be not solicitous for your life, what you shall eat, nor for your body, what you shall put on. Is not the life more than the meat and the body more than the raiment? Behold the birds of the air, for they neither sow, nor do they reap nor gather into barns: and your heavenly Father feedeth them. Are not you of more value than they? And which of you by taking thought can add to his stature one cubit? And for your raiment why are you solicitous? Consider the lilies of the field, how they grow: they labor not, neither do they spin. But I say to you that not even Solomon in all his glory was arrayed as one of these. And if the grass of the field, which is today and tomorrow is cast into the oven, God doth so clothe: how much more you, O ye of little faith? Be not solicitous therefore, saying: What shall we eat: or, what shall we drink: or, wherewith shall we be clothed? For after all these things do the heathens seek. For your heavenly Father knoweth that you have need of all these things. Seek ye therefore first the kingdom of God and His justice: and all these things shall be added unto you. Be not therefore solicitous for tomorrow: for the morrow will be solicitous for itself. Sufficient for the day is the evil thereof.

These examples serve to show that providence extends to all things, and gives to all beings what is suitable to their nature. God provides the birds of the air with their food and also has endowed them with instinct which directs them to seek out what is necessary and no more. If this is His way of dealing with the lower creation, surely He will have a care for us.

If providence provides what is needful for the birds of the air, how much more attentive will it be to the needs of such as we, who have a spiritual, immortal soul, with a destiny incomparably more sublime than that of the animal creation. The heavenly Father knows what we stand in need of. What, then, must our attitude be? First of all we must seek the kingdom of God and His justice, and then whatever is necessary for our bodily subsistence will be given us over and above. Those who make it their principal aim to pursue their final destiny (God the sovereign good who should be loved above all things), will be given whatever is necessary to attain that end, not only what is necessary for the life of the body, but also the graces to obtain life eternal.[1]

Our Lord refers to providence again in St. Matthew (10: 28): "Fear ye not them that kill the body and are not able to kill the soul: but rather fear him that can destroy both soul and body in hell. Are not two sparrows sold for a

[1] This is explained by St. Thomas, Ia, q. 22, a. 2: "We must say, however, that all things are subject to divine providence, not only in general, but even in their own individual selves. This is made evident thus. For since every agent acts for an end, the ordering of effects toward that end extends as far as the causality of the first agent extends. . . . But the causality of God extends to all being, not only as to the constituent principles of species, but also to the individualizing principles; not only of things incorruptible, but also of things corruptible. Hence all things that exist in whatsoever manner are necessarily directed by God toward some end; as the Apostle says: 'Those things that are of God are ordained by Him' (Rom. 13: 1). Since providence is nothing less than the type of the order of things to an end, we must say that all things are subject to it."

St. Thomas also says, Ia, q. 22, a. 3: "God has immediate providence over everything, even the smallest; and whatsoever causes He assigns to certain effects, He gives them the power to produce these effects. As to the execution of this order of providence, God governs things inferior by superior, not on account of any defection in His power, but in order to impart to creatures (especially to those of the higher order), the dignity of causality." Thus to men has been given dominion over domestic animals which, by their docile obedience, are of assistance to him in his labors.

What St. Thomas says in the Ia, q. 22, a. 4, may be summed up as follows: Providence does not destroy human liberty, but has ordained from all eternity that we should act freely. The divine action not only directs us to act, but directs us to act freely; it extends to the very free mode of our acts, which it produces in us and with our co-operation, insomuch as it is more intimately present to us than we are to ourselves. Cf. Ia, q. 19, a. 8.

farthing? And not one of them shall fall to the ground without your Father. But the very hairs of your head are all numbered. Fear not therefore: better are you than many sparrows." So again in St. Luke (12: 6–7).

Always it is the same *a fortiori* argument from the care the Lord has for the lower creation and thence leading us to form some idea of what the divine governance must be in the order of spiritual things.

As St. Thomas points out in his commentary on St. Matthew, what our Lord wishes to convey is this: *It is not the persecutor we should fear;* he can do no more than hurt our bodies, and what little harm he is capable of he cannot actually inflict without the permission of providence, which only allows these evils to befall us in view of a greater good. If it is true that not a single sparrow falls to the ground without our heavenly Father's permission, surely we shall not fall without His permission, no, nor one single hair of our head. This is equivalent to saying that providence extends to the smallest detail, to the least of our actions, every one of which may and indeed must be directed to our final end.

Besides the universality of providence, the New Testament brings out in terms no less clear *its infallibility* regarding everything that comes to pass. It is pointed out in the text just mentioned: "The very hairs of your head are all numbered." This infallibility extends even to the secrets of the heart and to our future free actions. In St. John (6: 64) we read: "The words that I have spoken to you are spirit and life. But there are some of you that believe not"; and the Evangelist adds: "For Jesus knew from the beginning who they were that did

not believe and who he was that would betray Him." Again
(13:11) during the last supper Jesus told those who were
present: "You are clean, but not all"; for, continues St. John,
"He knew who he was who would betray Him; and therefore He said: You are not all clean." St. Matthew also records
the words, "One of you is about to betray me." Now if Jesus
thus has certain knowledge of the secrets of hearts and, as
His prediction of persecutions shows, of future free actions,
they must surely be infallibly known to the eternal Father.

In St. Matthew (6:4–6), we are told: "When thou shalt
pray, enter into thy chamber and, having shut the door, pray
to thy Father in secret: and thy Father who seeth in secret
will repay thee." And later we find St. Paul saying to the
Hebrews (4:13): "Neither is there any creature invisible
in His sight: but all things are naked and open to His eyes,
to whom our speech is."

The teaching on *the necessity of prayer,* to which the
Gospel is constantly returning, obviously presupposes a providence extending to the very least of our actions. In St. Matthew (7:7–11) our Lord tells us: "If you then being evil,
know how to give good things to your children: how much
more will your heavenly Father who is in heaven give good
things to them that ask Him?" Here is another and stronger
argument for divine providence based on the attentive care
shown by a human father for his children. If he watches
over them, much more will our heavenly Father watch
over us.

Likewise, the *parable of the wicked judge* and the widow
in St. Luke (18:1–8) is an incentive to us to pray with perseverance. Annoyed by the persistent entreaties of the widow,

the judge finally yields to her just demands so that she may cease to be troublesome to him. "And the Lord said: Hear what the unjust judge saith. And will not God revenge his elect who cry to him day and night: and will he have patience in their regard?"

Our Lord proclaims the same truth in St. John (10: 27): "My sheep hear My voice. And I know them: and they follow Me. And I give them life everlasting: and they shall not perish forever. And no man shall pluck them out of My hand. That which My Father hath given Me is greater than all: and no one can snatch them out of the hand of My Father. I and the Father are one." These words point out emphatically the infallibility of providence concerning everything that comes to pass, including even our future free actions.

But what the Gospel message declares even more clearly is whether there is not after all some higher, some *eternal purpose* to which the divine governance directs all things, and further, that if it permits evil and sin—it cannot in any way be its cause—it does so only in view of some greater good.

In St. Matthew we read (5: 44): "Love your enemies: do good to them that hate you: and pray for them that persecute and calumniate you: that you may be the children of your Father who is in heaven, who maketh His sun to rise upon the good and bad and raineth upon the just and the unjust." And again in St. Luke (6: 36): "Be ye therefore merciful, as your heavenly Father is merciful." Persecution itself is turned to the good of those who endure it for the love of God: "Blessed are they that suffer persecution for justice' sake: for theirs is the kingdom of heaven. Blessed are ye when they

shall revile you and persecute you and speak all that is evil
against you, untruly, for My name's sake: be glad and rejoice,
for your reward is very great in heaven. For so they persecuted
the prophets that were before you" (Matt. 5: 10).

Here is the full light heralded from afar in the Book of Job
and more distinctly in this passage from the Book of Wisdom
(3: 1–8): "The souls of the just are in the hand of God . . .
in time they shall shine . . . they shall judge nations: and
their Lord shall reign forever."

Here is the full light of which we were given a glimpse
in the Book of Machabees (11: 7–9), where, as we have seen,
one of the martyrs, on the point of expiring, thus addresses
his persecutor: "Thou, O most wicked man, destroyest us
out of this present life: but the King of the world will raise
us up, who die for His laws, in the resurrection of eternal
life."

In the light of this revealed teaching, St. Paul writes to
the Romans (5: 3): "We glory also in tribulations, knowing
that tribulation worketh patience: and patience trial; and
trial hope; and hope confoundeth not; because the charity of
God is poured forth in our hearts, by the Holy Ghost who
is given to us." And again (8: 28): "We know that to them
that love God all things work unto good: to such as according to His purpose are called to be saints." This last text
sums up all the rest, revealing how this universal and infallible providence directs all things to a good purpose, not excluding evil, which it permits without in any way causing it.
And now there remains the question as to the sort of knowledge we can have of the plan pursued by the divine governance.

The light and shade in the providential plan

We have found clearly expressed in the Old Testament the truth that for us divine providence is an evident fact, yet that certain of its ways are unfathomable. This truth is brought out in still greater relief in the New Testament in connection with sanctification and eternal life.

Providence is an evident fact from the order prevailing in the universe, from the general working of the Church's life, and again from the life of the just taken as a whole. This is affirmed in the words of our Lord just quoted: "Behold the birds of the air, for they neither sow, nor do they reap, nor gather into barns: and your heavenly Father feedeth them. Are not you of much more value than they?" (Matt. 6: 26.) So again St. Paul (Rom. 1: 20): "The invisible things of Him from the creation of the world are *clearly seen, being understood by the things that are made,* His eternal power and divinity."

In the parables of the prodigal son, the lost sheep, the good shepherd, and the talents, our Lord also illustrates how providence is concerned with the souls of men. All that tenderness of heart shown by the father of the prodigal is already in an infinitely more perfect way possessed by God, whose providence watches over the souls of men more than any other earthly creature, in the lives of the just especially, in which everything is made to concur in their final end.

Jesus also proclaims how with His Father He will watch over the Church, and we now find verified these words of His: "Thou art Peter, and upon this rock I will build My Church. And the gates of hell shall not prevail against it" (Matt. 16: 18); "Going therefore, teach ye all nations: baptizing them in the name of the Father and of the Son and of the Holy Ghost; teaching them to observe all things whatsoever I have commanded you. And behold I am with you all days, even to the consummation of the world" (Matt. 28: 19–20). We are now witnessing in the spread of the Gospel in the nations throughout the five continents the realization of this providential plan, which in its general lines stands out quite distinctly.

In this plan of providence, however, there are also *elements of profound mystery,* and our Lord will have us to understand that to the humble and childlike, however, these mysterious elements will appear quite simple; their humility will enable them to penetrate even to the heights of God. First and foremost there is the mystery of the redemption, of the sorrowful passion and all that followed, a mystery which Jesus only reveals to His disciples little by little as they are able to bear it, a mystery that at the moment of its accomplishment will be a cause of confusion to them.

There is also *the whole mystery of salvation:* "I confess to Thee, O Father, Lord of heaven and earth, because Thou hast hidden these things from the wise and prudent and hast revealed them to little ones. Yea, Father: for so hath it seemed good in Thy sight" (Matt. 11: 25); "My sheep hear my voice. And I know them: and they follow me. And I give them life everlasting: and they shall not perish forever" (John 10: 27).

"There shall arise false christs and false prophets and shall show great signs and wonders, insomuch as to deceive (if possible) even the elect" (Matt. 24: 24); "Of that day and hour [the last] no one knoweth: no, not the angels in heaven, but the Father alone. [And the same must be said of the hour of our death.] Watch ye therefore, because you know not

what hour your Lord will come" (Matt. 24:36, 42). The
Apocalypse, which foretells these events in obscure and sym-
bolic language, remains still a book sealed with seven seals
(Apoc. 5:1).

Later on St. Paul lays stress on these mysterious ways of
Providence. "The foolish things of the world hath God
chosen, that He may confound the wise: and the weak things
of the world and the things that are contemptible, hath God
chosen, and things that are not, that He might bring to
nought the things that are; that no flesh should glory in His
sight" (I Cor. 1:27). It was through the Apostles, some of
whom were chosen from the poor fisherfolk of Galilee, that
Jesus triumphed over paganism and converted the world to
the Gospel, at the very moment when Israel in great part
proved itself unfaithful. God can choose whomsoever He
will without injustice to anyone.

Freely He made choice in former times of the people of
Israel, one among the various nations; from the sons of Adam
He chose Seth in preference to Cain, then Noe and afterwards Sem He preferred to his brothers, then Abraham; He
preferred Isaac to Ismael, and last of all Jacob. And now,
freely He calls the Gentiles and permits Israel in great part
to fall away. Here is one of the most striking examples of the
light and shade in the plan of providence; [2] it may be summed
up in this way. On the one hand *God never commands the
impossible,* but, to use St. Paul's words, *will have all men to
be saved* (I Tim. 2:4). On the other hand, as St. Paul says
again, "What hast thou that thou hast not received?" (I Cor.
4:7.) One person would not be better than another, were he
not loved by God more than the other, since His love for us

---

[2] That is the mystery St. Paul speaks of in the Epistle to the Romans, 9:6.

is the source of all our good.[3] These two truths are as luminous and certain when considered apart as their intimate reconciliation is obscure, for it is no less than the intimate reconciliation of infinite justice, infinite mercy, and supreme liberty. They are reconciled in the Deity, the intimate life of God; but for us this is an inaccessible mystery, as white light would be to someone who had never perceived it, but had seen only the seven colors of the rainbow.

This profound mystery prompts St. Paul's words to the Romans (11: 25-34):

Blindness in part has happened in Israel, until the fulness of the Gentiles shall come in. . . . But as touching the election, they [the children of Israel] are most dear for the sake of their fathers . . . that they also may obtain mercy. . . . O the depths of the riches of the wisdom and of the knowledge of God! How incomprehensible are His judgments, and how unsearchable His ways! For who hath known the mind of the Lord? Or who hath been His counsellor? . . . Of Him, and by Him, and in Him, are all things: to Him be glory forever.

But the only reason why these unfathomable ways of providence are obscure to us is that they are too luminous for the feeble eyes of our minds. Simple and humble souls easily recognize that, for all their obscurity and austerity, these exalted ways are ways of goodness and love. St. Paul points this out when he writes to the Ephesians (3: 18): "I bow my knees to the Father of our Lord Jesus Christ, of whom all paternity in heaven and earth is named . . . that you may be able to comprehend, with all the saints, what is the breadth

[3] Cf. St. Thomas, Ia, q.20, a.3: "Since God's love is the cause of goodness in things, no one thing would be better than another, if God did not will a greater good for it than for the other."

and length and height and depth, to know also the charity
of Christ, which surpasseth all knowledge: that you may
be filled unto all the fulness of God."

Amplitude in the ways of providence consists in their reaching to every part of the universe, to all the souls of men, to every
secret of the heart. In their length they extend through every
period of time, from the creation down to the end of time
and on to the eternal life of the elect. Their depth lies in the
permission of evil, sometimes terrible evil, and in view of
some higher purpose which will be seen clearly only in
heaven. Their height is measured by the sublimity of God's
glory and the glory of the elect, the splendor of God's reign
finally and completely established in the souls of men.

Thus providence is made manifest in the general outlines
of the plan it pursues, but its more exalted ways remain for
us a mystery. Nevertheless, little by little "to the righteous a
light rises in the darkness" (Ps. 111: 4). Every day we can get
a clearer insight into these words of Isaias (9: 2): "The people
that walked in darkness have seen a great light: to them that
dwelt in the region of the shadow of death, light is risen."
And gradually, if we are faithful, we learn more and more
each day to abandon ourselves to that divine providence
which, as the canticle Benedictus says, "directs our steps into
the way of peace" (Luke 1: 79).

Abandonment to the divine will is thus one of the fairest
expressions of hope combined with charity or love of God.
Indeed, it involves the exercise to an eminent degree of all
the theological virtues, because perfect self-abandonment to
providence is pervaded by a deep spirit of faith, of confidence,
and love for God. And when this self-abandonment, far from
inducing us to fold our arms and do nothing as is the case

with the Quietists, is accompanied by a humble, generous
fulfilment of our daily duties, it is one of the surest ways of
arriving at union with God and of preserving it unbroken
even in the severest trials. Once we have done our utmost to
accomplish the will of God day after day, we can and we
must abandon ourselves to Him in all else. In this way we
shall find peace even in tribulation. We shall see how God
takes upon Himself the guidance of souls that, while continuing to perform their daily duties, abandon themselves completely to Him; and the more He seems to blind their eyes,
the saints tell us, the more surely does He lead them, urging
them on in their upward course into a land where, as St.
John of the Cross says, the beaten track has disappeared,
where the Holy Ghost alone can direct them by His divine
inspirations.

CHAPTER XVIII

PROVIDENCE AND PRAYER

When we reflect on the infallibility of God's foreknowledge and the unchangeableness of the decrees of providence, not infrequently a difficulty occurs to the mind. If this infallible providence embraces in its universality every period of time and has foreseen all things, what can be the use of prayer? How is it possible for us to enlighten God by our petitions, to make Him alter His designs, who has said: "I am the Lord and I change not"? (Mal. 3: 6.) Must we conclude that prayer is of no avail, that it comes too late, that whether we pray or not, what is to be will be?

On the contrary, the Gospel tells us: "Ask, and it shall be given you" (Matt. 7: 7). A commonplace with unbelievers and especially with the deists of the eighteenth and nineteenth centuries, this objection in reality arises from an erroneous view as to the primary source of efficacy in prayer and the purpose for which it is intended. The solution of the objection will show the intimate connection between prayer and providence, since (1) it is founded upon providence, (2) it is a practical recognition of providence, and (3) it co-operates in the workings of providence.

Providence, the primary cause of efficacy in prayer

We sometimes speak as though prayer were a force having the primary cause of its efficacy in ourselves, seeking by way of persuasion to bend God's will to our own; and forthwith the mind is confronted with the difficulty just mentioned, that no one can enlighten God or prevail upon Him to alter His designs.

As clearly shown by St. Augustine and St. Thomas (IIa IIae, q. 83, a. 2), the truth is that prayer is not a force having its primary source in ourselves; it is not an effort of the human soul to bring violence to bear upon God and compel Him to alter the dispositions of His providence. If we do occasionally make use of these expressions, it is by way of metaphor, just a human way of expressing ourselves. In reality, *the will of God is absolutely unchangeable,* as unchangeable as it is merciful; yet in this very unchangeableness the efficacy of prayer, rightly said, has its source, even as the source of a stream is to be found on the topmost heights of the mountains.

In point of fact, before ever we ourselves decided to have recourse to prayer, it was willed by God. From all eternity God willed it to be one of the most fruitful factors in our spiritual life, a means of obtaining the graces necessary to reach the goal of our life's journey. To conceive of God as not foreseeing and intending from all eternity the prayers we address to Him in time is just as childish as the notion of a God subjecting His will to ours and so altering His designs.

Prayer is not our invention. Those first members of our race, who, like Abel, addressed their supplications to Him, were inspired to do so by God Himself. It was He who caused it to spring from the hearts of patriarchs and prophets; it is He who continues to inspire it in souls that engage in prayer. He it is who through His Son bids us, "Ask, and it shall be given you: seek and you shall find: knock, and it shall be opened unto you" (Matt. 7:7).

The answer to the objection we have mentioned is in the main quite simple in spite of the mystery of grace it involves. *True prayer,* prayer offered with the requisite conditions, *is infallibly efficacious* because God has decreed that it shall be so, and God cannot revoke what He has once decreed.

It is not only what comes to pass that has been foreseen and intended (or at any rate permitted) by a providential decree, but the manner also in which it comes to pass, the causes that bring about the event, the means by which the end is attained.

Providence, for instance, has determined from all eternity that there shall be no harvest without the sowing of seed, no family life without certain virtues, no social life without authority and obedience, no knowledge without mental effort, no interior life without prayer, no redemption without a Redeemer, no salvation without the application of His merits and, in the adult, a sincere desire to obtain that salvation.

In every order, from the lowest to the highest, God has had in view the production of certain effects and has prepared the necessary causes; with certain ends in view He has prepared the means adequate to attain them. For the material harvest He has prepared a material seed, and for the spiritual harvest a spiritual seed, among which must be included prayer.

Prayer, in the spiritual order, is as much a cause destined from all eternity by providence to produce a certain effect, the attainment of the gifts of God necessary for salvation, as heat and electricity in the physical order are causes that from

all eternity are destined to produce the effects of our everyday experience.

Hence, far from being opposed to the efficacy of prayer,
the unchangeableness of God is the ultimate guaranty of
that efficacy. But more than this, prayer must be the act by
which we continually acknowledge that we are subject to
the divine governance.

Prayer, an act of worship paid to Providence

The lives of all creatures are but a gift of God, yet only
men and angels can be aware of the fact. Plants and animals
receive without knowing that they are receiving. It is the
heavenly Father, the Gospel tells us, who feeds the birds
of the air, but they are unaware of it. Man, too, lives by the
gifts of God and is able to recognize the fact. If the sensual
lose sight of it, that is because in them reason is smothered
by passion. If the proud refuse to acknowledge it, the reason
is that they are spiritually blinded by pride causing them to
judge all things not from the highest of motives but from
what is often sheer mediocrity and paltriness.

If we are of sound mind, we are bound to acknowledge
with St. Paul that *we possess nothing but what we have received*: "What hast thou that thou hast not received?" (I
Cor. 4:7.) Existence, health and strength, the light of intelligence, any sustained moral energy we may have, success
in our undertakings, where the least trifle might mean failure
—all these are the gifts of Providence. And, transcending reason, faith tells us that the grace necessary for salvation and
still more the Holy Ghost whom our Lord promised are pre-
eminently the gift of God, the gift that Jesus refers to in

these words of His to the Samaritan woman, "If thou didst know the gift of God" (John 4: 10).

Thus when we ask of God in the spirit of faith to give health to the sick, to enlighten our minds so that we may see our way clearly in difficulties, to give us His grace to resist temptation and persevere in doing good, this prayer of ours is an act of worship paid to Providence.

Mark how our Lord invites us to render this daily homage to Providence, morning and evening, and frequently in the course of the day. Recall to mind how He, after bidding us, "Ask and it shall be given you" (Matt. 7: 7), goes on to bring out the goodness of Providence in our regard: "What man is there among you, of whom if his son shall ask bread, will he reach him a stone? Or if he shall ask him a fish, will he reach him a serpent? If you then being evil, know how to give good gifts to your children: how much more will your Father who is in heaven give good things to them that ask Him?" (Matt. 7: 7, 9–11.) Our Lord's statement carries its own proof. If there is any kindness in a father's heart, does it not come to him from the heart of God or from His love?

Sometimes indeed God might be said to reverse the parts, when through His prevenient actual graces He urges us to pray, to render due homage to His providence and obtain from it what we stand most in need of. Recall, for instance, how our Lord led on the Samaritan woman to pray: "If thou didst know the gift of God and who He is that saith to thee: Give me to drink: thou perhaps wouldst have asked of Him, and He would have given thee living water . . . springing up into life everlasting" (John 4: 10, 14). The Lord entreats us to come to Him; He waits for us patiently, always eager to listen to us.

The Lord is like a father who has already decided to grant some favor to His children, yet prompts them to ask it of Him. Jesus first willed that the Samaritan woman should be converted and then gradually caused her to burst forth in heartfelt prayer; for sanctifying grace is not like a liquid that is poured into an inert vessel; it is a new life, which the adult will receive only if he desires it.

Sometimes God seems to turn a deaf ear to our prayer, especially when it is not sufficiently free from self-interest, seeking temporal blessings for their own sake rather than as useful for salvation. Then gradually grace invites us to pray better, reminding us of the Gospel words: "Seek ye first the kingdom of God and His justice: and all these things shall be added unto you" (Matt. 6: 33).

Indeed at times it seems that God repulses us as if to see whether we shall persevere in our prayer. He did so to the Canaanite woman. The harshness of His words to her seemed like a refusal: "I was not sent but to the sheep that are lost of the house of Israel . . . It is not good to take the bread of the children and to cast it to the dogs." Inspired undoubtedly by grace that came to her from Christ, the woman replied: "Yea, Lord: for the whelps also eat of the crumbs that fall from the table of their masters." "O woman," Jesus said, "great is thy faith. Be it done to thee as thou wilt" (Matt. 15: 23, 26–28). And her daughter was delivered from the demon that was tormenting her.

When we really pray, it is an acknowledgment, a practical and not merely abstract or theoretical acknowledgment, that we are under the divine governance, which infinitely transcends the governance of men. Whether our prayer takes the form of adoration or supplication or thanksgiving or reparation, it should thus unceasingly render to providence that homage which is its due.

Prayer co-operates in the divine governance

Prayer is not in opposition to the designs of Providence and does not seek to alter them, but actually co-operates in the divine governance, for when we pray we begin to wish in time what God wills for us from all eternity.

When we pray, it may seem that the divine will submits to our own, whereas in reality it is our will that is uplifted and made to harmonize with the divine will. All prayer, so the Fathers say, is an uplifting of the soul to God, whether it be prayer of petition, of adoration, of praise, or of thanksgiving, or the prayer of reparation which makes honorable amends.

One who prays properly, with humility, confidence, and perseverance, asking for the things necessary for salvation, does undoubtedly co-operate in the divine governance. Instead of one, there are now two who desire these things. It is God of course who converted the sinner for whom we have so long been praying; nevertheless we have been God's partners in the conversion. It is God who gave to the soul in tribulation that light and strength for which we have so long besought Him; yet from all eternity He decided to produce this salutary effect only with our co-operation and as the result of our intercession.

The consequences of this principle are numerous. First, the more prayer is in *conformity with the divine intentions,* the more closely does it co-operate in the divine governance. That there may be ever more of this conformity in our prayer, let us every day say the Our Father slowly and with great attention; let us meditate upon it, with love accompanying our faith. This loving meditation will become contemplation, which will ensure for us the hallowing and glorifying of God's name both in ourselves and in those about us, the coming of His kingdom and the fulfilment of His will here on earth as in heaven. It will obtain for us also the forgiveness of our sins and deliverance from evil, as well as our sanctification and salvation.

From this it follows that our prayer will be the purer and more efficacious when we *pray in Christ's* name and offer to God, in compensation for the imperfections of our own love and adoration, those acts of love and adoration that spring from His holy soul.

A Christian who says the Our Father day by day with gradually increasing fervor, who says it from the bottom of his heart, for others as well as for himself, undoubtedly co-operates very much in the divine governance. He co-operates far more than the scientists who have discovered the laws governing the stars in their courses or the great physicians who have found cures for some terrible diseases. The prayer of St. Francis, St. Dominic, or, to come nearer to our own times, St. Teresa of the Child Jesus, had an influence certainly not less powerful than that of a Newton or a Pasteur. One who really prays as the saints have prayed, co-operates in the saving not only of bodies but of souls. Every soul, through its higher faculties, opens upon the infinite, and is, as it were, a universe gravitating toward God.

Close attention to these intimate relations between prayer and providence will show that prayer is undoubtedly a more potent force than either wealth or science. No doubt science accomplishes marvelous things; but it is acquired by human means, and its effects are confined within human limits. Prayer, indeed, is a supernatural energy with an efficacy coming from God and the infinite merits of Christ, and from actual grace that leads us on to pray. It is a spiritual energy more potent than all the forces of nature together. It can obtain for us what God alone can bestow, the grace of contrition and of perfect charity, the grace also of eternal life, the very end and purpose of the divine governance, the final manifestation of its goodness.

At a time when so many perils threaten the whole world, we need more to reflect on the necessity and sublimity of true prayer, especially when it is united with the prayer of our Lord and of our Lady. The present widespread disorder must by contrast stimulate us constantly to reflect that we are subject not only to the often unreasoning, imprudent government of men, but also to God's infinitely wise governance. God never permits evil except in view of some greater good. He wills that we co-operate in this good by a prayer that becomes daily more sincere, more humble, more profound, more confident, more persevering, by a prayer united with action, in order that each succeeding day shall see more perfectly realized in us and in those about us that petition of the Our Father: "Thy will be done on earth as it is in heaven." At a time when Bolshevism is putting forth every effort against God, it behooves us to repeat it again and again with ever deepening sincerity, in action as well as in word, so that as time goes on God's reign may supersede the reign of greed and pride. Thus in a concrete, practical way we shall at once see that God permits these present evils only because He has some higher purpose in view, which it will be granted us to see, if not in this world, at any rate after our death.

PART IV

SELF-ABANDONMENT TO PROVIDENCE

CHAPTER XIX

Why and in What Matters We Should Abandon Ourselves to Providence

The doctrine of self-abandonment to divine providence is a doctrine obviously founded on the Gospel, but it has been falsely construed by the Quietists, who gave themselves up to a spiritual sloth, more or less renounced the struggle necessary for the attainment of perfection, and seriously depreciated the value and necessity of hope or confidence in God, of which true self-abandonment is a higher form.

But it is possible also to depart from the Gospel teaching on this point in a sense entirely opposite to that of the Quietists with their idle repose, by going to the other extreme of a useless disquiet and agitation.

Here as elsewhere the truth is the culminating point lying between and transcending these two extreme conflicting errors. It behooves us therefore to determine exactly the meaning and import of the true doctrine of self-abandonment to the will of God if we are to be saved from these sophistries, which have no more than a false appearance of Christian perfection.

We shall first see why it is we should practice this self-abandonment to Providence, and then in what matters. After that we shall see what form it should take and what is the attitude of Providence toward those who abandon themselves completely to it.

We shall get our inspiration from the teaching of St. Francis de Sales,[1] Bossuet,[2] Père Piny, O.P.,[3] and Père de Caussade, S.J.[4]

Why we should abandon ourselves to divine providence

The answer of every Christian will be that the reason lies in *the wisdom and goodness of Providence.* This is very true; nevertheless, if we are to have a proper understanding of the subject, if we are to avoid the error of the Quietists in renouncing more or less the virtue of hope and the struggle necessary for salvation, if we are to avoid also the other extreme of disquiet, precipitation, and a feverish, fruitless agitation, it is expedient for us to lay down four principles already somewhat accessible to natural reason and clearly set forth in revelation as found in Scripture. These principles underlying the true doctrine of self-abandonment, also bring out the motive inspiring it.

The first of these principles is that everything which comes to pass has been *foreseen by God from all eternity,* and has been willed or at least permitted by Him.

---

[1] *Treatise on the Love of God,* tr. by Mackey, O.S.B., Bk. VIII, chap. 3: "How we are to conform ourselves to the divine will which is called the signified will." Again, chaps. 4–7 and chap. 14: "A short method to know God's will"; Bk. IX, chap. 1: "Of the union of our will with that divine will which is called the will of good pleasure." Again, chaps. 2–6 and chap. 15. See also *Spiritual Conferences,* tr. by Mackey, O.S.B., Conference II, "On Confidence," and Conference XV, "On the Will of God."

[2] *Discours sur l'acte d'abandon à Dieu;* also *Etats d'oraison,* Bk. VIII, chap. 9.

[3] *Le plus parfait, ou Des voies intérieures la plus glorifiante pour Dieu et la plus sanctifiante pour l'âme,* published in 1683, new edition with notes by Père Noble, O.P. The author shows how this interior way involves the practice of the liveliest faith, the most confident hope, and the purest love; he shows, too, that it is a way which is suited to every interior soul.

[4] *Abandonment to divine providence,* new edition, including the letters of the author and revised with the addition of appendices by Père H. Ramière, 2 vols. Abridged ed., 1 vol. English translation by E. J. Strickland.

Nothing comes to pass either in the material or in the spiritual world, but God has foreseen it from all eternity; because with Him there is no passing from ignorance to knowledge as with us, and He has nothing to learn from events as they occur. Not only has God foreseen everything that is happening now or will happen in the future, but whatever reality and goodness there is in these things He has willed; and whatever evil or moral disorder is in them, He has merely permitted. Holy Scripture is explicit on this point, and, as the councils have declared, no room is left for doubt in the matter.

The second principle is that nothing can be willed or permitted by God that does not contribute to *the end He purposed in creating,* which is the manifestation of His goodness and infinite perfections, and the glory of the God-man Jesus Christ, His only Son. As St. Paul says (I Cor. 2:23), "All are yours. And you are Christ's. And Christ is God's."

In addition to these two principles, there is a third, which St. Paul states thus (Rom. 8:28): "We know that to them that love God all things work together unto good: to such as, according to His purpose, are called to be saints" and persevere in His love. God sees to it that *everything contributes to their spiritual welfare,* not only the grace He bestows on them, not only those natural qualities He endows them with, but sickness too, and contradictions and reverses; as St. Augustine tells us, even their very sins, which God only permits in order to lead them on to a truer humility and thereby to a purer love. It was thus He permitted the threefold denial of St. Peter, to make the great Apostle more humble, more mistrustful of self, and by this very means become stronger and trust more in the divine mercy.

These first three principles may therefore be summed up in this way: Nothing comes to pass but God has foreseen it, willed it or at least permitted it. He wills nothing, permits nothing, unless for the manifestation of His goodness and infinite perfections, for the glory of His Son, and the welfare of those that love Him. In view of these three principles, it is evident that our trust in Providence cannot be too childlike, too steadfast. Indeed, we may go further and say that this trust in Providence should be blind as is our faith, the object of which is those mysteries that are non-evident and unseen (*fides est de non visis*) for we are certain beforehand that Providence is directing all things infallibly to a good purpose, and we are more convinced of the rectitude of His designs than we are of the best of our own intentions. Therefore, in abandoning ourselves to God, all we have to fear is that our submission will not be wholehearted enough.[5]

In view of Quietism, however, this last sentence obliges us to lay down a fourth principle no less certain than the principles that have preceded. The principle is, that obviously self-abandonment does not dispense us from *doing everything in our power* to fulfil God's will as made known in the commandments and counsels, and in the events of life; but so long as we have the sincere desire to carry out His will thus made known from day to day, we can and indeed we must abandon ourselves for the rest to the divine will of good pleasure, no matter how mysterious it may be, and thus avoid a useless disquiet and mere agitation.[6]

[5] By the gift of fear, hope is prevented from turning to presumption, as magnanimity is prevented by humility from degenerating into pride. Cf. St. Thomas, IIaIIae, q.19, a.9, 10; q.160, a.2; q.161, a.1; q.129, a.3 ad 4um. They are complementary virtues which, by their interconnection, balance and strengthen one another, and thus they increase together.

[6] Cf. St. Francis de Sales, *The Love of God*, Bk. VIII, chap. 5: "Of the con-

This fourth principle is expressed in equivalent terms by the Council of Trent (Sess. VI, cap. 13), when it declares that we must all have firm hope in God's assistance and put our trust in Him, being careful at the same time to keep His commandments. As the well-known proverb has it: "Do what you ought, come what may."

All theologians explain what is meant by *the divine will as expressed:* expressed, that is, in the commandments, in the spirit underlying the counsels, and in the events of life.[7] They add that, while conforming ourselves to His expressed will,[8] we must abandon ourselves to His divine will of good pleasure, however mysterious it may be, for we are certain beforehand that in its holiness it wills nothing, permits nothing, unless for a good purpose.

We must take special note here of these words in the Gospel of St. Luke (16: 10): "He that is faithful in that which is least is faithful also in that which is greater." If every day

---

formity of our will with that will of God which is made known to us by His commandments"; Bk. IX, chap. 1: "Of the union of our will with that divine will which is called the will of good pleasure." So also chaps. 2–6.

Bossuet, *Etats d'oraison,* Bk. VIII, chap. 9, says: "Christian indifference being out of the question where the expressed will of God is concerned, we must restrict it, as St. Francis de Sales does, to certain events controlled by His will of good pleasure, whose sovereign commands determine the daily occurrences in the course of life."

Dom Vital Lehodey, *Holy Abandonment,* tr. by Luddy, O. Cist., p. 123, says: "In short, the good pleasure of God is the domain of abandonment, His expressed will, of obedience."

[7] Cf. St. Thomas, Ia, q. 19, a. 11, 12: "On the will of expression in God." Certain events, such as the death of another, have great significance. As St. Thomas points out (*ibid.*), sins also are permitted by God—personal sins, like the threefold denial in St. Peter's life, which God permitted so as to make him more humble; sins also that others commit against us, acts of injustice which God permits that we may derive spiritual profit from them, as He permitted the persecutions against the Church.

[8] Cf. St. Thomas, IaIIae, q. 19, a. 10: "Whether it is necessary for the human will, in order to be good, to be conformed to the divine will, as regards the things willed?"

we do what we can to be faithful to God in the ordinary routine of life, we may be confident that He will give us grace to remain faithful in whatever extremity we may find ourselves through His permission; and if we have to suffer for Him, He will give us the grace to die a heroic death rather than be ashamed of Him and betray Him.

These are the principles underlying the doctrine of trusting self-abandonment. Accepted as they are by all theologians, they express what is of Christian faith in this matter. The golden mean is thus above and between the two errors mentioned at the beginning of this section. By constant fidelity to duty, we avoid the false and idle repose of the Quietist, and on the other hand by a trustful self-abandonment we are saved from a useless disquiet and a fruitless agitation. Self-abandonment would be sloth did it not presuppose this daily fidelity, which indeed is a sort of springboard from which we may safely launch ourselves into the unknown. Daily fidelity to the divine will as expressed gives us a sort of right to abandon ourselves completely to the divine will of good pleasure as yet not made known to us.

A faithful soul will often recall to mind these words of our Lord: "My meat is to do the will of Him that sent me" (John 4:34). The soul finds its constant nourishment in the divine will as expressed, abandoning itself to *the divine will as yet not made known,* much as a swimmer supports himself on the passing wave and surrenders himself to the oncoming wave, to that ocean that might engulf him but that actually sustains him. So the soul must strike out toward the open sea, into the infinite ocean of being, says St. John Damascence, borne up by the divine will as made known there and then and abandoning itself to that divine will upon which all successive moments of the future depend. The future is with God, future events are in His hands. If the merchants to whom Joseph was sold by his brethren had passed by one hour sooner, he would not have gone into Egypt, and the whole course of his life would have been changed. Our lives also are dependent on events controlled by God. Daily fidelity and trusting self-abandonment thus give the spiritual life its balance, its stability and harmony. In this way we live our lives in almost continuous recollection, in an ever-increasing self-abnegation, and these are the conditions normally required for contemplation and union with God. This, then, is the reason why our life should be one of self-abandonment to the divine will as yet unknown to us and at the same time supported every moment by that will as already made known to us.

In this union of fidelity and self-abandonment we have some idea of the way in which asceticism, insisting on fidelity or conformity to the divine will, should be united with mysticism, which emphasizes self-abandonment.

In what matters we should abandon ourselves to divine Providence

Once we have complied with the principles just laid down, when we have done all that the law of God and Christian prudence demand, our self-abandonment should then embrace everything. What does this involve? In the first place, *our whole future,* what our circumstances will be tomorrow, in twenty years and more. We must also abandon ourselves to God in all that concerns *the present,* in the midst of the difficulties we may be experiencing right now; even *our past* life, our past actions with all their consequences should be abandoned to the divine mercy.

We must likewise abandon ourselves to God in *all that affects the body,* in health and sickness, as well as in all that affects *the soul,* whether it be joy or tribulation, of long or brief duration. We must abandon ourselves to God in all that concerns the good will or malice of men.[9] Says St. Paul:[10]

If God be for us, who is against us? He that spared not His own Son, but delivered Him up for us all, how hath He not also, with Him, given us all things? . . . Who then shall separate us from the love of Christ? Shall tribulations? Or distress? Or famine? Or nakedness? Or danger? Or persecutions? Or the sword? . . . I am sure that neither death, nor life, nor angels, nor principalities, nor powers, nor things to come, nor might, nor height, nor depth, nor any other creature, shall be able to separate us from the love of God which is in Christ Jesus our Lord.

Could there be a more perfect self-abandonment in the spirit of faith, hope, and love? This is an abandonment embracing all the vicissitudes of this world, all the upheavals that may convulse it, embracing life and death, the hour of death, and the circumstances, peaceful or violent, in which we breathe forth our last sigh.

The same thought has been expressed in the psalms: "Fear the Lord . . . for there is no want to them that fear Him. The rich have wanted, and have suffered hunger: but they that seek the Lord shall not be deprived of any good (Ps. 33:10); "O how great is the multitude of Thy sweetness, O Lord, which Thou hast hidden for them that fear Thee!

[9] Père de Caussade, *L'abandon,* Vol. II, App. I, p. 279.
[10] Rom. 8: 31–39.

Which Thou hast wrought for them that hope in Thee. . . .
Thou shalt hide them in the secret of Thy face from the disturbance of men. Thou shalt protect them in Thy tabernacle
from the contradiction of tongues" (Ps. 30: 20–21).

And again Job: "I have not sinned: and my eye abideth in
bitterness. Deliver me, O Lord, and set me beside Thee and
let any man's hand fight against me" (17: 3).

Thus, as recorded in the Book of Daniel (13: 42), the
daughter of Helcias, the worthy Susanna, abandoned herself to God under the vile calumnies of the two ancients.
"O eternal God," she cries, "who knowest hidden things, who
knowest all things before they come to pass, Thou knowest
that they have borne false witness against me: and behold
I must die, whereas I have done none of these things which
these men have maliciously forged against me." It is recorded
in the prophecy how the Lord heard the prayer of this noble
woman: "And when she was led to be put to death, the Lord
raised up the holy spirit of a young boy whose name was
Daniel. And he cried out with a loud voice: I am clear of
the blood of this woman. Then all the people, turning themselves toward him, said: What meaneth this word that thou
hast spoken?" Inspired by God, the young Daniel then
showed how her two accusers had borne false witness. Separating them one from the other, he questioned them apart in
the presence of the people, and thus all unintentionally they
showed by their contradictory statements that they had lied.

What is our practical conclusion to be? It is this, that in
doing our utmost to carry out our daily duties we must for
the rest abandon ourselves to divine providence, and that
with the most childlike confidence. And if we are really striv-

ing to be faithful in little things, in the practice of humility, gentleness, and patience, in the daily routine of our lives, God on His part will give us grace to be faithful in greater and more difficult things, should He perchance ask them of us; then, in those exceptional circumstances, He will give to those that seek Him exceptional graces.

In psalm 54: 23 we are told: "Cast thy care upon the Lord, and He shall sustain thee: He shall not suffer the just to waver forever. . . . But I will trust Thee, O Lord."

Imbued with these same sentiments, St. Paul writes to the Philippians (4: 4): "Rejoice in the Lord always: again, I say, rejoice. Let your modesty be known to all men. The Lord is nigh. Be nothing solicitous: but in everything, by prayer and supplication, with thanksgiving, let your petitions be made known to God. And the peace of God, which surpasseth all understanding, keep your hearts and minds in Christ Jesus."

Again, in order to exhort us to have confidence, St. Peter tells us in his First Epistle (5: 5):

Be ye humbled therefore under the mighty hand of God, that He may exalt you in the time of visitation: casting all your care upon Him, for He hath care of you. Be sober and watch: because your adversary the devil, as a roaring lion, goeth about seeking whom he may devour. Whom resist ye, strong in faith: knowing that the same affliction befalls your brethren who are in the world. But the God of all grace, who hath called us into His eternal glory in Christ Jesus, after you have suffered a little, will Himself perfect you and confirm you and establish you.

"Blessed are they that trust in Him" (Ps. 2: 13). "They that hope in the Lord," says Isaias, "shall renew their strength. . . . They shall walk and not faint" (40: 31).

We have a perfect model of this abandonment to divine providence in St. Joseph, in the many difficulties that beset him at the moment of our Lord's birth at Bethlehem, and again when he heard the mournful prophecy of the aged Simeon, and during all the time that elapsed from the flight away from Herod into Egypt until the return to Nazareth.

Following his example, let us live our lives in that same spirit, fulfilling our daily duties, and the grace of God will never be wanting. By His grace we shall be equal to anything He asks of us, no matter how difficult it may sometimes be.

CHAPTER XX

The Manner in Which We Must Abandon Ourselves to Providence

We have said that it is because of the wisdom and goodness of providence that we should put our trust in it and abandon ourselves completely to it; and further, that, provided we fulfil our daily duties, this self-surrender should then embrace everything, all that concerns both soul and body, remembering that if we are faithful in small things grace will be given us to be faithful in what is greater.

Now let us see what forms this confidence and self-abandonment must take according to the nature of events as these do or do not depend on the will of man; let us see what spirit should animate it, what virtues should inspire it.

On the various ways of abandoning oneself to providence according to the nature of the event [1]

In order to have a proper understanding of the doctrine of holy indifference, it is well to point out, as spiritual writers frequently do,[2] that our self-abandonment must be in dif-

---

[1] Cf. St. Francis de Sales, *The Love of God,* Bk. VIII, chap. 5; Bk. IX, chaps. 1–7.

[2] Cf. St. Francis de Sales, *loc. cit.,* and *Spiritual Conferences,* II, XV; De Caussade, *Abandon,* II, 279 (App. 2). Cf. also Dom Vital Lehodey, *Holy Abandonment,* Part III: "On abandonment in the natural goods of the body (health and sickness)," pp. 166 ff.; "on abandonment of those of the mind (the unequal distribution of these gifts)," pp. 191 ff.; "on abandonment of one's own good estimation in others (humiliations and persecutions)," pp. 207 ff.; "on abandonment in the

ferent ways in so far as events independent of the human will call for a type of self-abandonment different from that required by the injustice done to us by men, or our personal sins and their consequences.

Where it concerns *events independent of the human will* (such as accidents impossible to foresee, incurable diseases), our self-abandonment cannot be too absolute. Resistance here would be useless and would only serve to make us more unhappy; whereas, by accepting them in the spirit of faith, confidence and love, these unavoidable sufferings will become very meritorious.[3] In times of affliction, as often as we say, "Thy will be done," we acquire new merit, and thus what is a real trial becomes a means of great sanctification. Moreover, even in trials that may come upon us, but which perhaps will never materialize, self-abandonment is still of great profit. In preparing to sacrifice his son with perfect self-abandonment, Abraham gained much merit, even though in the event God ceased to demand it of him. By the practice of self-abandonment trials present and to come thus become means of sanctification, the more so as it is inspired by a more intense love for God.

Where it concerns *sufferings brought upon us through the injustice of men,* their ill will, their unfairness in their deal-

spiritual varieties of the common way (failures and faults, trials and consolations)," pp. 244 ff.; "abandonment in the spiritual varieties of the mystical way," pp. 244 ff.

[3] There are instances where a life has been completely changed by trials, as may be seen from the biography of Abbé Girard, entitled, *Vingt-deux ans de martyr.* After receiving the diaconate, this saintly priest contracted tuberculosis of the bones and for twenty-two years was confined to his bed in the cruelest suffering, which he offered up each day for the priests of his generation. Here was one who to his great grief was never able to celebrate mass, and yet he was daily united to our Lord's sacrifice perpetuated on the altar. Far from breaking up his vocation, sickness transfigured it.

ings with us, their calumnies, what must our attitude be?

St. Thomas,[4] speaking of the injuries and undeserved re-proaches, the insults and slanders that affect only our person, declares we must be ready to bear them with patience in compliance with our Lord's words: "If one strike thee on thy right cheek, turn to him also the other" (Matt. 5: 39). But, he continues, there are occasions when some answer is called for, either for the good of the person who injures us, to put a stop to his insolence, or to avoid the scandal such slanders and calumnies may cause. If we do feel bound to retaliate and offer some sort of resistance, let us put ourselves unreservedly in God's hands for the success of the steps we take. In other words, we must deplore and reprove these acts of injustice not because they are wounding to our self-love and pride, but because they are an offense against God, en-dangering the salvation of the guilty parties and of those who may be led astray by them.

So far as we are concerned, we should see in the injustice men do to us the action of divine justice permitting this evil in order to give us an opportunity of expiating other and very real failings, failings with which no one reproaches us. It is well also to see in this sort of trial the action of divine mercy, which would make of it a means to detach us from creatures, to rid us of our inordinate affections, our pride and lukewarmness, and thus oblige us to have immediate recourse to a fervent prayer of supplication. Spiritually these acts of injustice are like the surgeon's knife, very painful at times but a great corrective. The suffering they cause must bring home to us the value of true justice; not only must it lead us

[4] Cf. St. Thomas, IIaIIae, q.72, a.3; q.73, a.3 ad 3um.

to be just in our dealings with our neighbor, but it must give birth in us to the beatitude of those who, as the Gospel says, hunger and thirst after justice and who shall indeed have their fill.

And so, instead of upsetting and embittering us, men's contempt for us may have a very salutary effect, by impressing us with the utter vanity of all human glory and with the sublimity of the glory of God as the saints have understood it. It is the way leading to that true humility which causes us to accept contempt and to love to be treated as objects worthy of contempt.[5]

Lastly, what is to be our attitude regarding all those vexations of every kind that are the result not of the injustice of others, but of our own failings, our own indiscretions and weaknesses?

In these *failings of ours* and their consequences, we must distinguish the element of disorder and guilt from the salutary humiliations resulting from them. Whatever our self-love may have to say, we can never regret too keenly any inordinateness there may have been in our actions, on account of the wrong it has done to God, and the harm it has done to our own soul and, as an almost invariable consequence, to the soul of our neighbor. As for the *salutary humiliation* resulting from it, we must accept it with complete self-abandonment according to the words of the psalm (118: 71-77): "It is good for me that Thou hast humbled me: that I may learn Thy justifications. The law of my mouth is good to me, above thousands of gold and silver. . . . I know, O Lord, that Thy judgments are equity: and in Thy truth

[5] Cf. St. Thomas, "On the degrees of humility," IIa IIae, q. 161, a. 6.

Thou has humbled me. O let Thy mercy be for my comfort.
. . . Let Thy tender mercies come unto me, and I shall live:
for Thy law is my meditation."

These humiliations resulting from our personal failings are
the true remedy for that exaggerated estimate of ourselves to
which we so often cling in spite of the disapproval and
contempt others show for us. It even happens that pride
hardens us to humiliations from a purely external source, and
causes us to offer to ourselves the incense others refuse us.
This is one of the most subtle and dangerous forms of self-
love and pride, and, to correct it, the divine mercy makes use
of those humiliations which are the result of our own failings; in its loving kindness it makes those very failings contribute to our progress. Hence, while laboring to correct
ourselves, we should accept these humiliations with perfect
self-abandonment. "It is good for me that Thou hast humbled me, O Lord." It is the way leading to a practical realization of those profound words of the *Imitation,* so fruitful to
one who has really understood them: "Love to be unknown
and accounted as nought." By this doctrine we must live
according as the occurrences do or do not depend on ourselves.

The spirit that should animate our self-abandonment
to Providence

Is it a spirit that depreciates our hope of salvation on the
plea of advanced perfection, as the Quietists claimed? Quite
the contrary: it must be a spirit of deep faith, confidence,
and love.

The will of God, as expressed by His commandments, is
that we should hope in Him and labor confidently in the

work of our salvation in the face of every obstacle. This expressed will of God pertains to the domain of obedience, not of self-abandonment. This latter concerns the will of His good pleasure on which depends our still uncertain future, the daily occurrences in the course of our life, such as health and sickness, success and misfortune.[6]

To sacrifice our salvation, our eternal happiness, on the plea of perfection, would be absolutely contrary to that natural inclination for happiness which, with our nature, we have from God. It would be contrary to Christian hope, not only to that possessed by the common run of the faithful, but also to that of the saints, who in the severest trials have hoped on "against all human hope," to use St. Paul's phrase (Rom. 4: 18), even when all seemed lost. Nay, to sacrifice our eternal beatitude in this way would be contrary to charity itself, by which indeed we love God for His own sake and desire to possess Him that we may eternally proclaim His glory.

The natural inclination we have from God which leads us to desire happiness is not a disorder, for it already contains the initial tendency to love God the sovereign good more than ourselves. As St. Thomas has pointed out,[7] in our own organism the hand naturally tends to prefer the interests of the body to its own and to sacrifice itself, if necessary, for the safety of the body. And our Lord Himself says that the hen instinctively gathers her little ones under her wing, ready to sacrifice herself if necessary to save them from the hawk, the reason being that, all unconsciously, she prefers the welfare of the species to her own. In a higher form this same natural

[6] Cf. St. Francis de Sales, *The Love of God*, Bk. IX, chap. 5, and Bossuet, *Etats d'oraison*, Bk. VIII, chap. 9.

[7] Cf. St. Thomas, Ia, q. 60, a. 5.

tendency is to be found in man: in loving what is highest in himself He loves his Creator even more; to cease to desire our perfection and salvation would be to turn our back upon God.[8] There can be no question, therefore, of our sacrificing the desire for salvation and eternal happiness, as the Quietists imagined, on the plea of advanced perfection.

Far from it: self-abandonment involves the exercise in an eminent degree of the three theological virtues, faith, hope, and charity, as it were fused into one.[9]

It is nevertheless true to say that God purifies our desire from the self-love with which it may be tinged by leaving us in some uncertainty about it and so inducing us to love Him more exclusively for His own sake.[10]

We should abandon ourselves to God in *the spirit of faith*, believing with St. Paul (Rom. 8: 28) that "all things work together unto good" in the lives of those who love God and persevere in His love. Such an act of faith was that made by holy Job who, when deprived of his wealth and his children, remained submissive to God, saying: "The Lord gave, the Lord hath taken away. . . . Blessed be the name of the Lord" (Job 1: 21).

In the same spirit Abraham prepared to sacrifice his son in obedience to God's command, abandoning himself in the deepest faith to the divine will of good pleasure in all that concerned the future of his race. We are reminded of this by St. Paul when he tells us in the Epistle to the Hebrews

---

[8] That such is the teaching of St. Thomas, we have shown at length elsewhere. Cf. *L'Amour de Dieu et la Croix de Jésus*, I, 77–150.

[9] Certain authors have spoken of the virtue of self-abandonment. In reality the act of self-abandonment has its source not in a special virtue, but in the three theological virtues combined with the gift of piety.

[10] Cf. Piny, *Le plus parfait*, chap. 7.

(11:17): "By faith Abraham, when he was tried, offered Isaac: and he that had received the promises offered up his only begotten son (to whom it was said: in Isaac shall thy seed be called), accounting that God is able to raise up even from the dead." Far less exacting are the trials we have to endure, though on account of our weakness they sometimes seem to weigh heavily upon us.

At any rate, let us believe with the saints that whatever the Lord does He does well, when He sends us humiliations and spiritual dryness as when He heaps honors and consolations upon us. As Father Piny remarks,[11] nowhere is there a deeper or more lively faith than in the conviction that God arranges everything for our welfare, even when He appears to destroy us and overthrow our most cherished plans, when He allows us to be calumniated, to suffer permanent ill-health, and other afflictions still more painful.[12] This is great faith indeed, for it is to believe the apparently incredible: that God will raise us up by casting us down; and it is to believe this in a practical and living way, not merely an abstract and theoretical way. We find verified in our lives these words of the Gospel: "Every one that exalteth himself [like the Pharisee] shall be humbled: and he that humbleth himself [like the publican] shall be exalted" (Luke 18:14). Also we find verified these words of the Magnificat: "He hath put down the mighty from their seat and hath exalted the humble. He hath filled the hungry with good things: and the rich He hath sent empty away" (Luke 1:52). Every one of us must by hu-

---

[11] *Ibid.*

[12] In the lives of many saints we see how the appalling calumnies they had to endure became, by God's permission, the occasion of a marvelous increase in their love for Him.

mility be numbered among these little ones, among those that hunger for divine truth which is the true bread of the soul.

While fulfilling our daily duties, then, we must abandon ourselves to almighty God in a spirit of deep faith, which must also be accompanied by an absolutely childlike confidence in His fatherly kindness. *Confidence* (*fiducia* or *confidentia*), says St. Thomas,[13] is a steadfast or intensified hope arising from a deep faith in the goodness of God, who, according to His promises, is ever at hand to help us—*Deus auxilians.*[14]

As the psalms declare: "Blessed are they that trust in the Lord" (2: 12); "They that trust in the Lord shall be as Mount Sion: he shall not be moved forever that dwelleth in Jerusalem" (124: 1); "Preserve me, O Lord, for I have put my trust in Thee" (15: 1); "In Thee, O Lord, have I hoped, let me not be confounded" (30: 1).

St. Paul (Rom. 4: 18) reminds us how Abraham, in spite of his advanced years, believed in the divine promise that he would be the father of many nations, and adds: "Against hope, he believed in hope. . . . In the promise also of God he staggered not by distrust: but was strengthened in faith, giving glory to God: most fully knowing that whatsoever He has promised, He is able to perform."

We, too, while fulfilling our daily duties, should look to our Lord for the realization of these words of His: "My sheep hear My voice: and I know them, and they follow Me . . . and no man shall pluck them out of My hand" (John

---

[13] Cf. St. Thomas, IIa IIae, q. 129, a. 6.

[14] We are especially reminded of this, the formal motive of hope, in the name of Jesus, which means Savior, and in various titles given to the Blessed Virgin: Help of Christians, Refuge of Sinners, Our Lady of Perpetual Help.

10: 27). As Father Piny notes,[15] to do one's duty in all earnestness and then to resign oneself with entire confidence into our Lord's hands is the true mark of a member of His flock. What better way can there be of hearkening to the voice of the good Shepherd than by constantly acquiescing in all that He demands of us, lovingly beseeching Him to have pity on us, throwing ourselves confidently into the arms of His mercy with all our failings and regrets? By so doing, we are at the same time placing in His hands all our fears for both the past and the future. This holy self-abandonment is not at all opposed to hope, but is childlike confidence in its holiest form united with a love becoming ever more and more purified.

Love in its purest form, in fact, depends for its support upon the will of God, after the example of our Lord who said: "My meat is to do the will of Him that sent Me, that I may perfect His work" (John 4: 34); "Because I came down from heaven, not to do My own will, but the will of Him that sent Me" (John 5: 30). Thus no more perfect or nobler or purer way of loving God can be found than to make the divine will our own, fulfilling God's will as expressed to us and then abandoning ourselves entirely to His good pleasure. For souls that follow this road, God is everything: eventually, they can say in very truth: "My God and my all." God is their center; they find no peace but in Him, by submitting all their aspirations to His good pleasure and accepting tranquilly all that He does. At times of greatest difficulty St. Catherine of Siena would remember the Master's words to her: "Think of Me and I will think of thee."

Rare indeed are the souls that attain to such perfection as

---

[15] Cf. Piny, *Le plus parfait,* chap. 8.

this. And yet it is the goal at which we all must aim. St. Francis de Sales says:

Our Lord loves with a most tender love those who are so happy as to abandon themselves wholly to His fatherly care, letting themselves be governed by His divine providence, without any idle speculations as to whether the workings of this providence will be useful to them, to their profit, or painful to their loss, and this because they are well assured that nothing can be sent, nothing permitted by this paternal and most loving heart, which will not be a source of good and profit to them. All that is required is that they should place all their confidence in Him.[16] . . . When, in fulfilling our daily duties, we abandon everything, our Lord takes care of everything and orders everything. . . . The soul has nothing else to do but to rest in the arms of our Lord like a child on its mother's breast. When she puts it down to walk, it walks until she takes it up again, and when she wishes to carry it, she is allowed to do so. It neither knows nor thinks where it is going, but allows itself to be carried or led wherever its mother pleases. So this soul lets itself be carried when it lovingly accepts God's good pleasure in all things that happen, and walks when it carefully effects all that the known (expressed) will of God demands.[17]

Then it can truly say with our Lord: "My meat is to do the will of Him that sent Me" (John 4: 34). Therein it finds its peace, which even now is in some sort the beginning of eternal life within us—*inchoatio vitae aeternae.*

[16] Read, for instance, the life of Blessed Cottolengo. There it will be seen what a tender love God had for this soul so admirably resigned to providence, and how almighty God blessed his *piccola casa* in Turin, where assistance is given daily to ten thousand poor. Here is one of the most striking instances of God's goodness to us. If the stars in the heavens chant the glories of God, much more do works of mercy such as this.

[17] St. Francis de Sales, *Spiritual Conferences,* tr. by Mackey, O.S.B., Conference II, p. 25. The interior conviction expressed in this passage, as proceeding from the theological virtues and the gifts of the Holy Ghost, far surpasses any theological speculation.

CHAPTER XXI

Providence and the Duty of the Present Moment

"All whatsoever you do in word or in work, all things do ye in the name of the Lord Jesus Christ, giving thanks to God and the Father by Him" (Col. 3: 17). To understand more clearly how we should live from day to day trusting in God, and in a spirit of self-abandonment, it is well to pay close attention to the duty of the present moment and the graces offered us to fulfil it.

We will speak first of the duty which presents itself at every moment, as the saints have understood it, and then we will clarify their attitude from the teaching of Scripture and theology, which is applicable to us all.

The duty of the present moment as the saints understood it

The duty at any given moment conveys, frequently under a modest exterior, the expression of God's will regarding ourselves and our individual lives. Thus it was our Lady lived her life of union with God, by accomplishing His will in the daily routine of duties of her simple life, a life outwardly commonplace like that of any other person in her lowly rank. Thus, too, did the saints live, doing the will of God as it was revealed to them from one moment to the other, without allowing themselves to be upset by unforeseen reverses. Their secret consisted in submitting constantly to the divine action in the shaping of their lives. In that action they recognized all they had to do and suffer, duties to be accomplished, crosses to be borne. They were persuaded that what is happening at the moment is a sign that either God wills or permits it for the good of those seeking Him. Even the evil they experienced taught them something: by taxing their patience it showed them by contrast what must be done to avoid sin and its disastrous consequences. Thus the saints see in the sequence of events a sort of providential schooling. Moreover, they are convinced that behind the succession of external happenings runs a parallel series of actual graces which are continually being offered to enable us to draw great spiritual profit from these events, whether painful or pleasing. The sequence of events, if looked at in the right perspective, is an instructive course on the things of God, a sort of extension of revelation or application of the Gospel truths continuing down to the end of time.

A distinction is made in almost every sphere between theoretical, abstract teaching and practical or applied teaching. The same holds good in the spiritual order, where, in His own way, almighty God imparts these two kinds of instruction, the one in the Gospel and the other in the course of our lives.

This important truth about life is often completely disregarded. As a rule, no sooner do we meet with contradictions and reverses than we utter nothing but complaints and murmurings. We find that this illness has come upon us just when there is so much to be done; that something indispensable is denied us; that someone is depriving us of the necessary means, or placing insurmountable obstacles in our way as regards the good we must accomplish or the apostolate to which we have devoted ourselves.

In these or even more painful circumstances the saints would confess that fundamentally the one thing necessary is *to do the will of God from day to day.* God never commands the impossible. Each moment has a duty which God makes really possible for every one of us and in the fulfilment of which He appeals to our love and generosity.

If, then, as a result of our failings, something happens to distress us, it is a providential lesson which we must accept in all humility and thus derive some profit from it. If, through no fault of our own, God permits us to be deprived of certain help, this is because that help is not really necessary for our sanctification and salvation. The saints find that in a sense nothing is wanting to them unless it be a greater love for God. If only we knew the inner meaning of those incidents we call hindrances, contradictions, reverses, disappointments, misfortunes, and failures, we should of course deplore any disorder they might involve (and the saints deplored it, were pained by it far more than we), but we should also reproach ourselves for complaining and give more consideration to the higher purpose God is pursuing in all that He wills and even in His divine permission of evil.[1]

---

[1] In the Second Book of Kings it is related how Semei, a kinsman of Saul, reviled the prophet David, casting stones at him and cursing him. When one of David's officers would have gone out to slay the reviler, David said: "Let him alone and let him curse: for the Lord hath bid him curse David. And who is he that shall dare say, Why hath he done so? . . . Let him alone that he may curse as the Lord hath bidden him. Perhaps the Lord may look upon my affliction, and the Lord may render me good for the cursing of this day" (II Kings 16: 6 ff.). This reminds us of our Lord's words during His passion when, counseling Peter to be calm, He allowed Himself to be led away by the armed soldiery with Judas at their head and healed Malchus, whom Peter had wounded with his sword. We meet with many such incidents in the lives of the saints, where the unforeseen opportunity is seized upon so soon as it presents itself.

Should we wonder that the ways of providence are sometimes mysterious and that reason is disconcerted at the mystery? "The just man liveth by faith" (Rom. 1:17), says the Scripture, and in particular he lives by the mystery of providence and its ways. Eventually he realizes that, far from being contradictory, the mystery cannot be rejected without every phase of our life becoming a contradiction.

More than once the Scripture declares: "The Lord killeth and maketh alive; He bringeth down to hell and bringeth back again."[2]

The more the divine action makes us die to sin and its consequences, the more it detaches us from all that is not God Himself, and the more it vivifies us. It has been said that sometimes grace is a destroyer; yet, in its workings within us, it does not destroy, but perfects any good there is in nature, restoring and sublimating it. We may say of grace as was said of God: "It killeth and maketh alive" (I Kings 2:6).

As Père de Caussade remarks, when explaining these ways of Providence,[3] "The more obscure the mystery is to us, the more light it contains in itself"; for its obscurity is due to a radiance too intense for our feeble vision.

Moreover, what happens to each of us personally from one moment to the other by the will and permission of Providence, is of greater instruction for us. Therein we may see the expression of the divine will in our regard at the present moment. In this way, too, within us is formed that *experimental knowledge* of God's dealings with us, a knowledge without which we can hardly direct our course aright in

[2] See I Kings 2:6; Deut. 32:39; Tobias 13:2; Wis. 16:13.
[3] *Abandonment to Divine Providence*, Bk. I, chap. 2, p. 25.

spiritual things or do any lasting good to others.[4] In the spiritual order more than anywhere else real knowledge can be acquired only by suffering and action. Though our Lord's holy soul from the moment of His coming into the world enjoyed the beatific vision and an infused knowledge, yet He willed also to have an experimental knowledge, that knowledge which is acquired from day to day and enables us to view things under that special aspect which contact with reality gives when they have been infallibly foreseen. We foresee that a very dear friend who is sick has not long to live, yet when death does come and if our eyes are open to see, it will provide a new lesson in which God will speak to us as time goes on. This is the school of the Holy Ghost, in which His lessons have nothing academic about them, but are drawn from concrete things. And He varies them for each soul, since what is useful for one is not always so for another. Although we must not be superstitious and think we see a deep meaning in what is merely accidental and of no significance, let us in all simplicity listen to what Providence has to say to each one of us personally in these concrete lessons it gives. We must not treat this doctrine in a purely material and mechanical way; it is a question of being supernaturally-minded in everything, in all simplicity and without disputings or foolish questionings.

The author just quoted says:[5]

The will of God in the present moment is an ever bubbling source of sanctity. . . . All you who thirst, learn that you have not far

---

[4] Herein is the explanation of all that supernatural good which saints like the Curé of Ars have done for souls. With no great theological learning, he nevertheless had the deepest insight into God's dealings with souls of every condition, and thus, with very little time for reflection, he would in one day give to hundreds of persons the sound counsel which their immediate needs required.

[5] *Ibid.*, p. 27.

to go to find the fountain of living waters; it gushes forth quite close
to you right now; therefore hasten to find it. Why, with the fountain so near, do you tire yourselves with running about after every
little rill? . . . O unknown Love! It seems as though Your wonders were finished and nothing remained but to copy Your an-
cient works, and to quote Your past discourses. And no one sees
that Your inexhaustible activity is a source of new thoughts, of
fresh sufferings, and further actions . . . of new saints.

The heart of Jesus is a "source of graces ever new."

As age succeeds age the saints have no need to copy the
lives or writings of those who have gone before; they need
only to live their lives in continuous self-abandonment to
God's secret inspirations. In this they and their predecessors
are alike, in spite of differences peculiar to the age and the
individual. Could we but see the divine light it contains, the
present moment would remind us that everything may contribute to our spiritual advancement in the love of God, as
means or instrument, or at least as occasion, by way of trial
or by way of contrast. In the order intended by Providence
this present moment is in some way related to our last end,
to the one thing necessary; and thus each instant of fleeting
time has some sort of relation with the unique instant of unchanging eternity.

Could we but grasp this truth, then not only the time of
mass or our hours of prayer and visits to the Blessed Sacrament would be a source of sanctification to us, but *every
hour of the day* would take on a supernatural significance
and remind us that we are on our way to eternity. Hence
the pious practice of blessing each hour as it begins, calling
down the divine benediction upon it. At every moment we
should be at God's service; there is no moment of the day

that has not some duty for us to fulfil, some duty toward God or our neighbor, the duty at least of patiently waiting when external action is no longer possible. Every minute must find us hallowing the name of God as though there were nothing more to keep us here in time, as though the next moment must see our entry into eternity.

In the World War this was the attitude of the more spiritually-minded when under gunfire. In those three-minute intervals before firing recommenced, they would say to themselves: "One moment, perhaps, and then death," and they would live the present moment as though it were the prelude to eternity.

This, too, was the attitude of the saints, not only in exceptional circumstances, but in the ordinary routine of their lives: they never lost the sense of God's presence. Now light is thrown on this attitude of theirs by the Gospel principles we mentioned and which are as applicable to us as to them.

The teaching of Scripture and theology on the duty of the present moment

In his First Epistle to the Corinthians, St. Paul wrote (10: 31): "Whether you eat or drink, or whatsoever else you do, do all for the glory of God"; and to the Colossians he said (3: 17): "All whatsoever you do in word or in work, all things do ye in the name of the Lord Jesus Christ, giving thanks to God and the Father by Him."

Our Lord Himself said (Matt. 12: 34-36): "Out of the abundance of the heart the mouth speaketh. A good man out of a good treasure bringeth forth good things: and an evil man out of an evil treasure bringeth forth evil things. But I say to you, that every idle word that men speak, they shall render an account of it in the day of judgment."

The full significance of this doctrine is elucidated by St. Thomas (Ia IIae, q. 18, a. 9), who teaches that in the concrete, *hic et nunc, no deliberate act is morally indifferent;* every one of our deliberate acts is either good or bad. The reason is that every deliberate act in a rational being should itself be rational or directed to a morally good end, and in the Christian every deliberate act should be directed at least virtually to God. If this is done, then the act is good, otherwise it is bad; no other alternative is possible. Our very recreations and amusements, the walks we take, all must have some morally good purpose. To take a walk is of course indifferent when considered in the abstract; to walk in one direction rather than in another may also be indifferent. But our walk must have in view a rational purpose: for example, to repair or renew our strength so as to apply ourselves once again to our appointed task. And thus our very amusements assume a moral significance and value in our lives as rational beings.

To adopt the metaphor of a well-known preacher, our deliberate acts are like drops of rain falling on a mountain peak at the watershed. Some water flows to the right into one river and so eventually to the ocean; the rest flows to the left to join another river flowing down to another sea far off in the opposite direction. So also it is with our deliberate acts: they are either directed to what is good and so eventually to God, or they are directed to evil. Not one of these acts, when presented in the concrete reality of life, is indifferent.

This teaching may at first sight appear severe. That is not so: a virtual or implicit intention is all that is needed, renewed each morning at prayer-time and as often as the Holy Ghost inspires us to lift up our hearts to God.

Nay more, it is a consoling doctrine, for it follows that in the lives of the just every deliberate act that is not sinful is at once morally good and meritorious, whether it be easy or difficult, trivial or heroic.

Again, when rightly understood and really lived, this doctrine is a source of sanctification. It leads to the reflection that *what God does at any particular moment is well done* and is a sign of His will. Thus Job, deprived of all things, saw in this the will of God trying Him for his sanctification; thus instead of cursing this most painful episode of his, he blessed the name of the Lord. Let us, then, learn to recognize in what is happening every moment something positively intended by God, or at any rate divinely permitted, and always directed to some higher good purpose. In this way, no matter what happens, we shall always be at peace.

The whole doctrine is summed up by St. Francis de Sales in these few words: "Every moment comes to us pregnant with a command from God, only to pass on and plunge into eternity, there to remain forever what we have made it."

To see thus constantly in the duty of the present moment the expression of the divine will comes principally from the gift of wisdom, which enables us in a manner to see in God, the first cause and last end, every event whether painful or pleasing. That is why, as St. Augustine says, this gift corresponds to the beatitude of the peacemakers: that is, the beatitude of those who preserve their peace where many another will be troubled and who will often restore to those who are in deep trouble the peace they have lost. "Blessed are the peacemakers, for they shall be called the children of God" (Matt. 5:9).

CHAPTER XXII

The Grace of the Present Moment and Fidelity in Little Things

We were saying that the duty we must accomplish with every succeeding hour is the expression of God's will for each one of us individually *hic et nunc* and thus conveys a certain practical instruction very valuable for sanctification. It is the Gospel teaching as applied to the various circumstances of our lives, a real object-lesson imparted by almighty God Himself.

If we could only look on each moment from this point of view, as the saints did, we should see that to each moment there is attached not only a duty to be performed, but also a grace to be faithful in accomplishing that duty.

The spiritual riches contained in the present moment

As fresh circumstances arise, with their attendant obligations, fresh actual graces are offered us in order that we may derive the greatest spiritual profit from them. Above the succession of external events that go to make up our life, there runs a parallel series of actual graces offered for our acceptance, just as the air comes in successive waves to enter our lungs and so make breathing possible.

This succession of actual graces which we either agree to make use of for our spiritual benefit, or, on the other hand, neglect to do so, constitutes the history of each individual soul as it is written down in the book of life, in God, to be laid open some day for our inspection. It is thus that our Lord continues to live in His mystical body, and especially in His saints, in whom He continues a life that will know no end, a life that at every moment requires new graces and new activities.

Our Lord has said:

I will ask the Father, and He shall give you another Paraclete, that He may abide with you forever, the Spirit of truth, whom the world cannot receive, because it seeth Him not, nor knoweth Him: but you shall know Him; because He shall abide with you, and shall be in you. . . . He will teach you all things, and bring all things to your mind, whatsoever I shall have said to you (John 14: 16, 26).

To those who will listen, the Holy Ghost is in all things their guide from day to day, and by His grace He engraves the law of God upon the soul, doing this either directly Himself or through the preaching of the Gospel. St. Paul tells the Corinthians: "Do we need (as some do) epistles of commendation to you or from you? You are our epistle . . . being manifested, that you are the epistle of Christ, ministered by us, and written not with ink, but with the spirit of the living God: not in tables of stone, but in the fleshy tablets of the heart" (II Cor. 3: 1–3). And thus in the souls of men is being written the interior history of the Church, to be continued down to the end of time. It is this history which is set out symbolically in the Apocalypse, and only at the last day will it be read with clarity of perception.

This is how Père de Caussade puts it in the following remarkable passages:

Oh, glorious history! grand book written by the Holy Spirit in this present time! It is still in the press to turn out holy souls. There is never a day when the type is not arranged, when the ink is not applied, when the pages are not printed. We are still in the dark night of faith. The paper is blacker than the ink. . . . It is written in characters of another world, and there is no understanding it except in heaven. . . . If the transposition of twenty-five letters is incomprehensible as sufficing for the composition of an almost infinite number of different volumes, each admirable of its kind, who can explain the works of God in the universe? . . . Teach me, divine Spirit, to read in this book of life. I desire to become Thy disciple and, like a little child, to believe what I cannot understand and cannot see.[1]

What great truths are hidden even from Christians who imagine themselves most enlightened! . . . To effect this union with Him, God makes use of the worst of His creatures as well as of the best, and of the most distressing events as well as of those which are pleasant and agreeable. Our union with Him is even the more meritorious as the means enabling us to maintain it are the more repugnant to nature.[2]

The present moment is ever filled with infinite treasures; it contains more than you have capacity to hold. Faith is the measure. Believe, and it will be done to you accordingly. Love also is the measure. The more the heart loves, the more it desires; and the more it desires, so much the more will it receive. The will of God presents itself to us at each moment as an immense ocean that no human heart can fathom; but what the heart can receive from this

---

[1] *Abandonment to Divine Providence,* Bk. I, chap. 2, sec. 5, p. 23.

[2] *Ibid.* sec. 3, p. 26. At least this is often the case, though an act that is in no way disagreeable may often be very meritorious, such as the prayer of a saint in times of consolation.

ocean is equal to the measure of our faith, confidence and love. The whole creation cannot fill the human heart, for the heart's capacity surpasses all that is not God. The mountains that are terrifying to look at, are but atoms for the heart. The divine will is an abyss of which the present moment is the entrance. Plunge into this abyss and you will always find it infinitely more vast than your desires. Do not flatter anyone, nor worship your own illusions; they can neither give you anything nor take anything from you. You will receive your fulness from the will of God alone, which will not leave you empty. Adore it, put it first, before all other things. . . . Destroy the idols of the senses. . . . When the senses are terrified, or famished, despoiled, crushed, then it is that faith is nourished, enriched, and enlivened. Faith laughs at these calamities as the governor of an impregnable fortress laughs at the futile attacks of an impotent foe.[3]

When the will of God is made known to a soul, and has made the soul realize His willingness to give Himself to it—provided that the soul, too, gives itself to God—then under all circumstances the soul experiences a great happiness in this coming of God, and enjoys it the more, the more it has learnt to abandon itself at every moment to His most adorable will.[4]

God is like the ocean, sustaining those who in all confidence surrender themselves to Him and do everything in their power to follow His inspirations as a ship will respond to a favorable breeze. This is what our Lord meant when He said: "The spirit breatheth where he will and thou hearest his voice: but thou knowest not whence he cometh and whither he goeth. So is everyone that is born of the Spirit" (John 3:8).

How sublime is this doctrine! As the present minute is

[3] *Ibid*. sec. 3, p. 19.
[4] *Ibid*.

passing, let us likewise bear in mind that what exists is not merely our body with its sensibility, its varying emotions of pain and pleasure; but also our spiritual and immortal soul, and the actual grace we receive, and Christ who exerts His influence upon us, and the Blessed Trinity dwelling within us. We shall then have some idea of the infinite riches contained in the present moment and the connection it has with the unchanging instant of eternity into which we are some day to enter. We should not be satisfied with viewing the present moment along the horizontal line of time, as the connecting link between a vanished past and an uncertain temporal future; we ought rather to view it along that vertical line of time which links it up with the unique instant of unchanging eternity. Whatever happens, let us say to ourselves: At this moment God is present and desires to draw me to Himself. In one of the most painful moments of St. Alphonsus' life, when the beloved congregation he had just founded seemed all but lost, he heard these words from the lips of a lay friend of his: "God is always present, Father Alphonsus." Not only did he renew his courage, but that hour of pain became one of the most fruitful of his life.

Let us in all reverses give heed to the actual graces offered us with each passing minute for the fulfilment of present duty. We shall thus realize more and more how great must be our fidelity in little things as well as in great.

Fidelity in little things

Our Lord tells us (Luke 16: 10): "He that is faithful in that which is least is faithful also in that which is greater." Again, in the parable of the talents He says to each of the faithful servants: "Well done, good and faithful servant, because thou hast been faithful over a few things, I will place thee over many things: enter thou into the joy of thy Lord" (Matt. 25: 21). We have here a most important lesson on the value of trivial things, one very often ignored by those who are naturally high-minded, who take the first step on the wrong path when their sense of dignity degenerates into pride. We cannot lay too much stress on this point in considering the fidelity we ought to show to the grace of the present moment.

As often noted, in many cases where souls have given themselves to God in all sincerity and have made generous, even heroic efforts to prove their love for Him, a critical moment comes when they must abandon a too personal way of judging and acting—though it may be of a high order—so as to enter upon the path of true humility, that "little humility" which loses sight of self and looks henceforward on God alone.

At that moment two widely different courses are possible: either the soul seeks for itself the course to take and pursues it, or it fails to do so, sometimes going so far astray in its upward path as to go back again without being altogether aware of it.

To see this path of true humility is to discover in our everyday life, from morning to night, opportunities of performing seemingly trivial acts for the love of God. But the frequent repetition of these acts is of immense value and leads to a delicacy of attitude to God and our neighbor which, if constant and truly sincere, is the mark of perfect charity.

The acts then demanded of the soul are very simple and pass by unnoticed. There is nothing in them for self-love to take hold of. God alone sees them, and the soul thinks it is offering Him, so to speak, nothing at all. And yet these acts, St. Thomas says,[5] are like drops of water continually falling on the same spot: eventually they bore a hole in the rock. The same real effect is gradually produced by the assimilation of the graces we receive. They penetrate the soul and its faculties, at the same time sublimating them and gradually bringing everything to the required supernatural focus. Without this fidelity in little things actuated by the spirit of faith and love, humility, patience and gentleness, the contemplative life will never penetrate the active, the ordinary everyday life. Contemplation will be confined, as it were, to the summit of the intellect, where it is more speculative than contemplative; it will fail to permeate our whole existence and manner of life and will remain almost completely barren whereas it should become every day more fruitful.

This is a matter of supreme importance. St. Francis de Sales more than once speaks of it.[6] St. Thomas says the same

[5] Cf. St. Thomas, IIa IIae, q.24, a.6 ad 2um.

[6] *Introduction to the Devout Life,* Part III, chap. 1: "Opportunity is seldom given for the exercise of fortitude, magnanimity, or munificence; but meekness, temperance, modesty, and humility are virtues wherewith all the actions of our life should be tempered. There are other virtues more excellent, it is true, but the practice of these is more necessary. Sugar is more excellent than salt, but salt is more necessary and more general in its use. Therefore we should always have a goodly supply of these general virtues ready to hand, since we need them almost continually.

"In the exercise of the virtues we should always prefer that which is most conformable with our duty, not that which is most agreeable to our taste. . . . Each one should practice those virtues in particular which are most required for the state of life to which he is called.

"Of the virtues that have no immediate connection with our particular duty, we must prefer the more excellent to the more ostentatious. Comets usually appear greater than stars and to our eyes occupy far greater space, whereas in reality they are not to be compared with the stars either in magnitude or quality. . . . Hence it is that the ordinary run of men usually prefer corporal alms to spiritual . . . bodily mortifications to meekness . . . modesty and other mortifications of the heart, though these are far more excellent."

Ibid. chap. 2: "Yea, Philothea, the King of glory does not reward His servants thing in another way when he teaches, as we have already seen, that in the concrete reality of life *no deliberate act is hic et nunc morally indifferent.*[7] In a rational being every deliberate act should be rational, should have an "honorable" end in view, and in the Christian every act should be directed at least virtually to God as to the supreme object of love. This truth brings out the importance of the multifarious actions we have to perform day by day. Perhaps they are trivial in themselves, nevertheless they are of great importance relative to God and the spirit of faith and love, of humility and patience that should actuate us in performing them and offering them to Him.

This critical moment of which we are speaking marks a difficult crisis in the spiritual life of many fairly advanced souls, who then run the risk of falling back again.

If a soul that has shown itself generous or even heroic, after reaching this point is still far too personal in its manner of judging and acting and does not see the need of a change, it continues on its way with a merely acquired impetus, and its prayer and activities are no longer what they should be. There is a real danger here. The soul may become stunted and its development arrested like one dwarfed through some deformity. Or it may take a false direction. Instead of true humility, it may almost unawares develop a sort of refined pride, which scarcely appears at first except in the small details of daily life. For that reason this will remain unknown to a spiritual director living apart from those he directs. This pride will steadily take the form of an amused condescension,

according to the dignity of the offices they hold, but according to the love and humility with which they exercise them."

[7] Cf. St. Thomas, IIaIIae, q. 18, a. 9.

and subsequently develop into an acerbity of manner in our relations with our neighbor, permeating the whole life of the day and thus stultifying everything. This acerbity may lead to rancor and contempt for our neighbor, whom nevertheless we should love for God's sake.

A soul that has come to this pass will not easily be led to make those holy considerations which are necessary for it to return to the point whence it went astray. Such a soul should be recommended to our Lady's care; in many cases she alone can lead it back into the right path.[8]

The remedy for this evil is to make the soul very attentive to the grace of the moment and faithful in trivial things.

To quote Père de Caussade once more:

Actions are not determined by ideas or by a confusion of words which by themselves would only serve to excite pride. . . . We must make use only of what God sends us to do or to suffer, and not forsake this divine reality to occupy our minds with the historical wonders of the divine work instead of gaining an increase of grace by our fidelity. The marvels of this work, which we read about for the purpose of satisfying our curiosity, often only tend to disgust us with things that seem trifling but by which, if we do not despise them, the divine love effects very great things in us. Fools that we are! We admire and bless this divine action in the writings that relate its history; and when it is ready to continue this writing on our hearts, we keep moving the paper and prevent it writing by our curiosity, that we may see what it is doing in and around us. . . . For love of Thee, O my God, and for the discharge of my

---

[8] If by God's grace such a soul recovers itself and begins to follow the way of true humility, it may resume its upward course from the point it had already reached, without being obliged to start again from the beginning. The reason is that even after mortal sin, the soul whose repentance is proportionate to the offense will recover the grace it has lost in the same degree as it had reached before the fall. Cf. St. Thomas, IIIa, q.89, a.2, c. et ad 2um; a.5 ad 3um.

debts, I will confine myself to the one essential business, that of the present moment, and thus enable Thee to act.[9]

This is what is meant by the common saying, *Age quod agis*. And so, if we are really doing our utmost day by day to be faithful to God in little things, He will certainly give us strength to be faithful to Him in difficult and very painful circumstances, if through His permission that should be our lot. Thus will be realized the words of the Gospel: "Sufficient for the day is the evil thereof"; [10] "He that is faithful in that which is least, is faithful also in that which is greater." [11]

[9] *Abandonment to Divine Providence,* Bk. I chap. 2, sec. 12, p. 35.
[10] Matt. 6: 34.
[11] Luke 16: 10.

CHAPTER XXIII

THE ATTITUDE OF PROVIDENCE TOWARD THOSE WHO ABANDON THEMSELVES COMPLETELY TO IT

Fidelity to daily duty by docile correspondence to the graces offered us every moment, soon receives its reward in that special assistance which Providence gives to those who practice this childlike self-surrender. This assistance, it may be said, is shown mainly in three ways, which it will be well to emphasize: thus Providence gives special guidance to those souls in their darkness; it defends them against whatever is hostile to their spiritual welfare; and it intensifies their interior life more and more.

In what way God guides those souls that abandon themselves to Him

He enlightens them through the gifts of wisdom and understanding, knowledge and counsel, which with sanctifying grace and charity we received in baptism and to a greater degree in confirmation. In imperfect souls these gifts, together with those of piety, fortitude, and filial fear, are, so to speak, shackled by more or less inordinate inclinations, so that such souls are living but a superficial life, which prevents them from being attentive to the inspirations of the Master of the interior life.

These gifts have been likened to the sails of a boat by which it readily accommodates itself to the least stir of a favorable wind. In imperfect souls, however, the sails are furled and will not respond to the breeze. On the other hand, when the soul does what it can to fulfil its daily obligations and steer its bark as it should, abandoning itself to God, He visits it with His inspirations, at first latent and confused, which if well received, become more and more frequent, more insistent and luminous.

Then, amidst the joyful and painful events of life, the clash of temperaments, in times of spiritual dryness, amidst the snares of the devil or of men, their suspicion and their jealousies, the soul in its higher regions at any rate remains always at peace. It enjoys this serenity because it is intimately persuaded that God is guiding it and, in abandoning itself to Him, it seeks only to do His will and nothing more. Thus it sees Him everywhere under every external guise and makes use of everything to further its union with Him. Sin itself, by its very contrast, will recall the infinite majesty of God.

Then is increasingly realized the words of the Apostle St. John to the faithful for whom he wrote his First Epistle: "Let the unction you have received from God abide in you. And you have no need that any man teach you: but as His unction teacheth you of all things, and is truth, and is no lie" (I John 2:27).

The soul has then less need of reasonings and methods in its prayer and meditation, or for its guidance; it has become more simplified in its mode of thought and desire. It follows rather the interior action of God in its soul, which makes itself felt not so much by the impression of ideas, as through the instinct or the necessity imposed by circumstances where only one course is possible. It perceives at once the depth of meaning in some phrase from the Gospels which has not previously impressed it. God gives it an understanding of the Scriptures such as He gave to the two disciples on the way to Emmaus. The simplest sermons are a source of enlightenment and it discovers treasures in them; for God makes use of these means that He Himself may enlighten the soul, just as a great artist may use the most ordinary implement, the cheapest pencil, to execute a great masterpiece, a wonderful picture of Christ or the Blessed Virgin.

In God's dealings with souls that abandon themselves to Him, much remains obscure, mysterious, disconcerting, impenetrable; but He makes it all contribute to their spiritual welfare, and some day they will see that what at times to them was the cause of profound desolation was the source of much joy to the angels.

Moreover, God enlightens the soul by means of this very darkness and just when He appears to blind it. When the things of sense, which once so charmed and fascinated us, are obliterated, then the grandeur of spiritual things begins to be seen. A fallen monarch, like Louis XVI after losing his throne, sees more clearly than ever before the sublimity of the Gospel and of the many graces he has received in the past. Formerly he scarcely gave them a thought, being too absorbed in the external splendors of his kingdom. And now it is the kingdom of heaven that is revealed to him.

An important law in the spiritual world is that *the transcendent darkness of divine things* is in a sense more illuminating than the obviousness of earthly things. We have an illustration of this in the sensible order. Surprising as the truth may at first appear, we see much farther in the darkness of the night than in the light of day. The sun, in fact, must first be hidden before we can see the stars and have a glimpse of the unfathomable depths of the sky. The spectacle presented to us on a starry night is sometimes incomparably more beautiful than anything to be seen on even the sunniest day. In the daytime, doubtless, our view may extend far over the surrounding country, and even to the sun itself, though its light takes eight minutes to reach us. But in the darkness of the night we see at a single glance thousands of stars, although the light from even the nearest requires four and a half years to reach us. From the spiritual point of view the same holds true: as the sun prevents our seeing the stars, so in human life there are things which by their glare obstruct our view of the splendors of the faith. It is fitting, then, that from time to time in our lives Providence should subdue this glare of inferior things so as to give us a glimpse of something far more precious for our soul and our salvation.

Indeed, in the spiritual order, as in the physical, there is often an alternation of day and night; it is mentioned more than once in the *Imitation*. If we are saddened at the approach of twilight, God could well answer us by saying: How can I otherwise reveal to you all those thousands of stars which can be seen only at night?

Thus is verified the truth of our Lord's words when He said: "He that followeth me walketh not in darkness" (John 8:12). The light of faith dispels the lower darkness of ignorance, sin, and damnation, says St. Thomas.[1] Moreover, since this divine darkness is owing to a higher light which is too intense for our feeble vision, it does enlighten us in its own fashion and gives us a glimpse into the abyss of the

[1] S. Thomas, *in Joann*. 8: 12.

heavens, into the deep things of God, into the mystery of the ways of Providence. St. Paul says: [2]

We speak wisdom among the perfect: yet not the wisdom of the world, neither of the princes of this world that come to nought. But we speak the wisdom of God in a mystery, a wisdom which is hidden, which God ordained before the world, unto our glory: which none of the princes of this world knew. For if they had known it, they would never have crucified the Lord of glory. But, as it is written: That eye hath not seen, nor ear heard: neither hath it entered into the heart of man, what things God hath prepared for them that love him. But to us God hath revealed them by His Spirit. For the Spirit searcheth all things, yea, the deep things of God.

God has His own way of enlightening souls concerning His intimate life and the secrets of His ways. Sometimes He seems to blind them, yet, in reality, just when an inferior light disappears, then it is that He gives them a more sublime light. For the saint, the darkness of death is followed immediately by the light of glory. Those around him are saddened to see this present life coming so quickly to an end; he is happy to see it drawing to its close, for it means his entry into everlasting life.

If at times in our lives everything seems desperate, and, as Tauler says, the masts have gone overboard and the ship is reduced to a mere hulk in the midst of the tempest, then is the moment to abandon ourselves to God fully and completely, without reserve. If we do so with all our heart, God will at once take into His own hands the immediate direction of our lives, for He alone can save us. "The Lord leadeth the

[2] See I Cor. 2: 6.

just by right ways and showeth him the kingdom of God"
(Wis. 10: 10).

*The soul that abandons itself to God is defended by Him
against the enemies of its spiritual welfare*

This is what St. Paul tells us in the Epistle to the Romans
(8: 31): "If God be for us, who is against us? He that spared
not even His own Son, but delivered Him up for us all, how
hath He not also, with Him, given us all things." The Book
of Wisdom says of the just who in confidence abandon themselves to God: "With His right hand He will cover them,
and with His holy arm He will defend them" (5: 17).

All things are controlled by Providence; the least circumstance, however insignificant, is in its hands. With Providence there is no such thing as chance; and so by some little
unforeseen incident it can easily upset the cunning calculations of those hostile to spiritual good. We have an example
of this in the life of Joseph, who was sold by his brethren.
Had not the Ismaelite merchants, by chance apparently,
passed by just when his brothers had decided to put him
to death, he would have been left there in the cistern where
they had thrown him. But it was then and not an hour later,
as was ordained by God from all eternity, that the merchants
arrived on the scene, and Joseph was thus sold into slavery.
And so, being led into Egypt, he was later to be a benefactor
to those who had wished to destroy him. Let us recall also
the story of Esther, of the prophet Daniel, and of many others.
Similar and more striking are the circumstances surrounding
the birth of our Lord. Herod had organized all the forces at
his disposal to put the Messias to death and had then re-

quested the wise men from the East to obtain for him precise information about the child. But, "having received an answer in sleep that they should not return to Herod, they went back another way to their own country" (Matt. 2: 12). "Then Herod, perceiving that he was deluded by the wise men, . . . sending, killed all the men children that were in Bethlehem and in all the borders thereof" (*ibid.*, 2: 16), but an angel, appearing in sleep to Joseph, commanded him to save the child from the king's wrath and flee into Egypt.

In the lives of the just it is not miraculous that their guardian angels intervene at God's command to inspire some holy thought in them, whether they be asleep or awake; it is a providential occurrence by no means rare in the lives of those who abandon themselves completely to God. In the Book of Psalms (90: 10) we are told: "There shall be no evil come to thee: nor shall the scourge come near thy dwelling. For the Lord hath given His angels charge over thee, to keep thee in all thy ways. In their hands they shall bear thee up, lest thou dash thy foot against a stone." We must not tempt God, of course; but in the fulfilment of our daily duties we must resign ourselves humbly into His hands, and those who thus abandon themselves to Him, He will protect as a mother protects her children. If He allows persecution, often bitter persecution, to come upon them, as He did in the case of His own Son, nevertheless He will not allow the just to lose courage, but will sustain them in invisible ways and, if in a moment of weakness they should fall, as Peter did, He will raise them up again and lead them on to the haven of salvation.

The soul that abandons itself to God instead of resisting its enemies, so the saints tell us, finds in them useful allies. Says Père de Caussade:[3]

There is nothing that is more entirely opposed to worldly prudence than simplicity; it turns aside all schemes without comprehending them, without so much as a thought about them. . . . To have to deal with a simple soul is, in a certain way, to have to deal with God. What can be done against the will of the Almighty and His inscrutable designs? God takes the cause of the simple soul in hand. It is unnecessary to study the intrigues of others against it. . . . The divine action makes the soul adopt such just measures as to surprise even those who wish to take it by surprise. It profits by all their efforts. . . . They are the galley-slaves who bring the ship into port with hard rowing. All obstacles turn to the good of this soul. . . . All it has to fear is lest it should take part in a work and so disturb it . . . in which it has nothing to do but peacefully to observe the work of God, and follow with simplicity the attractions He gives it. . . . The soul in the state of abandonment can abstain from justifying itself by word or deed. The divine action justifies it.

Thus it is in the lives of the saints, and, in due proportions, the way they have followed ought to be ours also.

Not infrequently we hear people who are beset by difficulties say in a flippant sort of way: "Why worry?" That is a sheer materialistic and egotistic conception of the doctrine we are here considering. The animating principle of this doctrine is a trustful self-abandonment to Providence. If this trustful self-abandonment is no longer present, as in such recipes for life as that "why worry?" then nothing is left but a body without a soul, a formula of no greater value than the moral energy of the person who utters it. When one has departed

[3] *Abandonment to Divine Providence*, pp. 81–83.

from this way of salvation, all that is left of the noblest maxims on life is a dead formula that will serve as an excuse for anything. Yet to all is offered the light of life in the Gospel. The consecrated host elevated every morning on our altars is offered up for all, and all can unite themselves with this oblation. In place of that confidence in God which should accompany our daily task, for us to substitute an arrogant assurance based on purely human calculations is a tremendous misfortune. Man then sets himself up in the place of God; he destroys the theological virtues within him. He is poles asunder from the doctrine we are considering here, which is pre-eminently that of life.

God quickens more and more the interior life of souls that abandon themselves to Him

Not only is He their protector and guide, but He quickens them by His grace, by the virtues and the gifts of the Holy Ghost, and also through the fresh inspirations He is continuously sending them. Moreover, He is quickening them even when He appears to strip them, even to death itself, according to these words of St. Paul: "To me to live is Christ: and to die is gain" (Phil. 1:21). For many life consists in sport or art or some intellectual activity, such as science or philosophy. But for such souls as we are speaking of, life is simply Christ, or as St. Paul says, union with Christ. Christ is their life, says St. Thomas,[4] in the sense that He is the constant motive of their most profound vital activity. It is for Him they live and act continuously; not for any human purpose but in very truth for the Lord, who quickens them more and more, making this life of theirs depend upon just

---

[4] *Comment. in Epist. ad Philipp.* 1:21.

those things that apparently must destroy them, even as Christ Himself made of His cross the most potent instrument of our salvation.

This profound teaching was expressed with remarkable clearness by a seventeenth century Dominican, Père Chardon, in his book, *La Croix de Jésus*.[5] He points out that the divine action, in gradually detaching us from all that is not God, sometimes in most painful ways, tends by that very detachment to unite us more and more closely to Him. Loss is thus turned into gain. As grace increases within us, it becomes at once a source of separation and of union; the progressive separation is simply the reverse side of the union. Says Chardon:

For fear lest a too frequent enjoyment of consolations should arrest the soul's inclination to Himself, God interrupts the flow of the stream in order to make the soul yearn more ardently for the source. . . . He withdraws His graces to give Himself instead. He steals gently through the soul, making Himself master of the faculties and all their concerns that He may cause it to rejoice in the one necessary good, which must be loved only in that same solitude in which the supremacy of its being is isolated from all else.

Thus with the disappearance of an inferior light and life, another light appears, to illuminate our life in a way far more sublime.

When an apostle is struck down with paralysis in the midst of his apostolate and in the prime of life, people often imagine that his influence is at an end, whereas it ought to be, as it often is, the beginning of something higher, the direct external apostolate giving place to that hidden yet profound apostolate which exerts its influence on souls through prayer

[5] See 3ᵉ Entretien, chaps. 8 ff.

and self-immolation in Christ and thereby causes to overflow upon them the chalice of superabounding redemption.

Act of self-abandonment

This whole doctrine is beautifully summed up in the following anonymous prayer inspired by St. Augustine:

O my God, I leave myself entirely in Thy hands. Turn and turn
again this mass of clay, as a vessel that is fashioned in the potter's
hand (Jer. 18:6). Give it a shape; then break it if Thou wilt: it is
Thine, it has nothing to say. Enough for me that it serves all Thy
designs and that nothing resists Thy good pleasure for which I was
made. Ask, command. What wouldst Thou have me to do? What
wouldst Thou have me not to do? Lifted up, cast down, in persecution, in consolation, in suffering, intent upon Thy work, good
for nothing, I can do no more than repeat with Thy holy Mother:
"Be it done unto me according to Thy word."

Give me that love which is beyond all loves, the love of the cross
—not those heroic crosses with a glory that might foster self-love,
but those ordinary crosses which we bear with so much distaste—
those daily crosses with which our life is strewn and which at every
moment we encounter on our way through life: contradictions,
neglect, failures, opposition, false judgments, the coldness or im-
pulsiveness of some, the rebuffs or contempt of others, bodily infirmities, spiritual darkness, silence and interior dryness. Only then
wilt Thou know that I love Thee, even though I neither know nor
feel it myself; and that is enough for me.

This is truly holiness of a high order. Were there but a
few such moments of great affliction in our lives, we should
then have reached the topmost heights and have come very
nigh to God. Now every moment God is inviting us to live

this way and lose ourselves in Him. Especially at such moments as these it can be truly said: "The Lord leadeth the just by right ways and showeth him the kingdom of God" (Wis. 10: 10).

CHAPTER XXIV

PROVIDENCE AND THE WAY OF PERFECTION

If one thing more than another should interest us in the providential plan, it is the way of perfection traced out by God from all eternity. The itinerary of this ascent has been described by all the great spiritual writers, but some have given special consideration to its relations with Providence. Among these is St. Catherine of Siena. We propose to give here the main outlines of her testimony on this subject, which she received from on high.

If we choose St. Catherine's testimony in preference to that of other saints, this is because she has a broad view of concrete realities, and thus we can easily apply what she says to the spiritual needs of persons in every state of life. Moreover, her style, though never descending from the sublime, is so realistic and practical that it is suited to every type of mind. It almost attains to the loftiness and simplicity of the Gospels.

It has often been remarked how perfect is the harmony between the teaching of St. Thomas and that expounded by St. Catherine in her ecstasies and written down by her secretaries, in that book which has been called the *Dialogue*.

Nowhere is this doctrinal harmony more striking than on this subject of Christian perfection and the path which, in the designs of Providence, must lead to it. As evidence of this we shall consider the following points:

1) In what especially does perfection consist?

2) Is perfection a matter of strict precept or is it simply a matter of counsel?

3) Is the light of faith sufficient for Christian perfection, or is there also required the light which comes from the gift of wisdom? And is this light normally in proportion to our degree of charity, of our love for God?

4) In the designs of Providence, what purifications are necessary for us to arrive at perfection? Can we acquire it without passing through the so-called passive purifications, the patient and loving endurance of the crucifixion of the senses and the spirit?

5) Is every interior soul called by Providence to an infused contemplation of the mysteries of faith illumined by the gift of wisdom, and to that union with God which is the result of this contemplation and which is widely different from such extraordinary graces as revelations and visions? In other words, according to the providential plan is the highest point reached normally in the development of the life of grace here on earth (the normal prelude to our heavenly life), of the ascetical order, or does it pass to the mystical order? Is our own activity under the influence of grace its distinctive characteristic, or is it rather our docility in responding to the inspirations of the Holy Ghost?

In reply to these questions we will quote from the *Dialogue* certain passages that deal expressly with this subject.

In what Christian perfection especially consists

Does it consist mainly in bodily mortifications or in practices of piety or in the knowledge of divine things? St. Catherine of Siena replies with St. Thomas (IIa IIae, q. 184, a. 1) that *Christian perfection consists principally in charity,* primarily in the love of God and secondarily in the love of our neighbor.

This doctrine is very clearly expressed in the *Dialogue* (chapter 11),[1] where we read:

> Some time ago, if thou remember, when thou wert desirous of doing great penance for my sake, asking, "What can I do to endure suffering for Thee, O Lord?" I replied to thee, speaking in thy mind, "I take delight in few words and many works." I wished to show thee that he who merely calls on me with the sound of words, saying: "Lord, Lord, I would do something for Thee," and he who desires for my sake to mortify his body by many penances, but does not renounce his own will, was wrong in thinking this to be pleasing to me. . . . I, who am infinite, seek infinite works, that is, unlimited surgings of the heart.[2] I wish therefore that the works of penance, and of other corporal exercises, should be observed merely as means, and not as the fundamental perfection of the soul. For if the principal affection of the soul were placed in penance, I should receive a finite thing like a word, which, when it has issued from the mouth, is no more, unless it has issued with affection of soul, which conceives and brings forth virtue in truth. It is by means of this interior virtue that the finite operation, which I have called a word, is united with the affection of love.

If it is otherwise we shall have no more than the material side of perfection; the soul and inspiration of the interior life will no longer be there. In the same passage she tells us: "We must not make our final end to consist in penance, or in any external act; these, as I have said, are finite works. . . . It is good at times for us to discontinue them, whether this arise from necessity or from

---

[1] *The Dialogue of the Seraphic Virgin Catherine of Siena,* tr. by Algar Thorold, pp. 22–23.

[2] In us an act of the love of God, being the act of a creature, must always be finite, but is infinite by reason of its object and motive.

obedience (whereas there must never be any interruption in that life which consists in the love of God). . . . The soul ought therefore to adopt them as means, and not as an end . . . they please when they are performed as the instruments of virtue, and not as a principal end in themselves." This last sentence brings out the necessity of avoiding the opposite extreme in neglecting bodily mortification as practiced by all the saints.

Merit consists in the virtue of love alone, directed by the light of true discretion, without which the soul is worth nothing. Discretion gives me this love endlessly, boundlessly, since I am the supreme and eternal truth. The soul can therefore place neither laws nor limits to her love for me; but her love for her neighbor, on the contrary, is ordered in certain conditions. It is within the scope of charity not to cause the injury of sin to self so as to be useful to others; for if one single sin sufficed for the production of an act of great consequence, it would not be a charity dictated by prudence to commit it.

Holy discretion ordains that the soul should direct all her powers unreservedly to my service with a manly zeal and that her love for her neighbor be such that she would lay down a thousand times, if it were possible, the life of her body for the salvation of souls, prepared to endure whatever torments so that her neighbor may have the life of grace.

This, then, is what *Christian perfection consists* in especially, principally *in a generous love for God,* and secondarily *in a love for our neighbor* which is not just affection, but translates itself into action.

This is why St. Catherine of Siena loves to speak of charity as giving life to all the virtues,[3] as rendering their acts meritorious of eternal life.[4] It is the mother of them all; it is the

---

[3] *Dialogue*, chaps. 5 and 7; pp. 10, 13, 14.
[4] *Ibid.*, chaps. 3 and 4; pp. 4, 8.

bridal garment of God's servants; [5] it is like a tree which, when planted in the soil of humility, lifts high to the heavens its blossoms and its abundance of fruit, the fruit of eternal life.[6] The saint frequently insists on the impossibility of separating love for our neighbor from the love of God, the love of our neighbor being simply the radiation of the love we have for God, its sure sign and token.[7] The love of our neighbor, she adds, cannot be really efficacious unless we love him in God and for His sake. It is compared to a vessel filled at a fountain: "If a man carry away the vessel and then drink from it, the vessel becomes empty, but if he keeps his vessel standing at the fountain while he drinks, it always remains full." [8]

If you wish friendship to endure, if you would continue long to refresh yourself from the cup of friendship, then leave it to be filled continuously at the fount of living water, otherwise it will no longer be capable of satisfying your thirst.

We find precisely the same teaching in the *Summa Theologica* of St. Thomas. For him, too, *perfection consists principally in charity,* which gives life to all the virtues and unites us to our last end, to God the author of grace; for by charity we love God more than ourselves, more than all else, and for His sake everything that is at all worthy of love.

Without charity nothing is of any value for eternal life. No knowledge, not even the knowledge of divine things can bear any fruit unless it is united with the love of God. Such knowledge, says the saint, may be infected with the poison

[5] *Ibid.,* chap. 1; p. 2.
[6] *Ibid.,* chap. 9; p. 20.
[7] *Ibid.,* chaps. 6, 7, 89, 90; pp. 10, 13, 16, 169 f.
[8] *Ibid,* chap. 64; p. 117.

of pride,[9] and frequently it will obtain far more light from prayer than from study, that light of life, at once simple yet sublime, the source of contemplation, by which knowledge is unified and rendered fruitful.

Perfection and the precept of love

Does this perfection, consisting in a high degree of charity, come under the commandments or is it merely a matter of counsel?

The teaching of St. Thomas is that this perfection comes under the supreme commandment, not however as something to be realized immediately but as the ideal at which all Christians must aim, each according to his condition, some in the religious life, others in the world.[10] The Angelic Doctor declares explicitly that Christian *perfection consists essentially in a generous fulfilment of the commandments,* especially of those two commandments that concern the love of God and of our neighbor; the actual practice of the three counsels, poverty, chastity, and obedience is only accidental, enabling us to arrive at a perfect love for God more readily and more surely. Such perfection, in fact, is still attainable even in the married state and in the midst of worldly occupations, as is evidenced in the lives of a number of the saints.[11]

This same teaching we find in St. Catherine of Siena. In her *Dialogue* she points out that the supreme commandment has no limits, as its phrasing shows: "Thou shalt love the Lord thy God with thy whole heart and with thy whole soul and with all thy strength and with all thy mind" (Luke

[9] *Ibid.,* chaps. 85 and 96; pp. 158–160, 186 f.
[10] Cf. St. Thomas, IIa IIae, q. 184, a. 3, c. et ad 2um.
[11] *Ibid.*

10: 27). This law of love is not binding merely up to a certain degree beyond which charity becomes simply a matter of counsel; every Christian is bound to aim at perfection in love. We read in the *Dialogue:* "Thou seest how discreetly every soul . . . should pay her debts, that is, should love me with an infinite love and without measure." [12] Indeed, St. Catherine distinctly states that, although it is possible to observe the commandments without the actual exercise of the three evangelical counsels, nevertheless the perfect fulfilment of the commandments is impossible without the spirit animating the counsels, that spirit of detachment from creatures which is simply one aspect of the love of God and which must always increase in us.

This point is well expressed by the saint in God's words to her:

Inasmuch as the counsels are included in the commandments, no one can observe the latter who does not observe the former, at least in spirit, that is to say, that they possess the riches of the world humbly and without pride, as lent to them and not their own; for they are only given to you for your use, through My goodness, since you only possess what I give you and can retain only what I allow you to retain. I give you as much of them as I see to be profitable for your salvation, and in this way should you use them, for a man, so using them . . . observes the counsels in spirit, having cut out of his heart the poison of disordinate love and affection.[13]

As St. Paul said, we should use these things as though we used them not. This means "to possess the things of this world not as their servants but as their lords," and not be

---

[12] *Dialogue,* chap. 11; p. 25.
[13] *Ibid.,* chap. 47; p. 89.

enslaved by them as a miser by his wealth.[14] Thus in every
state of life we shall so walk as to gain eternal life, advanc-
ing daily in charity as the supreme commandment requires,
and as Eucharistic communion enables us to do by strengthening the soul in the measure of its desires.[15]

By following this path the soul may reach the perfection
of charity even in this world, may reach such a pure and
mighty love for God and souls that it will be prepared to
accept insults, contempt, affronts, ridicule, persecution, everything, for the honor of our Lord and the salvation of
one's neighbor.[16]

Perfection and the light which the gift of wisdom imparts in prayer: the visitation of the Lord

To attain this high degree of charity in which Christian
perfection principally consists, are the light of faith and the
use of vocal prayer sufficient? Must we not have recourse besides to mental prayer, in which the Holy Ghost illuminates
the soul by the light of His gifts?

Prayer, the saint tells us, is one of the great means of arriving at perfection.[17] *True prayer,* founded in the knowledge
of God and of self, *consists in the fervor of desire.*[18] Vocal

---

[14] It is in this spirit that St. Francis drank in the beauty of an Umbrian landscape; thus, too, the great contemplatives of the Netherlands, like Ruysbroeck, delighted in the indefinable charm of Flanders and its wide, silent plains with their
tender and varied verdure, to be seen nowhere else, and their avenues of poplars
waving in the breeze.

Thus do the people of the East delight in the beauty of the starry skies at night
and follow the course of the planets among the fixed stars, counting out the hours
on this great clock of the skies. "The heavens show forth the glory of God"
(Ps. 18: 1).

[15] *Dialogue,* chaps. 2, 110; pp. 3, 218.

[16] *Ibid.,* chaps. 76, 77, 140; pp. 142, 144, 319.

[17] *Ibid.,* chap. 65; p. 120.

[18] *Ibid.,* chap. 66; pp. 121, 125.

prayer must be accompanied by mental prayer, or it will be like a body without a soul.[19] Again, we must abandon vocal for mental prayer when God invites us to do so. We read in the *Dialogue:*

The soul should season the knowledge of herself with the knowledge of My goodness, and then vocal prayer will be of use to the soul who makes it, and pleasing to Me, and she will arrive, from the vocal imperfect prayer, exercised with perseverance, at perfect mental prayer; but if she simply aims at reciting a certain number of stereotyped phrases, and for vocal prayer abandons mental prayer, she will never arrive at it. . . . Let her be attentive when I visit her mind sometimes in one way and sometimes in another, in a flash of self-knowledge or of contrition for sin, sometimes in the broadness of My charity, and sometimes by placing before her mind, in diverse ways, according to My pleasure and the desire of the soul, the presence of My truth. . . . The moment she is aware of My imminent presence she must abandon vocal prayer; then, My visitation past, if there should be time, she can resume the vocal prayers, which she had resolved to say . . . of course provided it were not the divine office which clerics and religious are bound and are obliged to say. . . . If they at the hour appointed for saying it should feel their minds drawn and raised by desire, they should so arrange as to say it before or after My visitation. . . . And so, by practice and perseverance, she will taste prayer in truth and the food of the blood of My only begotten Son, and therefore I told thee that some communicated virtually with the body and blood of Christ, although not sacramentally; that is, they communicate in the affection of charity, which they taste by means of holy prayer, little or much, according to the affection with which they pray. They who proceed with little prudence and without method taste little, and they who proceed with much, taste much. For the more

[19] *Ibid.,* chap. 66; p. 122.

the soul tries to loosen her affection from herself, and fasten it in Me with the light of the intellect, the more she knows; and the more she knows, the more she loves and, loving much, she tastes much.[20]

St. Catherine shows clearly how those who have reached the state of union have their understanding illumined by an infused supernatural light.

"The eye of the intellect," she says,[21] "is lifted up and gazes into My Deity, when the affection behind the intellect is nourished and united with Me. This is a sight which I grant to the soul, infused with grace, who, in truth, loves and serves Me." It is in this sense that we say generally that St. Thomas received much more enlightenment in prayer than from study.[22] It is that infused contemplation which we shall find St. John of the Cross speaking of later on and which usually, he says, is granted to the more advanced and to the perfect.[23] St. Catherine continues:

The doctors, confessors, virgins, and martyrs, all of them had this infused knowledge and received their inspiration therefrom, each in a different way, according to the demands of their own or their neighbor's salvation. . . . This supernatural light is given by grace

[20] *Ibid.*, pp. 124 f.

[21] *Ibid.*, chap. 84; p. 157.

[22] This does not mean that St. Thomas acquired through prayer a knowledge of new conclusions, new theses; it means that among the principles he habitually contemplated there were some that stood out in prayer in all their transcendence as the crown and summit of doctrine illuminating all the rest. It was in prayer, for instance, that he saw clearly the transcendence and universality of the principle he formulates in Ia, q.20, a.3: "Since the love of God is the cause of goodness in creatures, none would be better than another, were it not more beloved of God." In this principle is virtually contained the whole treatise on predestination and grace, which is no more than a corollary drawn from it.

[23] St. John of the Cross, *Dark Night*, Bk. I, chap. 14 (*init.*): "Progressives and proficients are in the illuminative way; there God nourishes and strengthens the soul by *infused contemplation.*"

to the humble who are desirous of receiving it . . . but the proud blind themselves to this light, because their pride and the cloud of self-love prevents them from seeing this light. Wherefore, in examining the books of the Scripture, they interpret it merely in a literal sense. They get not to the marrow of it, because they have deprived themselves of the light by which the Scripture was written and is interpreted.[24]

We see it to be the general rule, as St. Thomas already declared,[25] that this vital illumination proceeding from the gift of wisdom is bestowed to a degree corresponding to that of charity. Hence St. Catherine continues: "Under the guidance of this light we love, because love follows the intellect. The greater the knowledge, the greater the love, and the greater the love, the greater the knowledge. Thus the one feeds the other." [26] If those who write about Raphael or Michelangelo let nothing pass in the effort to exhaust their subject, then surely we should neglect nothing that will enable us to probe more deeply into the Gospel and really live by the holy mass.

"The tongue is at a loss to recount the joy felt by him who goes on this, the true road, for even in this life he participates in that good which has been prepared for him in eternal life." [27] As St. Thomas says: "It is a certain commencement of eternal life." [28]

This state of union is described in chapter 89, where it is distinguished absolutely from the visions and revelations spoken of in chapter 70. In this state are combined an

[24] *Dialogue,* chap. 85; pp. 158–159.
[25] Cf. St. Thomas, Ia IIae, q.68, a.5: There is a connection between the gifts and charity, and thus they develop together. Especially intimate is the relation between the gift of wisdom and charity (cf. IIa IIae, q.45, a.2–5).
[26] *Dialogue,* chap. 85; p. 160.
[27] *Ibid.,* chap. 28; p. 54.
[28] Cf. St. Thomas, IIa IIae, q.24, a.3 ad 2um.

experimental knowledge of our own poverty and a quasi-experimental knowledge of God's infinite goodness; they are, says the saint, like the lowest and the highest points on a circle that will continue to expand until we enter heaven.[29] This graceful image brings out clearly the intimate connection between these two kinds of experimental knowledge, and shows the great difference between them and that knowledge which is purely abstract and speculative. We have here the very essence of the spiritual life.

In the same chapter we read:

> Growing, and exercising herself in the light of self-knowledge, she (the soul) conceives displeasure at herself and finally perfect hatred, at the same time acquiring a true knowledge of My goodness, and thereby being inflamed with love. She begins to unite herself to Me, and to conform her will to Mine, and experiences a joy and a compassion hitherto unknown. The joy she experiences is that of loving Me; . . . at the same time she lovingly grieves at the offense committed against Me, and at the loss of her fellow-creature. . . . She is in a state of desolation at not being able to give glory as she would wish, and in the agony of her desire she finds it delightful to satiate herself at the table of the holy cross.[30]

This brings us to the very center of the mystery of redemption.

The contemplation involved in this union with God distinctive of the Christian life in its full perfection is evidently an infused contemplation, for in chapters 60 and 61 we read:

> If My servants are confused at the knowledge of their imperfection, if they give themselves up to the love of virtue, if they dig up with hatred the root of spiritual self-love . . . they will be so pleasing to

---

[29] *Dialogue*, chaps. 89, 4, 72; pp. 166, 6, 135.
[30] *Ibid.*, chap. 89; p. 166.

Me . . . that I will manifest Myself to them. . . . My charity is manifested in two ways; first, in general, to ordinary people. The second mode of manifestation . . . is peculiar to those who have become My friends. . . . When I reveal Myself to her it makes itself felt in the very depths of the soul, by which such souls taste, know, prove and feel it. Sometimes I even reveal Myself to the soul by arousing in her sentiments of love, and endowing her with the spirit of prophecy.[31]

But, as is evident from chapter 70, this last favor is no longer normal but extraordinary.

Providential trials and union with God

Obviously the union with God we have been considering presupposes mortification or active purification, which we must impose upon ourselves in order to extinguish within us the concupiscence of the flesh, the concupiscence of the eyes, and the pride of life. But, over and above this, does it presuppose passive purifications or the patient and generous acceptance of crosses?

Most certainly it does. Nothing could be more definite than St. Catherine's teaching on this point when she speaks of temptation, of the trials of the just, and of the different sorts of tears, which must be carefully distinguished according as they proceed from the love of self or from pure love.

When faced with temptation, the soul can always resist in virtue of the merits of the blood of the Savior; God never commands the impossible. These temptations, when they are resisted, bring a deeper knowledge of ourselves and of God's goodness and strengthen us in virtue.[32]

[31] *Ibid.*, chaps. 60 and 61; pp. 111–112.
[32] *Ibid.*, chaps. 43, 59, 146; pp. 78, 108, 336.

Again, *God sends trials to purify us from our failings* and imperfections, and to put us to the necessity of growing in His love when there is no longer air to breathe but in Him.[33] The way the soul welcomes these trials is the test of its perfection.[34] Then, after shedding the unfruitful tears of self-love and those caused by servile fear which dreads the punishment rather than the sin, the soul by degrees comes to experience the tears of pure love. Thus in chapter 89 the saint tells us:

Inasmuch as she (the soul) has not yet arrived at great perfection, she often sheds sensual tears, and if thou askest Me why, I reply: because the root of self-love is not sensual love, for that has already been removed (by mortification and the preliminary trials) . . . but it is a spiritual love with which the soul derives spiritual consolations or loves some creature spiritually. . . . Therefore, when such a soul is deprived of the thing she loves, that is, internal or external consolation (the former coming from Me, the latter from the creature), and when temptations and the persecutions of men come on her, her heart is full of grief. And, as soon as the eye feels the grief and suffering of the heart, she begins to weep with a tender and passionate sorrow, pitying herself with the spiritual compassion of self-love. . . . But growing, and exercising herself in the light of self-knowledge, she conceives displeasure at herself and finally perfect self-hatred. . . . Immediately her eye . . . cries with hearty love for Me and for her neighbor, grieving for the offense against Me and her neighbor's loss. . . . Her heart is united to Me in love. . . . This is the last stage in which the soul is blessed and sorrowful. Blessed she is through the union which she feels herself to have with Me, tasting the divine love; sorrowful through the offenses which she sees done to My goodness and greatness, for

[33] *Ibid.,* chaps. 24, 45; pp. 47, 85.
[34] *Ibid.,* chap. 95; p. 183.

she has seen and tasted the bitterness of this in her self-knowledge, by which self-knowledge, together with her knowledge of Me, she arrived at the final stage. Yet this sorrow is no impediment to the unitive state.[35]

We are reminded by it how our Lord's own afflictions were ever united to a perfect peace, even on the cross.[36]

The purifications leading up to this state of union are plainly those same passive purifications which are treated of later on at such great length by St. John of the Cross. In proof of this it will be sufficient to read chapter 24: "How God prunes the living branches united to the stem in order to make them bear abundant fruit"; chapter 43: "Of the advantage of temptations"; chapter 45: "Who those are whom the thorns germinated by the world do not harm"; and finally chapter 20: "How, without enduring trials with patience, it is impossible to please God."

Conclusion: the general call

What conclusion are we to come to? The passages we have just quoted, lead to the following conclusions: This union with God which normally constitutes the full perfection of the Christian life is something more than a purely active

---

[35] Cf. *Dialogue*, chap. 89; pp. 166 f. Cf. also chap. 91 on the tears of fire, those wholly interior tears the saints shed at the sight of souls being lost; they cannot weep sensible tears, which would bring them some relief. There are thus five sorts of tears (cf. chap. 88; p. 164): (a) the tears of worldlings over the loss of the things of this world; (b) the tears of slaves who are wholly dominated by servile fear and weep over the chastisement they have incurred; (c) the tears of mercenary servants who do indeed weep over sin, but also over the loss of consolations; (d) the tears of the perfect who weep over the offense given to God and the loss of souls; (e) the tears of the absolutely perfect who weep besides over their exile, which deprives them of the vision of God and an indissoluble union with Him.

[36] Cf. St. Thomas, IIIa, q. 46, a. 8.

union, the result of our own personal activity under the influence of grace; it is also a passive union, the result of our docility to the Holy Ghost and the divine inspirations we receive through His sevenfold gifts, and these again normally increase with charity.

Thus the soul will normally arrive at the contemplative way in prayer, in reading the Scriptures and in assisting at mass, contemplating ever more profoundly the infinite value of the sacrifice of the altar, which perpetuates in substance the sacrifice of the cross. It will arrive also at the contemplative way of exercising the apostolate, in which, far from losing its union with God, it will preserve that union so that others may acquire it.

Is every interior soul called to this state of union? St. Catherine gives the answer to this question when she explains, in chapter 53, these words of our Lord: "If any man thirst, let him come to Me and drink. . . . Out of his belly shall flow rivers of living water" (John 7:37-38). The *Dialogue* says:

You were all invited generally and in particular, by My Truth, My Son, when, with ardent desire, He cried in the temple, saying: "Whosoever thirsteth, let him come to Me and drink." [37] . . . So that you are invited to the fountain of living water of grace, and you must come to Me, therefore, through My Son, with perseverance, keeping by Him who was made for you a bridge, not being turned back by any contrary wind that may arise, either of prosperity or of adversity, and to persevere until you find Me, who am the giver of the water of life, by means of this sweet and amorous Word, My only begotten Son. . . . The first condition required is for you to have thirst, because only those who thirst are invited: "Whosoever

[37] The reference here is to an individual call, not merely a general one. For many, however, the call remains remote; it becomes an immediate call only for those who are prepared to listen.

thirsteth, let him come to Me and drink." He who has no thirst will not persevere, for fatigue causes him to stop, persecution frightens him and no sooner does it begin to assail him than he retreats. He is afraid because he is alone. . . . You must then have thirst. . . . A man who is full of love and that of his neighbor, suddenly finds himself the companion of many royal virtues. Then the appetite of the soul is disposed to thirst. Thirst, I say, for virtue, and the honor of My name and salvation of souls. . . . Wherefore then he follows on with anxious desire, thirsting after the way of truth, in which he finds the fountain of the water of life, quenching his thirst in Me, the ocean of peace.[38]

St. Catherine expresses the same idea under another symbol in chapter 26, where the Father bids her pass over the bridge that binds earth to heaven, which is none other than Christ, the way, the truth, and the life. "These pierced feet of the Savior are steps by which thou canst arrive at His side, which manifests to thee the secret of His heart. . . . Then the soul is filled with love, seeing herself so much loved. Having passed the second step, the soul reaches out to the third, that is, to the mouth, where she finds peace."

Lastly, what is the sign by which we may recognize that the soul has arrived at perfect love? The Lord explains this to Catherine from chapter 74 to chapter 79:

It now remains to be told thee how it can be seen that souls have arrived at perfect love. This is seen by the same sign that was given to the holy disciples after they had received the Holy Spirit, when they came forth from the house, and fearlessly announced the doctrine of My Word, My only begotten Son, not fearing pain, but rather glorying therein. Those who are enamored of My honor, and famished for the food of souls, run to *the table of the Holy Cross.*

[38] Cf. *Dialogue,* chaps. 53, 54; pp. 100–103.

Their only ambition is to suffer and endure untold hardships in the service of their neighbor. They run eagerly in the path of Christ crucified, for it is His doctrine they accept, and they slacken not their pace on account of the persecutions, injuries, or pleasures of the world. They pass by all these things with fortitude and tranquil perseverance, their heart transformed by charity, tasting this sweetness of this food of the salvation of souls and ready to endure all things. This proves that the soul is in perfect love, loving without consideration of self. . . . If these souls love themselves, they do so for My sake, caring only for the praise and glory of My name. . . . In the midst of injuries it is patience that is resplendent, asserting her royal prerogative. . . . Such as these do not feel any separation from Me, whereas in the case of others, I come and go, not that I withdraw from them My grace, but the feeling of My sensible presence. I do not act thus to these most perfect ones who have arrived at a very high degree of perfection and are entirely dead to their own will, but I remain continually with them by My grace, giving them that feeling of My sensible presence.

Here obviously we have the exercise of charity and the gift of wisdom, each in an eminent degree, through which, St. Thomas says,[39] we are given a quasi-experimental knowledge of God present within us. This, surely, is the mystical life, the culminating point of the life of grace as it normally develops and the prelude to the heavenly life.

Those acquainted with the spiritual teaching of St. Thomas will realize how closely it agrees with the ascetic utterances of St. Catherine of Siena. In our opinion they are the expression of the traditional doctrine, which is content to lay stress on the right points in the reading of the Gospels and Epistles. "He that abideth in charity abideth in God, and God in Him"

[39] Cf. St. Thomas, IIa IIae, q. 45, a. 2.

(I John 4: 16); "His unction teacheth you of all things" (*ibid.*, 2: 27); "The Spirit Himself giveth testimony to our spirit that we are the sons of God. And if sons, heirs also; heirs indeed of God and joint heirs with Christ: yet so, if we suffer with Him, that we may also be glorified with Him" (Rom. 8: 16–17); "For you are dead: and your life is hid with Christ in God. When Christ shall appear, who is your life, then you also shall appear with Him in glory" (Col. 3: 3–4).

Have we forced the sense of these passages from the *Dialogue?* On the contrary, it is better to acknowledge that they cannot be comprehended fully. As Raphael was wont to say, "to comprehend is to equal," and to grasp the full meaning of the passages quoted, the same spirit of faith, the same exalted charity would be necessary as was possessed by St. Catherine of Siena.

Such, according to this witness, is the way of perfection God has traced out from all eternity in His providential plan to lead souls to their final destiny. It is the way that leads to the fountain of living water. "If any man thirst, let him come to Me and drink. . . . Out of his belly shall flow rivers of living water"; "He that shall drink of the water that I will give him shall not thirst forever" (John 7: 37–38; 4: 13).

PART V

Providence, Justice, and Mercy

CHAPTER XXV

Providence and Divine Justice

Now that we have spoken of providence in itself and its attitude to souls, we may suitably consider it in its relations with divine justice and with divine mercy. As in us prudence is connected with justice and the rest of the moral virtues, which it directs, so also in God *providence is united with justice and mercy,* these being the two great virtues of the love of God in our regard. Mercy has its foundation in the sovereign good in so far as it is of itself diffusive and tends to communicate itself externally. Justice, on the other hand, is founded in the indefeasible right of the sovereign good to be loved above all things.

These two virtues, says the psalmist, are found combined in all the works of God: "All the ways of the Lord are mercy and truth" (Ps. 24: 10). But, as St. Thomas remarks,[1] in certain of the divine works, as when God inflicts chastisement, justice stands out the more prominently, whereas in others, in the justification or conversion of sinners, for example, it is mercy that is more apparent.

This justice, which we attribute analogically to God, is not that commutative justice which regulates mutual dealings between equals: we cannot offer anything to God that does not belong to Him already. It is a distributive justice, analogous

---

[1] Cf. St. Thomas, Ia, q. 21, a. 4.

to that which a father shows toward his children or a good monarch toward his subjects. Thus, by reason of this justice of His, God first of all sees to it that every creature receives whatever is necessary for the attainment of its end. Secondly, He rewards merit and metes out punishment to sin and vice, especially if the sinner does not ask for mercy.

We shall do well to consider how providence directs the action of justice (1) during the course of our earthly existence, (2) at the moment of death, and (3) after death.

Providence and justice in the course of our earthly existence

Providence and justice combine in this present life to give us whatever is necessary to reach our true destiny: that is, to enable us to live an upright life, to know God in a supernatural way, to love and to serve Him, and so obtain eternal life.

There is a great inequality, no doubt, in circumstances, natural and supernatural, among men here on earth. Some are rich, others are poor; some are possessed of great natural gifts, whereas others are of a thankless disposition, weak in health, of a melancholy temperament. But God never commands the impossible; no one is tempted beyond his strength reinforced by the grace offered him. The savage of Central Africa or Central America has received far less than we have; but if he does what he can to follow the dictates of conscience, Providence will lead him on from grace to grace and eventually to a happy death; for him eternal life is possible of attainment. Jesus died for all men, and among those who have the use of reason only those are deprived of the grace necessary for salvation who by their resistance reject it. Since He never commands the impossible, God offers to all the means necessary for salvation.

Moreover, not infrequently *providence and justice will make up for the inequality* in natural conditions by their distribution of supernatural gifts. Often the poor man in his simplicity will be more pleasing to God than the rich man, and will receive greater graces. Let us recall the parable of the wicked rich man recorded in St. Luke (16: 19–31):

There was a certain rich man who was clothed in purple and fine linen and feasted sumptuously every day. And there was a certain beggar named Lazarus, who lay at his gate, full of sores, desiring to be filled with the crumbs that fell from the rich man's table. And no one did give him: moreover the dogs came and licked his sores. And it came to pass that the beggar died and was carried by the angels into Abraham's bosom. And the rich man also died. . . . And lifting up his eyes when he was in torments, he saw Abraham . . . and he cried and said: Father Abraham, have mercy on me. . . . And Abraham said to him; Son, remember that thou didst receive good things in thy lifetime, and likewise Lazarus evil things: but now he is comforted and thou art tormented.

This is to declare in effect that, where natural conditions are unequal, providence and justice will sometimes make up for it in the distribution of natural gifts. Again, the Gospel beatitudes tell us that one who is bereft of this world's enjoyments will in some cases feel more powerfully drawn to the joys of the interior life. This is what our Lord would have us understand when He says: "Blessed are the poor in spirit. . . . Blessed are the meek . . . that suffer persecution for justice' sake: for theirs is the kingdom of heaven." [2]

[2] Cf. The Canticle of Anna, I Kings 2: 1–10, and the *Magnificat*.

The love of Jesus goes out to those servants of His nailed to the cross, because then they are more like Him through the effective oblation they make of their entire being for the salvation of sinners. In them He continues to live; in them He may be said to prolong down to the end of time His own prayers and sufferings, and above all His love, for perfect love consists in the complete surrender of self.

For some there comes a time when every road in life is barred against them; humanly speaking, the future holds out no prospect whatever to them. In some cases this is the moment when the call comes to something higher. Some there are who spend long years confined to a bed of pain; for these henceforth there is no way open but the way of holiness.[3]

And so providence and justice, while giving to each one what is strictly necessary, will often make up for any disparity in natural conditions by the bestowal of grace. They reward us, even in this life, for the merits we have gained, reminding us, too, of our solemn duties by salutary warnings and well-

---

[3] We have an instance of this in recent years in the saintly Abbé Girard of Coutances, whose life of suffering is described by Miriam de Girard in *Vingt-deux ans de martyr*.

In other cases, atrocious calumnies have been the occasion of immense spiritual progress. During the pontificate of Pius X there lived in Rome a deeply Christian man, Aristides Leonori, an architect, who was responsible for a number of beautiful churches in various countries. In Rome he had established a work for the protection of young orphans. One of them falsely accused him before the civil courts of a most vile offense, having been bribed to do so by those hostile to this charitable work. Leonori, his hair whitened in a single night, appeared before the court and listened to the accusation now made publicly against him by this youth for whom he had done so much. When he had ended, Leonori looked steadily at him and simply said: "What could have induced you to say such things, my friend, after all I have done for you since you were a child?" At this the youth could no longer restrain his emotion and burst into tears, confessing that he had been paid to bring this lying charge against Leonori and thus destroy his work. There most decidedly Leonori found the royal road of the cross. He was a great friend of Pius X and died in the odor of sanctity.

deserved corrections, which are no more than medicinal punishments for the purpose of bringing us back into the right
path. In this way will a mother correct her child if she loves
it with a really enlightened, ardent love. When these salutary corrections are well received, we make expiation for our
sins, and God takes the opportunity of inspiring us with a
more sincere humility and a purer, stronger love. There is
a sharp distinction between souls according to their willingness or unwillingness to listen to these warnings from
God.

Providence and justice at the moment of death

As a general rule those who have paid heed during life to
the warning of God's justice and to the indefeasible right of
the sovereign good to be loved above all things are not taken
unawares when death comes, and in that supreme moment
they find peace. Wholly otherwise is it usually with those
who have refused to give ear to the divine warnings and who
during life have confounded hope with presumption.

If there is one thing that is dependent on Providence, it is
the hour of our death. "Be ye also ready," says our Lord, "for
at what hour you think not the Son of man will come" (Luke
12: 40). The same is true of the manner of our death and the
circumstances surrounding it. It is all completely unknown
to us; it rests upon Providence, in which we must put all our
trust, while preparing ourselves to die well by a better life.

Looked at from the point of view of divine justice, what a
vast difference there is between the death of the just and that
of the sinner! In the Apocalypse (20: 6, 14) the death of the
sinner is called a "second death," for he is already spiritually

dead to the life of grace, and if the soul departs from the body in this condition it will be deprived of that supernatural life forever. May God preserve us from that second death. The unrepentant sinner, says St. Catherine,[4]

is about to die in his injustice, and appear before the supreme Judge with the light of faith extinguished in him, which he received burning in holy baptism (but which he has blown out with the wind of pride) and with the vanity of his heart, with which he sets his sails unfurled to all the winds of flattery. Thus did he hasten down the stream of the delights and dignities of the world at his own will, giving in to the seductions of his weak flesh and the temptations of the devil.

The remorse of conscience (which is not to be confused with repentance) is then aroused with such lively feelings, that it gnaws the very heart of the sinner, because he recognizes the truth of what at first he knew not, and his error is the cause of great confusion to him. . . . The devil torments him with infidelity in order to drive him to despair.[5]

What are we to say of this struggle which finds the sinner disarmed, deprived of his living faith now extinguished in him, deprived also of a steadfast hope, which he has failed to foster as he ought by committing himself daily to God and laboring for Him? The wretched sinner has placed all his hopes in himself, not realizing that everything he possessed was but lent and must one day be accounted for. He is deprived, too, of the flame of charity, of the love of God which he has now utterly lost. He finds himself alone in his spiritual nakedness, bereft of all virtue. Having turned a deaf ear to the many warnings given during life, now, whichever way he turns, he sees nothing but cause for confusion. Due consideration was not given to divine justice during life; now it is the full

---

[4] *Dialogue,* chap. 36; p. 67.
[5] *Ibid.,* chap. 132; p. 288.

weight of that justice which makes itself felt, while the enemy of all good seeks to persuade the sinner that for him henceforth there is no mercy. How we should pray for those who are in their agony! If we do, then others will pray for us when our last moment comes.

In those last moments mercy still accommodates itself to the sinner, as it did to Judas when our Lord said at the last supper (Matt. 26:24): "Woe to that man by whom the Son of man shall be betrayed. It were better for him, if that man had not been born." Our Lord has not yet said who it is that is about to betray Him: He is too tender-hearted to reveal it. And then, the Gospel continues, "Judas that betrayed Him answering said: Is it I Rabbi? He saith to him: Thou hast said it." In delaying to put the question until the rest of the Apostles had done so, Judas feigns innocence, as if that were possible with one who even in this world reads the secrets of the heart. Notice, says St. Thomas commenting on these words, with what gentleness Jesus continues to call him friend and answers: "Thou hast said it"; as if to say, "It is you, not I, who say so, who are revealing it." Once again our Lord shows Himself full of compassion and mercy, closing His eyes to the sins of men so as to give them one more salutary warning and lead them to repentance. In Him are realized those touching words of the Scripture: "The Lord is compassionate and merciful" (Ps. 102:8); "overlooking the sins of men for the sake of repentance" (Wis. 11:24); "Let the meek hear and rejoice" (Ps. 33:3).

In view of these final warnings from God, we may well ask how the sinner dare accuse God of being a tyrant. No, it is the sinner who is his own tyrant; it is the sinner who has no consideration for himself; and none for God either, since he refuses Him the joy of applying to him what He said of the prodigal: "This my son was lost and is found" (Luke 15:24).

If the sinner will only disburden his conscience by a sincere confession, making acts of faith, of confidence in God, and contrition, at the last moment the divine mercy will enter in to temper justice and will save him. By reason of God's mercy every man may cling to hope at death if he so wills, if he offers no resistance. Remorse will then give place to repentance.

Otherwise the soul succumbs to remorse and abandons itself to *despair,* a sin far more heinous than any of the preceding, as in that neither infirmity nor the allurements of sensuality can excuse, a sin by which the sinner esteems his wickedness as outweighing God's divine mercy. And once in this despair, the soul no longer grieves over sin as an offense against God, it grieves only over its own miserable condition, a grief very different from that which characterizes attrition or contrition.

Blessed is the sinner who like the good thief then repents, reflecting that, as St. Catherine says,[6] "the divine mercy is greater without comparison than all the sins which any creature can commit."

Happier still is the just soul that throughout life has given due thought to the loving fulfilment of duty and, after the merits won and the struggle sustained here on earth, yearns for death in order to enjoy the vision of God, even as St. Paul

[6] *Ibid.,* p. 290.

desired "to be dissolved and to be with Christ" (Phil. 1: 23). As a rule a great peace fills the soul of the just in their last agony, a peace the more profound the greater their perfection; and this is often most true of those who during life have had the greatest dread of the divine justice. For them death is peaceful because their enemies have been vanquished during life.[7] Sensuality has been reduced to subjection under the curb of reason. Virtue triumphs over nature, overcoming the natural fear of death through the longing to attain their final end, the sovereign good. Being conformed to justice during life, conscience continues tranquil, though the devil seeks to trouble and alarm it.

At that moment, it is true, the value of this present time of trial, which is the price of virtue, will be more clearly seen, and the just soul will reproach itself for not having made better use of its time. But the sorrow it then experiences will not overwhelm it; it will be profitable in inducing the soul to recollect itself and place itself in the presence of the precious blood of our Savior, the Lamb of God who takes away the sins of the world. In the passage from time to eternity there is thus an admirable blending of God's mercy and justice. In his dying moments the just man anticipates the bliss prepared for him; he has a foretaste of his destiny which may sometimes be seen reflected in his countenance.

God's providence and justice in the next life

After death God's providence and justice intervene forthwith in *the particular judgment.* Revelation tells us so in the parable of the wicked rich man and the beggar Lazarus,

[7] *Ibid.,* chap. 131; p. 284.

whose souls were judged once and for all the moment they quitted this earth. Equally clear is St. Paul's teaching in more than one passage: "We must all be manifested before the judgment seat of Christ, that everyone may receive the proper things of the body, according as he hath done, whether good or evil";[8] "I have a desire to be dissolved and to be with Christ";[9] "I have finished my course. . . . As to the rest, there is laid up for me a crown of justice which the Lord the just judge will render to me in that day: and not only to me, but to them also that love His coming";[10] "It is appointed unto man once to die, and after this the judgment."[11]

It was the universal belief of the early Church that the martyrs entered at once into heaven and that unrepentant sinners, like the bad thief, received their punishment immediately after death.

The nature of this particular judgment is to be explained from the condition of the soul when separated from the body. Once the body has been left behind, the soul has direct vision of itself as a spiritual substance, in the same way that the pure spirit has direct vision of itself, and in that instant it is made aware of its moral condition. It receives an interior illumination rendering all discussion useless. God passes sentence, which is then transmitted by conscience, the echo of God's voice. The soul now sees plainly what is its due according to its merits and demerits, which then stand out quite distinctly before it. This is what the liturgy expresses symbolically in the *Dies Irae: Liber scriptus proferetur, in quo*

[8] See II Cor. 5: 10.
[9] Phil. 1: 23.
[10] See II Tim. 4: 8.
[11] Heb. 9: 27.

totum continetur. The soul will see whatever has been written down in the book of life concerning it.[12]

Justice will then mete out condign punishment for sins committed, to last for a time or for eternity. Mortal sin still unrepented at the moment of death will be henceforth like an incurable disease, but in something that cannot die, the immortal soul. The sinner has turned his back unrepentantly on the sovereign good, has in practice denied its infinite dignity as the last end, and has failed to revoke this practical denial while there was yet time. It is an irreparable disorder

---

[12] Immediately after the death of Gerontius, Newman puts these words into the mouth of the angel guardian:

> "When then—if such thy lot—thou seest thy Judge,
> The sight of Him will kindle in thy heart
> All tender, gracious, reverential thoughts.
> Thou wilt be sick with joy, and yearn for Him
> That one so sweet should e'er have placed Himself
> At disadvantage such, as to be used
> So vilely by a being so vile as thee.
> There is a pleading in His pensive eyes,
> Will pierce thee to the quick, and trouble thee,
> And thou wilt hate and loathe thyself; for, though
> Now sinless, thou wilt feel that thou hast sinned
> As never thou didst feel; and wilt desire
> To slink away, and hide thee from His sight;
> And yet wilt have a longing eye to dwell
> Within the beauty of His countenance.
> And those two pains, so counter and so keen—
> The longing for Him, when thou seest Him not;
> The shame of self at thought of seeing Him—
> Will be thy veriest, sharpest purgatory.
>
> .   .   .   .
>
> It is the face of the Incarnate God
> Shall smite thee with that keen and subtle pain;
> And yet the memory which it leaves will be
> A sovereign febrifuge to heal the wound;
> And yet withal it will the wound provoke,
> And aggravate and widen it the more."
> *The Dream of Gerontius,* 710–739.

and a conscious one. Remorse is there, but without repentance; pride and rebellion will continue forever and with them the punishment they deserve. But above all it involves the perpetual loss of the divine life of grace and the vision of God, of supreme bliss, the sinner clearly realizing that through his own fault he has failed forever to attain his destined end.[13]

Here the justice of God is seen to be infinite; it is a mystery that surpasses our understanding, as does the mystery of His mercy.

Here on earth the concepts or ideas we are able to have of divine justice and the rest of God's perfections must always remain limited, confined, and that in spite of the correction we apply in denying all limitation. These concepts represent the divine attributes as distinct from one another, though we did say that there is no real distinction between them. It follows that these restricted ideas harden the spiritual features of God somewhat, as the human features are hardened when we attempt to reproduce them in little squares of mosaic. Our concept of justice being distinct from that of mercy, divine justice appears to us not only infinitely just but absolutely unyielding, and His mercy appears to be sheer caprice.

In heaven, however, we shall see how the divine perfections, even those to all appearances directly opposed, are intimately blended, identified in fact, yet without destroying one another in the Deity, in God's intimate life, of which we shall then have distinct and immediate knowledge.

We shall then see that nowhere but in God do justice and mercy exist in their pure state, free from all imperfection, and that just as in us the cardinal virtues are interconnected

[13] Cf. St. Thomas, Ia IIae, q. 87, a. 3.

and inseparable, so also in Him justice cannot exist unless it is united with mercy, and conversely there can be no such thing as mercy apart from justice and providence.[14]

This is what is revealed to the saints from the moment of the particular judgment, which is immediately followed by their entry into glory.

There will be another manifestation of justice in the *general judgment* after the resurrection of the body, according to the words of the Creed: "I believe in Jesus Christ . . . who shall come to judge the living and the dead." Our Lord tells us (Matt. 24: 30–46): "All tribes of the earth . . . shall see the Son of man coming in the clouds of heaven with much power and majesty. And He shall send His angels with a trumpet and a great voice: and they shall gather together His elect from the four winds, from the farthest parts of the heavens to the utmost bounds of them." If Jesus had not been the Son of God, how could He, a poor village artisan, have uttered such words as these? It would have been the height of foolishness, whereas everything goes to show that it is the essence of wisdom.

This general judgment is evidently expedient, because man is not merely a private person, but is a social being, and this judgment will reveal to all men the rectitude of Providence and its ways, the reason also of its decisions and their outcome. Divine justice will then appear in all its sovereign perfection in contrast to the frequent miscarriage of human justice. Infinite mercy will be revealed in the case of repentant and pardoned sinners. Every knee will bend before Christ the Savior, triumphant now over sin, the devil, and death.

[14] Cf. St. Thomas, Ia IIae, q.65, a.1–3.

Then will appear also the glory of the elect: he who was humbled will now be exalted, and the kingdom of God will be established forever in the light of glory, in love and in peace.[15]

This is the kingdom we long for when day by day we say in the Our Father: "Thy kingdom come, Thy will [signified to us in Thy precepts and in the spirit of the counsels] be done on earth as it is in heaven." [16]

[15] Then will be realized those words from the Canticle of Anna, I Kings 2: 1–10: "The bow of the mighty is overcome: and the weak are girt with strength. The Lord killeth and maketh alive: He bringeth down to hell and bringeth back again. The Lord maketh poor and maketh rich: He humbleth and He exalteth. . . . He lifteth up the poor from the dunghill: that he may sit with princes, and hold the throne of glory." Here in the Old Testament is the prelude to the *Magnificat*.

[16] A young Jew, the son of an Austrian banker, who knew little of the Gospel beyond the *Our Father*, was one day given an opportunity of revenging himself on an enemy. But at the very moment the opportunity presented itself, there came to his mind the words, "Forgive us our trespasses as we forgive those who trespass against us." Instead of carrying out his revenge, he forgave his enemy completely with all his heart, and immediately his eyes were opened: he saw the Gospel in all its majesty and most firmly believed. He became a good Catholic and afterwards a priest and religious of the Order of St. Dominic. The kingdom of God was revealed to him the very moment he forgave.

CHAPTER XXVI

Providence and Mercy

We have been considering the relations between providence and divine mercy in the distribution of the means necessary for all to attain their end, in rewarding merit and chastising sin and wickedness. It now remains for us to speak of providence in its relation to divine mercy. God's mercy seems at first sight to differ so widely from His justice as to be directly contrary to it; it appears to set itself up in opposition to justice, intervening in order to restrict its rights. Yet in reality there can never be any opposition between two divine perfections; however widely they may differ from each other, the one cannot be the negation of the other. As we have already seen, they are so united in the eminence of the Deity, the intimate life of God, as to be completely identified.

Far from setting itself up in opposition to justice and putting restrictions upon it, mercy unites with it, but in such a way as to surpass it, as St. Thomas says.[1] In psalm 24: 10, we read: "All the ways of the Lord are mercy and truth (i. e., justice)," but, adds St. James, "Mercy exalteth herself above judgment [justice]." [2] In what sense is this to be understood? Says St. Thomas: [3]

[1] Cf. St. Thomas, Ia, q.21, a.4.
[2] James 2: 13.
[3] *Loc. cit.*

In this sense, that every work of justice presupposes and is founded upon a work of mercy, a work of pure loving kindness, wholly gratuitous. If, in fact, there is anything due from God to the creature, it is in virtue of some gift that has preceded it. . . . If He owes it to Himself to grant us grace necessary for salvation, it is because He has first given us the grace with which to merit. Mercy (or pure goodness) is thus, as it were, the root and source of all the works of God; its virtue pervades, dominates them all. As the ultimate fount of every gift, it exercises the more powerful influence, and for this reason it transcends justice, which follows upon mercy and continues to be subordinate to it."

If justice is a branch springing from the tree of God's love, then the tree itself is mercy, or pure goodness ever tending to communicate, to radiate itself externally.

We shall best understand this by a consideration of our own lives. Our best course will be to proceed, as we did with justice, by considering the relations between providence and mercy first of all in this present life, then at the moment of death, and lastly in the next life.

Providence and mercy in the course of our present life

If in this present life divine justice gives to each of us whatever is required for us to live rightly and so attain our end, mercy, on the other hand, gives far beyond what is strictly necessary, and it is in this sense that it surpasses justice.

In creating us, for example, God might have established us in a purely natural condition, endowing us with a spiritual, immortal soul, but not with grace. Out of pure goodness from the very day of creation He has granted us to participate supernaturally in His intimate life by bestowing on us sanctifying grace, the principle of our supernatural merits.

Again, after the fall, He might have left us in our fallen condition so far as justice is concerned. Or He might have raised us up from sin by a simple act of forgiveness conveyed through the mouth of a prophet after we had fulfilled certain conditions. But He has done something infinitely greater than this: out of pure mercy He gave us His only Son as a redeeming victim, and it is possible for us at all times to appeal to the infinite merits of the Savior. Justice loses none of its rights, but it is mercy that prevails.

Once Jesus had died for us, all we needed was to be guided by interior graces as well as by the preaching of the Gospel; but divine mercy has given us far more than this: it has given us the Eucharist, in which the sacrifice of the cross is perpetuated in substance on our altars and the fruits of that sacrifice are applied to our souls.[4]

Finally, those of us who have been born into Christian and Catholic families have received incomparably more from the divine mercy than the bare essentials God has given to the savage of Central Africa. With those essentials God has given to the savage, provided the first prevenient graces are not resisted, the savage will receive whatever further graces are required for salvation; but we have received much more than this from our very childhood. When we consider the matter, we realize that we have been led on by the invisible hands of Providence and Mercy, preserving us from many a false step and raising up each one of us individually when we have fallen.

Again, if divine justice rewards the merits we have acquired even in this life, *the gifts of mercy go far beyond anything we have deserved.*

---

[4] Cf. St. Catherine of Siena, *Dialogue,* chap. 30.

In the collect for the eleventh Sunday after Pentecost we pray: "Almighty and eternal God, who in the abundance of Thy goodness dost surpass the merits and even the desires of Thy suppliants: pour out Thy mercy upon us, forgive us the things our conscience must fear, and grant us what we cannot presume to ask. Through our Lord Jesus Christ, etc." [5]

The grace of absolution from mortal sin is not something that can be merited, it is a gratuitous gift. And how often has that grace been granted us!

Again, by no merit of ours could we obtain *the grace of communion;* it is the fruit of the sacrament of the Eucharist, which of itself produces that grace within us, even daily if we wish. And how many communions has not the divine mercy granted us! Let us bear in mind that if we are faithful in fighting against all attachment to venial sin, each successive communion becomes substantially more fervent than the last, since each successive communion must not only preserve but increase charity within us, thus disposing us to receive our Lord on the morrow with a substantial fervor, a readiness of desire not merely the same but more intense.

This *law of acceleration governing the love of God* in the souls of the just must, if we are alive to it, arouse our admiration. It will be seen that, just as the stone falls more rapidly as it approaches the earth which is attracting it, so is it with the souls of the just: the more nearly they approach to God and therefore the greater the force of His attraction, the more rapid must their progress be. We then grasp the meaning of these words of the psalm (32:5): "The earth is full of

---

[5] *Omnipotens sempiterne Deus, qui abundantia pietatis tuae et merita supplicum excedis et vota; effunde super nos misericordiam tuam: ut dimittas quae conscientia metuit, et adjicias quod oratio non praesumit. Per Dominum nostrum Jesum Christum Filium, etc.*

the mercy of the Lord." Even the sinner can say with the psalmist: "Return, O Lord, . . . we are filled in the morning with Thy mercy: and we have rejoiced, and are delighted all our days" (Ps. 89: 14).

If we could only see the whole span of our life as it is written down in the book of life, how many instances should we find where providence and mercy have intervened to piece together again the chain of our merits which again and again perhaps we have broken by our sins! But at the final moment mercy intervenes in a manner no less gracious.

Providence and mercy at the moment of death

If at that moment justice alone were to enter in, all those who had led a life of sin would die as they had lived. After so many warnings from Providence had been neglected, the final warning would receive no better response; remorse would not give place to a salutary repentance. Thanks to the mercy of God, however, this last appeal is more insistent. If His justice inflicts the punishment due to sin, here again His mercy will outstrip it by pardoning. To pardon means to "give beyond" what is due. The rights of justice are safeguarded, but mercy outweighs it by constantly inspiring the sinner, as death approaches, to make a great act of love for God, and of contrition, which will wipe away sin and the eternal punishment mortal sin incurs. And so, through the intervention of mercy, through the infinite merits of the Savior, through the intercession of Mary refuge of sinners, and of St. Joseph patron of the dying, *for many persons death is something very different from the way they lived.* These are the laborers of the eleventh hour whom the Gospel parable speaks of (Matt. 20:9); they receive eternal life, as do the rest, in proportion to the few meritorious acts they have performed before death, when already in their agony. Such was the death of the good thief who, touched by the loving-kindness of Jesus dying on the cross, was converted, and he had the happiness of hearing from the Savior's lips: "This day thou shalt be with Me in paradise" (Luke 23:43).

These interventions of mercy at the moment of death are one of the sublimest features of the true religion. This was often clearly enough shown during the World War, when a man, dying a tragic death after absolution, was saved, who in ordinary circumstances, in the midst of his occupations and pleasures, would perhaps have been lost.

So, too, where there are Catholic hospitals, many a poor soul, heeding the warning that the disease from which he is suffering is soon to carry him off, there prepares himself for a happy death. He listens to some sister speaking to him on this subject and then to the priest who finally reconciles him to God after thirty or forty years of a life spent practically in indifference, a life that has left much to be desired.

The divine mercy extends appealingly to every one of the dying. Jesus said: "Come to Me, all you that labor and are burdened: and I will refresh you" (Matt. 11:28). He dies for all men: as the beautiful prayers for those in their agony remind us, He is the Lamb of God who takes away the sins of the world.

The death of the repentant sinner is one of the greatest manifestations of divine mercy. Some striking examples of it are given us in the life of St. Catherine of Siena written by her confessor, Blessed Raymund of Capua.[6] Two condemned

---

[6] *Life,* chap. 7 (Bollandists, April 30, p. 918).

criminals, who were being tortured with hot pincers, were blaspheming ceaselessly, and then through her prayers the unhappy wretches received a vision of our Lord, who appeared covered with wounds, inviting them to repent and promising them forgiveness. At that same moment they begged earnestly for a priest and with heartfelt contrition confessed their sins. Thereupon their blasphemies were turned to praise, and they went joyfully to their death as to the gateway of heaven. Those who witnessed the incident were struck with amazement and could assign no reason for such a sudden change in their interior dispositions.

On another occasion the saint herself was present at the execution of the young nobleman, Nicholas Tuldo, who had been condemned to death for criticizing the government. When she saw how desperately he clung to life, refusing to accept what seemed to him so unjust a punishment, she herself prepared his soul to appear before God. Her account of the death-scene is given in a letter to her confessor, Raymund of Capua:

Seeing me at the place of execution, he began to smile, and wanted me to make the sign of the cross upon him. I did so and then I said to him: "On your knees, sweetness my brother. You are going to the marriage feast. You are about to enter into everlasting life." He prostrated himself with great gentleness, and I stretched out his neck; and bending over him, I reminded him of the blood of the Lamb. His lips said nought save "Jesus" and "Catherine." And so saying, I received his head in my hands, closing my eyes in the divine goodness, and saying, "I will."

Then I saw, as might the clearness of the sun be seen, the God-man, the wound in His side being open. He was permitting a transfusion of that blood with His blood, and adding the fire of holy desire given to that soul by grace to the fire of His divine charity.[7]

But if the death of the sinner is a manifestation of the divine mercy, far more beautiful is the death of the saint who has always remained faithful. His last moments are, as a rule, peaceful because he has vanquished his enemies during life and his soul is now prepared for the passage to eternity. Uniting himself with all the masses then being celebrated, he makes of his death a last sacrifice of reparation, adoration, thanksgiving, and supplication to obtain thereby that last grace of final perseverance which carries with it the assurance of salvation.

Providence and mercy after death

Mercy and justice, the Scripture tells us (Ps. 24: 10), combine in every one of God's works; but whereas mercy is the more prominent in some, as in the conversion of the sinner, in others justice predominates, as in the case of punishment due to sin.

Thus it is that, as St. Thomas says,[8] after death "mercy intervenes on behalf of the reprobate, in the sense that *the punishment they receive is less than they deserve.*" Were justice alone to enter in, they would suffer still more. St. Catherine of Siena is of the same mind.[9] Mercy is there to temper justice even for those who have fomented hatred among others, between class and class, nation and nation, even for the most perverse, for monsters like Nero, who have shown a refinement of malice, an obstinacy of will that spurned all advice.

[7] *Letters of St. Catherine of Siena,* tr. by Scudder, p. 113.
[8] See St. Thomas, Ia, q. 21, a. 4 ad 1um.
[9] *Dialogue,* chap. 30.

Obviously, with *the souls in purgatory* divine mercy is still more active, inspiring them with the loving desire to make reparation, which tempers a little that keen purifying pain they are undergoing and confirms them in their assurance of salvation.

In heaven divine mercy shines forth in the saints according to the intensity of their love for God. Our Lord will greet them with the words recorded in St. Matthew (25: 34):

Come, ye blessed of My Father, possess you the kingdom prepared for you from the foundation of the world. For I was hungry, and you gave Me to eat: I was thirsty, and you gave Me to drink: I was a stranger, and you took Me in: naked, and you covered Me: sick, and you visited Me: I was in prison, and you came to Me. Then shall the just . . . answer Him saying: Lord, when did we see Thee hungry . . . thirsty . . . and came to Thee? And the King answering shall say to them: Amen I say to you, as long as you did it to one of these My least brethren, you did it to Me.

What joy will be ours in that first instant of our entering into glory, when we shall receive the light of glory in order to see God face to face, in a vision that will know no end, whose measure will be the unique instant of changeless eternity.

How consoling is the thought of this infinite mercy, which transcends all wickedness and is inexhaustible. For this reason no relapse into sin, however shameful, however criminal, should cause a sinner to despair. There can be no greater outrage against God than to consider His loving kindness inadequate to forgive. As St. Catherine of Siena tells us, "His mercy is greater without any comparison than all the sins which any creature can commit." [10]

[10] *Dialogue,* chap. 32.

In this matter we should keep before our minds these words from the psalms, words that the liturgy is constantly putting before us:

The mercies of the Lord I will sing forever. . . . For Thou hast said: Mercy shall be built up forever in the heavens. Thy truth shall be prepared in them. . . . Thou art mighty, O Lord, and Thy truth is round about Thee, Thou rulest the power of the sea. . . . Thou hast humbled the proud one. . . .

The Lord is compassionate and merciful: longsuffering and plenteous in mercy. He will not always be angry: nor will He threaten forever. . . . For according to the height of the heaven above the earth, He hath strengthened His mercy toward them that fear Him. . . . As a father hath compassion on his children, so hath the Lord compassion on them that fear Him: for He knoweth our frame. He remembereth that we are dust.

Man's days are as grass: as the flower of the field so shall he flourish. For the spirit shall pass in him, and he shall not be. . . . But the mercy of the Lord is from eternity and unto eternity, upon them that fear Him.[11]

May the Lord deign that these words be revealed in us also, that we may glorify Him forever.

Rarely have the relations between mercy, justice, and providence been better expressed than in the *Dies Irae*.[12]

> Day of wrath and doom impending,
> David's word with Sibyl's blending!
> Heaven and earth in ashes ending!
>
> O, what fear man's bosom rendeth,
> When from heaven the Judge descendeth,
> On whose sentence all dependeth!

[11] Ps. 88: 2 ff.; Ps. 102: 8–17.
[12] Tr. by Irons; cf. *The Hymns of the Breviary and Missal.*

Death is struck, and nature quaking,
All creation is awaking,
To its Judge an answer making.

Lo! the book exactly worded,
Wherein all hath been recorded;
Thence shall judgment be awarded.

When the Judge His seat attaineth,
And each hidden deed arraigneth,
Nothing unavenged remaineth.

King of Majesty tremendous,
Who dost free salvation send us,
Fount of pity, then befriend us!

Think, kind Jesu! my salvation
Caused Thy wondrous incarnation;
Leave me not to reprobation.

Faint and weary Thou hast sought me,
On the cross of suffering bought me;
Shall such grace be vainly bought me?

Righteous Judge! for sin's pollution
Grant Thy gift of absolution,
Ere that day of retribution.

Through the sinful woman shriven,
Through the dying thief forgiven,
Thou to me a hope hast given.

Low I kneel, with heart submission,
Crushed to ashes in contrition;
Help me in my last condition!

Spare, O God, in mercy spare him!
Lord all-pitying, Jesu blest,
Grant them Thine eternal rest. Amen.

Let us acquire the habit of praying for those in their last agony, that the divine mercy may incline to them. Then others will assist us when the moment of our own death arrives. Where or how we shall die, we know not; it may be quite alone; but if we have prayed frequently for the dying, if again and again we have said with attention and from our hearts: "Holy Mary, Mother of God, pray for us sinners now and at the hour of our death," then at the supreme moment mercy will incline to us also.[18]

[18] In that fine book of his, *Le Docteur Angélique*, J. Maritain has set down this profound reflection: "How reconcile two apparently contradictory facts: the fact that modern history appears to be, as Berdyaev says, on the threshold of a new Middle Age in which the unity and universality of Christian culture will be recovered and extended this time to the whole universe, and the fact that the general trend of civilization seems to be toward the universalism of Antichrist and his iron rod rather than toward the universalism of Christ and His emancipatory law, and in any event to forbid the hope of a unification of the world in one universal Christian empire.

"As far as I am concerned, my answer is as follows: I think that two immanent tendencies intersect at every point in the history of the world . . . one tendency draws upward everything in the world which participates in the divine life of the Church, which is in the world but not of the world, and follows the attraction of Christ, the head of the human race.

"The other tendency draws downward everything in the world which belongs to the prince of the world. . . . History suffers these two internal strains as it moves forward in time, and human affairs are so subjected to a distension of increasing force until the fabric in the end gives way. So the cockle grows up along with the wheat; the capital of sin increases throughout the whole course of history and the capital of grace increases also and superabounds. Christian heroism will one day become the sole solution for the problem of life. . . . Then we shall doubtless see coincident with the worst condition in human history a flowering of sanctity." English tr. by J. F. Scanlan, *St. Thomas Aquinas, Angel of the Schools,* p. 86.

CHAPTER XXVII

PROVIDENCE AND THE GRACE OF A HAPPY DEATH

One of those vital questions that should be of the deepest interest to every soul, no matter what its condition, is the question of a happy death. On this subject St. Augustine wrote one of his last and finest works, the *Gift of Perseverance,* in which he gives his definite views on the mystery of grace.

By the Semi-Pelagians on the one hand and Protestants and Jansenists on the other, this vital question has been understood in widely different, even fundamentally opposite, senses. These two contrary heresies prompted the Church to define her teaching on this point more precisely and to declare the truth in all its sublimity as the transcendent mean between the extreme errors.

A brief summary of these errors will give us a better appreciation of the truth and a clearer understanding of what the grace of a happy death really is. We shall then see how this grace may be obtained.

The doctrine of the Church and the errors opposed to it

The *Semi-Pelagians* maintained that man can have the *initium fidei et salutis,* the beginning of faith and a good desire apart from grace, this beginning being subsequently confirmed by God. According to their view, not God but the sinner himself takes the first step in the sinner's conversion.

On the same principles the Semi-Pelagians maintained that, once justified by grace, man can persevere until death without a further special grace. For the just to persevere unto the end, it is enough, they said, that the *initium salutis,* this natural good will, should persist.

It amounted to this, that God not only wills all men to be saved, but wills it to the same extent in every case; and further, that precisely the element which distinguishes the just from the wicked—the *initium salutis* and those final good dispositions which are to be found in one and not in another, in Peter and not in Judas—is not to be referred to God as its author; He is simply an onlooker.

It meant the rejection of the mystery of predestination and the ignoring of those words of our Lord: "No man can come to Me, except the Father, who sent Me, draw him" (John 6: 44), words that apply both to the initial and to the final impulse of our hearts to God. "Without Me you can do nothing" (John 15: 5), our Lord said. As the Second Council of Orange recalled against the Semi-Pelagians, St. Paul added: "Who distinguisheth thee? Or what hast thou that thou hast not received?" (I Cor. 4: 7); "Not that we are sufficient to think anything of ourselves, as of ourselves; but our sufficiency is from God" (II Cor. 3: 5). If this is true of our every thought, still more true is it of the least salutary desire, whether it be the first or the last.

St. Augustine, too, pointed out that both the first grace and the last are in an especial way gratuitous. *The first prevenient grace cannot be merited* or in any way be due to a purely natural good impulse, since the principle of merit is sanctifying grace, and this, as its very name implies, is a gratuitous gift, a life wholly supernatural both for men and for angels.

Again, the final grace, *the grace of final perseverance,* is, as St. Augustine pointed out, *a special gift,* a grace peculiar to the elect, of whom our Lord said: "No one can snatch them out of the hand of My Father" (John 10:29). When this grace is granted, he added, it is from sheer mercy; if on the other hand it is not given, it is as a just chastisement for sin, usually for repeated sin, which has alienated the soul from God. We have it exemplified in the death of the good thief and that of the unrepentant one.

For St. Augustine the question is governed by two great principles. The first is that not only are *the elect* foreseen by God, but they are *more beloved* by Him. St. Paul had said: "Who distinguisheth thee? Or what hast thou that thou hast not received?" (I Cor. 4:17.) Later on we find St. Thomas saying that "since the love of God is cause of whatever goodness there is in things, no one thing would be better than another, if God did not will a greater good for one than for the other" (Ia, q. 20, a. 3).

The other principle, formulated by St. Augustine in express terms, is that *God never commands the impossible,* though in commanding He admonishes us to do what we can and to ask for grace to accomplish what we ourselves cannot do: *Deus impossibilia non jubet, sed in jubendo monet et facere quod possis et petere quod non possis.* These words, taken from his *De natura et gratia,*[1] are quoted by the Council of Trent [2] and bring out how God desires to make it really possible for all to be saved and observe His precepts, and how in fact He does so. As for the elect, He sees to it that they continue to observe His precepts until the end.

<hr>

[1] Chap. 43, n. 50.
[2] Denzinger, *Enchiridion Symbolorum,* n. 804.

How are these two great principles, certain and beyond dispute, to be intimately reconciled? Before receiving the beatific vision, no created intellect, of men or of angels, can perceive how this can be. It must first be seen how infinite justice, infinite mercy, and a sovereign liberty are reconciled in the Deity, and this requires an immediate vision of the divine essence.

As we know, these principles laid down by St. Augustine against Semi-Pelagianism were in substance approved by the Second Council of Orange. Thus it remains true that the grace of a happy death is a special grace peculiar to the elect.

At the opposite extreme to Semi-Pelagianism, Protestantism and Jansenism distorted the first principle formulated by St. Augustine by rejecting the second. On the pretext of emphasizing the mystery of predestination, they denied the all-embracing character of God's saving will, maintaining also that in some cases God commands the impossible, that at the moment of death it is not possible for all to be faithful to the divine precepts. We know what the first proposition of Jansenius was,[3] that certain of God's commandments are impossible for some even among the just, and this not merely when they are negligent or have not the full use of reason and will, but even when they have the desire to carry out these precepts and do really strive to fulfil them: *justis volentibus et conantibus.* Even for them the carrying out of certain precepts is impossible because they are denied the grace that would make it possible.

Such a proposition must drive men to despair and shows

---

[3] *Aliqua Dei praecepta hominibus justis volentibus et conantibus, secundum praesentes quas habent vires, sunt impossibilia, deest quoque illis gratia qua possibilia fiant.* Denzinger, n. 1092.

how wide is the gulf separating Jansenism from the true doctrine of St. Augustine and St. Thomas: *Deus impossibilia non jubet*. This grave error involves the denial of God's justice and hence of God Himself; *a fortiori* it denies His mercy and the offering of sufficient grace to all. Indeed it means the rejection of true human liberty (*libertas a necessitate*), so that finally sin becomes unavoidable and is sin no longer, and hence cannot without extreme cruelty be punished eternally.

From the same erroneous principles, Protestants were led to declare not only that predestination is gratuitous, but that good works, in the case of adults, are not necessary for salvation, faith alone sufficing. Hence that saying of Luther's: *Pecca fortiter et crede fortius:* sin resolutely, but trust even more resolutely in the application of Christ's merits to you and in your predestination. This is no longer hope, but is an unpardonable presumption. Jansenism and Protestantism, in fact, oscillate between presumption and despair, without ever being able to find true Christian hope and charity.

Against this heresy the Council of Trent defined [4] that "Whereas we should all have a steadfast hope in God, nevertheless (without a special revelation) no one can have absolute certainty that he will persevere to the end." The Council quotes the words of St. Paul: "Wherefore, my dearly beloved (as you have always obeyed . . .), with fear and trembling work out your salvation. . . . For it is God who worketh in you, both to will and to accomplish according to His good will" (Phil. 2: 12); "He that thinketh himself to stand, let him take heed, lest he fall" (I Cor. 10: 12). He must put all his trust in the Almighty, who is alone able to raise him up when he has fallen and keep the just upright in a corrupt

[4] Sess. VI, cap. 13, and canon 16: Denzinger, nn. 806, 826.

and perverse world. "And he shall stand: for God is able to make him stand" (Rom. 14:4).

And so the Church maintains the Gospel teaching in its rightful place above the vagaries of error, above the extreme heresies of Semi-Pelagianism and Protestantism. On the other hand, the elect are more beloved of God than are others and, on the other hand, God never commands the impossible, but in His love desires to make it really possible for all to be faithful to His commandments.

It remains true therefore, as against Semi-Pelagianism, that *the grace of a happy death is a special gift* [5] and, as against Protestantism and Jansenism, that among those who have the use of reason they alone are deprived of help at the last who actually reject it by resisting the sufficient grace offered them, as the bad thief resisted it, and that in the very presence of Christ the Redeemer.[6]

---

[5] The Council of Trent defined, Sess. VI, can. 22 (Denz. n. 832): "If anyone saith that the justified either is able to persevere without the special help of God in the justice received; or that with that help he is not able: let him be anathema." (Cf. nn. 804, 806.) The terms of the Council—"the grace of final perseverance is a special assistance"—must be rightly understood if all ambiguity is to be avoided. There is no necessity for a new action on the part of God, for, as will be pointed out shortly, conservation in grace is simply the continuation of its original production, not a new action. So also from the point of view of the soul, it is enough for the habitual grace to be preserved; there is no need for even one new actual grace, as happens in the case of the child that dies soon after baptism without ever making an act of the love of God. But, according to the Councils of Orange and Trent, what is a special gift, one granted to some and not to others, is the coincidence of the state of grace with death: the fact that grace is preserved up to that moment instead of God's permitting a fall. This coincidence of the state of grace with death is a great favor and is from God: when it is granted, it is the divine mercy that grants it, and in this sense it is a special gift.

[6] The Council of Trent says again, Sess. VI, cap. 11, 13 (Denzinger, nn. 804, 806): "God commands not impossibilities. . . . All ought to place and repose a most firm hope in God's help. For God, unless men be themselves wanting to His grace, as He has begun the good work, so will He perfect it (in them), to will and to accomplish" (Phil. 2:13).

This being so, how are we to obtain this immense grace of a happy death? Can we merit it? And if it cannot be merited in the strict sense, is it possible for us at any rate to obtain it through prayer? What are the conditions that such a prayer must conform to?

These are the two points we wish to develop, relying especially on what St. Thomas has written about them in Ia IIae, q. 114, a. 9.

Can we merit the grace of a happy death?

Are we able to merit it in the strict sense of the term "merit," which implies the right to a divine reward?

Final perseverance, a happy death, is no more than *the continuance of the state of grace* up to the moment of death, or at any rate it is the coincidence or union of death and the state of grace if conversion takes place at the last moment. In short, a happy death is death in the state of grace, the death of the predestinate or elect.

We now see why the Second Council of Orange declared it to be a special gift,[7] why, too, the Council of Trent declared the gratuitous element in it by saying that, "this gift cannot be derived from any other but from the One who is able to establish him who standeth that he stand perseveringly, and to restore him who has fallen."[8]

Whatever we are able to merit, though it comes chiefly from God, is not from Him exclusively; it proceeds also from our own merits, which imply the right to a divine reward.

---

[7] *Adjutorium Dei etiam renatis et sanctis semper est implorandum, ut ad finem bonum pervenire vel in bono possint opere perdurare* (Denzinger, n. 183).

[8] *Quod quidem (donum) aliunde haberi non potest, nisi ab eo qui potens est eum qui stat statuere ut perseveranter stet, et eum qui cadit restituere* (Denzinger, n. 806).

Hence we feel that the just must humbly admit that they have really *no right to the grace of final perseverance.*

St. Thomas demonstrates this truth by a principle as simple as it is profound, one that is now commonly received in the Church [9] (cf. Ia IIae, q. 114, a. 9). We may profitably pause to consider it for a moment; it will serve to keep us humble.

"The principle of merit," says St. Thomas, "cannot itself be merited (*principium meriti sub merito non cadit*)"; for no cause can cause itself, whether it be a physical cause or moral (as merit is). Merit, that act which entitles us to a reward, cannot reach the principle from which it proceeds. Nothing is more evident than that the principle of merit cannot itself be merited.

Now the gift of final perseverance is simply *the state of grace maintained up to the moment of death,* or at least at that moment restored. Furthermore, the state of grace, produced and maintained by God, is in the order of salvation the very principle of merit, the principle rendering our acts meritorious of an increase in grace and of eternal life. Apart from the state of grace, apart from charity whereby we love God with an efficacious love, more than ourselves, with a love founded at least on a right estimation of values, our salutary acts have no right to a supernatural reward. In such case these salutary acts, like those preceding justification, bear no proportion to such a reward; they are no longer the actions of an adopted son of God and of one who is His friend, heir to God and coheir with Christ, as St. Paul says. They proceed from a soul still estranged from God the last end, through

---

[9] Because of their exalted character, in the things of God the simplest are at the same time the most profound; but it is a simplicity wholly different from that which Voltaire spoke of when he said: "I am limpid as a brook because I have little depth."

mortal sin, from one having no right as yet to eternal life. Hence St. Paul writes (I Cor. 13: 1–3): "If I have not charity, I am nothing . . . it profiteth me nothing." Apart from the state of grace and charity, my will is estranged from God, and personally therefore I can have no right to a supernatural reward, no merit in the order of salvation.

Briefly, then, the principle of merit is the state of grace and perseverance in that state; but the principle of merit cannot itself be merited.

If the initial production of sanctifying grace cannot be merited, the same must be said of the preservation of anyone in grace, this being simply the continuation of the original production and not a distinct divine action. So says St. Thomas (Ia, q. 104, a. 1 ad 4um): "The conservation of the creature by God is not a fresh divine action, but the continuation of the creative act." Hence the maintenance of anyone in the state of grace can no more be merited than its original production.

To this profound reason many theologians add a second, which is a confirmation of it. Strictly *condign* merit (*meritum de condigno*) or merit founded in justice presupposes the divine promise to reward a certain good work. But God has never promised final perseverance or preservation from the sin of final impenitence to one who should keep His commandments for any length of time. Indeed it is precisely this obedience until death in which final perseverance consists; hence it cannot be merited by that obedience, for otherwise it would merit itself. We are thus brought back to our fundamental reason, that the principle of merit cannot be merited. Moreover, with due reservations, the same reason is applicable to congruous merit (*meritum de congruo*), that merit which is founded in the rights of friendship uniting us to God, the principle of which is again the state of grace.[10]

What it all comes to is this, that God's mercy, not His justice, has placed us in the state of grace and continues to maintain us therein.

The just, it is true, are able to merit eternal life, this being the term, not the principle of merit. Even so, if they are to obtain eternal life, it is still required that the merits they have won shall not have been lost before death through mortal sin. Now no acts of charity we perform give us the right to be preserved from mortal sin; it is mercy that preserves us from it. Here is one of the main foundations of humility.

Against this doctrine, now commonly accepted by theologians, a somewhat specious objection has been raised. It has been said that one who merits what is greater can merit what is less. Hence, since the just can merit eternal life *de condigno* and since this is something more than final perseverance, it follows that they can merit final perseverance also.

[10] It is a matter of discussion among theologians whether the gift of final perseverance can be the object of this congruous merit, which is founded not in justice but in the charity uniting us with God, *in jure amicabili,* in the rights of friendship existing between God and the just.

The best commentators of St. Thomas, relying on the principles formulated by him, state in reply that final perseverance cannot be the object of strict congruous merit, since the principle of this merit is a continued state of grace, and the principle of merit, as we have seen, cannot be merited.

Moreover, congruous merit strictly so-called, founded as it is in the rights of friendship, *in jure amicabili,* obtains infallibly the corresponding reward. God never refuses us what we have merited in this way, at any rate for ourselves personally. From which it would follow that, once come to the use of reason, all the just by their acts of charity would merit the gift of final perseverance and would in fact persevere to the end, which is not the case.

Nevertheless it remains true that the grace of a happy death may be the object of congruous merit understood in a wide sense, this being simply the impetratory value of prayer, which is founded not in justice or the rights of friendship, but in the liberality and mercy of God.

To this St. Thomas replies (*ibid.,* ad 2um et 3um): One who can do what is greater can do what is less, other things being equal, not otherwise. Now here there is a difference between eternal life and final perseverance: eternal life is not the principle of the meritorious act, far from it; eternal life is the term of that act. Final perseverance, on the other hand, is simply the continuance in the state of grace, and this, as we have already seen, is the principle of merit.

But, it is insisted, one who can merit the end can merit also the means to that end; but final perseverance is a means necessary to obtain eternal life and, therefore, like eternal life, can be merited.

Theologians in general reply by denying that the major premise is of universal application. Merit, indeed, is a means of obtaining eternal life, and yet it is not itself merited: it is enough that it can be had in other ways. Similarly, the grace of final perseverance can be obtained otherwise than by merit; it may be had through prayer, which is not directed to God's justice, as merit is, but to His mercy.

But, it is further insisted, if final perseverance cannot be merited, neither can eternal life, which is only the consequence of this. From what has already been said, we must answer that anyone in the state of grace may merit eternal life only on condition that the merits he has gained have not been lost or have been mercifully restored through the grace of conversion. Hence the Council of Trent states (Sess. VI, cap. 16 and can. 32), that the just man can merit eternal life, *si in gratia decesserit,* if he dies in the state of grace.

We are thus brought back to that saying of St. Augustine and of St. Thomas after him: where the gift of final perseverance is granted, it is through mercy; if it is not granted, it is in just chastisement for sin, and usually for repeated sin, which has alienated the soul from God.

From this we deduce many conclusions, both speculative [11] and practical. We shall draw attention only to the humility that must be ours as we labor in all confidence to work out our salvation.

What we have been saying is calculated from one point of view to inspire dread, but what we have still to say will give great consolation.

How the grace of a happy death may be obtained through prayer

What are the conditions to which this prayer must conform? If, strictly speaking, the gift of final perseverance cannot be merited, since the principle of merit does not merit itself, it may nevertheless be obtained through prayer, which is directed not to God's justice but to His mercy.

What we obtain through prayer is not always merited: the sinner, for example, who now is in the state of spiritual death, is able with the aid of actual grace to pray for and obtain sanctifying or habitual grace, which could not be merited, since it is the principle of merit.

It is the same with the grace of final perseverance: we cannot merit it in the strict sense, but we can obtain it through prayer for ourselves, and indeed for others also (cf.

---

[11] Since the grace of final perserverance is not merited, it is not because God has foreseen our merits that He bestows it upon us; from which it follows that predestination to glory is also gratuitous: it is not *ex praevisis meritis,* as St. Thomas says (Ia, q.23, a.5). If anyone wishes to maintain that it is *ex praevisis meritis,* then at least he must say that it is not "from merits foreseen as persisting unto the end apart from a special gift," *ex praevisis meritis absque speciali dono usque in finem perdurantibus.*

St. Thomas, *ibid.,* ad 1um). What is more, we can and indeed we ought to prepare ourselves to receive this grace by leading a better life.

Whatever the Quietists may have said, failure to ask for the grace of a happy death and to prepare ourselves to receive it argues a disastrous and stupid negligence, *incuria salutis.*

For this reason our Lord taught us to say in the Our Father: "Lead us not into temptation, but deliver us from evil"; and the Church bids us say daily: "Holy Mary, Mother of God, pray for us sinners now and at the hour of our death. Amen."

Can our prayer obtain this grace of a happy death infallibly? Relying on our Lord's promise, "Ask and you shall receive," theology teaches that prayer made under certain conditions is infallible in obtaining the gifts necessary for salvation, including therefore the final grace. What are the conditions required that prayer shall be infallibly efficacious? "They are four," St. Thomas tells us (IIa IIae, q. 83, a. 15 ad 2um): "We must ask for ourselves, the things necessary for salvation, with piety, with perseverance."

We are, in fact, more certain of obtaining *what we ask for ourselves* than when we pray for a sinner, who perhaps is resisting grace at the very moment we are praying for him.[12] But even though we ask for the gifts necessary for salvation, and for ourselves, prayer will not be infallibly efficacious unless it is made with piety, humility, and confidence, as well as with perseverance. Only then will it express the sincere,

---

[12] Nevertheless, if many of us are praying for the conversion of the sinner, or if our prayer continues not merely for days but for months and long years, it becomes more and more probable that God desires to hear us, since it is He who makes us persevere in our prayer.

profound, unwavering desire of our hearts. And here once
again together with our own frailty, appears the mystery of
grace; we may fail to persevere in our prayer as we may fail
in our meritorious works. This is why we say before communion at mass: "Never permit me, O Lord, to be separated
from Thee." Never permit us to yield to the temptation not
to pray; deliver us from the evil of losing the relish and desire for prayer; grant us that we may persevere in prayer
notwithstanding the dryness and the profound weariness we
sometimes experience.

Our whole life is thus shrouded in mystery. Every one of
our salutary acts presupposes the mystery of grace; every one
of our sins is a mystery of iniquity, presupposing the divine
permission to allow evil to exist in view of some higher good
purpose, which will be clearly seen only in heaven. "The
just man liveth by faith" (Rom. 1: 17). We need help to the
very end, not only that we may merit, but that we may pray
even. How are we to obtain the necessary help to persevere in
prayer? By bearing in mind our Lord's words: "If you ask the
Father anything in My name, He will give it to you. Hitherto
you have not asked anything in My name" (John 16: 23-24).

We must pray in the name of our Savior. That is the best
way of purifying and strengthening our intention, and will
do more than the sword of Brennus to turn the balance. We
must ask Him besides to make personal intercession on our
behalf. This intercession of His is continued from day to
day in the holy mass, wherein, as the Council of Trent says,
through the ministry of His priests He never ceases to offer
Himself and apply to us the merits of His passion.

Seeing that the grace of a happy death can be obtained
only through prayer and not merited, we should turn to that

most excellent and efficacious of all prayers, the prayer of our Lord, principal Priest in the sacrifice of the mass. It was for this reason Pope Benedict XV, in a letter to the director of the Archconfraternity of Our Lady For a Happy Death, earnestly recommended the faithful to have masses offered during life for the grace of a happy death. This is indeed the greatest of all graces, the grace of the elect; and if at that last moment we unite ourselves by an intense act of love with Christ's sacrifice perpetuated on the altar, we may even obtain remission of the temporal punishment due to our sins and thus be saved from purgatory.

Therefore, to obtain this grace of final perseverance, we should frequently *unite ourselves with the Eucharistic consecration,* the essence of the sacrifice of the mass, pondering on the four ends of sacrifice: adoration, supplication, reparation, and thanksgiving. Let us bear in mind that in this continuous oblation of Himself, our Lord is offering, as well the whole of His mystical body, especially those who suffer spiritually and thereby share a little in His own sufferings. This is a path that will carry us far if only we follow it perseveringly.[13]

[13] This point is well brought out in an excellent work recently published, *Sept retraites de la Mère Elizabeth de la Croix* (foundress of the Carmelite convent at Fontainebleau). In these retreats, the subject is simply the union of the soul that has consecrated itself to Jesus crucified for the glory of God and the salvation of souls. Constantly we meet with such passages as these: "Our Lord revealed to me the sentiments of His Sacred Heart and communicated them to me. . . . He said to me: 'The two chief motives that led Me to acquiesce in Pilate's condemnation of Me were the will and glory of My Father and a hunger for the salvation of men. Your whole life, in its smallest details, should be dominated by these two sentiments. Take upon yourself My own sufferings. . . . During this retreat, for yourself nothing, all for Me. My cross is to be found in pride, in sin; give Me a little help in carrying that cross. The fruit of My carrying the cross for you is that you desire nothing here below, that you be prepared to suffer always, that you desire all that the divine will desires, that you make expiation for the sins of men, of My priests and spouses especially, that you complain

This practice of uniting ourselves with the sacrifice of the mass, with the masses that all day long are being celebrated wherever the sun is rising upon the earth, is the best preparation for a happy death, the best preparation for that hour when for the last time in our lives we shall unite ourselves with the masses then being celebrated far and near. United then with the sacrifice of Christ perpetuated in substance upon the altar, our death will itself be a sacrifice of adoration both of God's supreme dominion, who is master of life and death, and of the majesty of Him who "leadeth down to hell and bringeth up again" (Tob. 13:2). It will be a sacrifice of supplication to obtain the final grace both for ourselves and for those who are to die in that same hour. It will also be a sacrifice of reparation for the sins of our life, and a sacrifice of thanksgiving for all the favors we have received since our baptism.

The sacrifice we thus offer with a burning love for God may well open to us forthwith the gates of heaven, as it did for the good thief dying there by the side of our Lord as He

of nothing, that you keep your soul fast to My own, that your heart be occupied solely with love for Me' (pp. 181 ff.). 'In this (when loaded with the cross) I am your model.' . . . At the offering of the bread and wine at mass our Lord Jesus Christ said to me: 'I offer you to My Father as victim embracing all that I intend in your regard . . . the needs of My Church . . . the perils in which souls are plunged and the ardor of My appeals.' At holy communion He said: 'I shall be your strength always.' 'My cross: that is the sign and token of the love I have for souls, of the love also that souls have for Me. You I have invited to share in the folly of the cross, to refuse to be bound to earth by a single thread . . . to follow Me through pain, insults, and ignominy . . . to be My spouse crucified unto death.' Again He said to Me: 'It was through calumny that I was condemned to be crucified. . . . The more your sufferings closely resemble Mine, the happier will you be: . . . it is the proof that you are loved more than others. Be kind of heart toward those who will bring or have already brought the cross to you.' . . . 'Suffer with Me in reparation for the glory of My Father and for the ransom of souls' " (pp. 184 ff.).

brought to its close the celebration of His bloody mass, the sacrifice of the cross.

Before this last hour of our life comes, we should cultivate the *practice of praying for the dying*. At the door of some chapels may be seen the little inscription: Pray for those who are to die while holy mass is being offered. A certain French writer was one day much struck by this inscription and thereafter every day prayed for the dying while he was attending mass. Later on he was overtaken by a serious illness, which lasted for years; unable any longer to go to mass, he offered up his sufferings each morning for those who were to die in the course of the day. He thus had the joy of obtaining a number of unexpected conversions *in extremis*.[14]

Let us also pray for the priests who assist the dying. It is a sublime ministry to assist a soul in its agony, in that last struggle. Pray that the priest may arrive in time and, if the sick man is already sunk in profound torpor, that he may obtain from heaven the necessary moment of consciousness. Pray that the priest may be able to prompt the sick man to make the great sacrifices God demands of him and that by his priestly prayer, offered in the name of Christ, in the name

---

14 We recommend on this point two books by Adolphe Retté: *Jusqu'à la fin du monde,* a living commentary on that sentence of Pascal's: "Jesus will continue in His agony until the end of the world," and *Oraisons du silence.* This latter work, from the fine passages it contains on solitude, poverty, detachment, suffering, peace, and the love of God, will prepare us for a happy death. It closes with these words: "May the rhythm of the hours yet remaining in my life here below be regulated solely by the sacred doxology, *Gloria Patri et Filio.* . . . Invocation full of strength, which makes me glad to have suffered and to go on suffering in Thy service, O Lord. Each time that I utter it with a contrite heart and with a right mind, I know that Thy grace will flow in upon my soul. . . . Grant that I may be crucified like the good thief on Thy right hand. Remember me, too, in Thy kingdom of heaven as Thou didst remember him." That prayer was heard. Adolphe Retté died a holy death.

of Mary and of all the saints, he may obtain for him the final grace, the grace of graces.

As the priest is giving this assistance to the dying, he some-times has the immense consolation of looking on, as it were, and watching our Lord save the soul as it suffers in that last moment. Hitherto perhaps he has prayed for a cure, but now that he sees the soul well prepared for death he ends by reciting confidently and with great peace that beautiful prayer of the Church:

Kyrie eleison, Christe eleison, Kyrie eleison. . . . Proficiscere, anima christiana, de hoc mundo, in nomine Dei Patris omnipotentis, qui te creavit, in nomine Jesu Christi Filii Dei vivi, qui pro te passus est, in nomine Spiritus Sancti, qui in te effusus est ("Go forth from this world, O Christian soul, in the name of God the Father Almighty, who created thee; in the name of Jesus Christ, Son of the living God, who suffered for thee; in the name of the Holy Ghost, who was poured out upon thee; in the name of the holy and glorious Virgin Mary, Mother of God; in the name of Blessed Joseph, predestined spouse of the Virgin; in the name of the angels and archangels . . . ; in the name of the patriarchs and prophets; in the name of the Apostles and the Evangelists; in the name of the holy martyrs and confessors; and of all the saints of God. May thy place be this day in peace and thy abode in holy Sion, through Our Lord Jesus Christ.

The mystery of salvation

And so for us a holy death throws light on the mystery of predestination, that terrible and yet gracious mystery which concerns the choice of the elect.

We now have a better grasp of those two great principles

formulated by St. Augustine and St. Thomas which we
quoted at the beginning of the chapter.

On the one hand, "since God's love is the cause of things,
*no one thing would be better than another, if God did not
will a greater good for one than for the other."* [15] No one
thing would be better than another by reason of some salutary act, whether it be the first or the last, easy or difficult, in
its inception or continuance, were he not more beloved of
God. This is what our Lord refers to when He says of the
elect, that "no man can snatch them out of the hand of My
Father" (John 10: 29). He was speaking here of the efficacy
of grace, which also led St. Paul to ask, "Who distinguisheth
thee? Or what hast thou that thou hast not received?" (I Cor.
4: 7.) Could we find anywhere a more profound lesson in
humility?

On the other hand, *God never commands the impossible,*
but love constrains Him to make the fulfilment of His precepts really possible for all, and especially for the dying; final
grace is denied them only when they reject it by resisting
the final appeal.

And therefore, say St. Augustine and St. Thomas, when
the grace of final perseverance is granted, as it was to the
good thief, it is through mercy; if it is not granted, it is as a
just chastisement for sin and usually for repeated sin; it is
a just chastisement, too, for the final act of resistance, as it
was with the impenitent thief, who was lost even as he hung
dying by the side of his Redeemer.

In the words of St. Prosper quoted by a council of the

[15] Cf. St. Thomas, Ia, q.20, a.3: *Cum amor Dei sit causa bonitatis rerum, non
esset aliquid alio melius, si Deus non vellet uni majus quam alteri. Ibid.,* a.4: *Ex
hoc sunt aliqua meliora, quod Deus eis majus bonum vult.* Here is the principle
of predilection.

ninth century, "If some are saved, it is the gift of Him who saves; if some perish, it is the fault of them that perish."[16]

Absolutely certain as are these two great principles when considered apart—the efficacy of grace and the possibility for all to be saved—how are they infinitely reconciled one with the other? Here is St. Paul's answer: "O the depth of the riches of the wisdom and of the knowledge of God! How incomprehensible are His judgments, and how unsearchable His ways!" (Rom. 11: 33.) No created intellect can perceive this intimate reconciliation before receiving the beatific vision. To perceive that is to perceive also how infinite justice, infinite mercy and a sovereign liberty are united and identified without any real distinction in the Deity, the intimate life of God, in precisely what is unutterable in Him, in that perfection which is exclusively His own and naturally incommunicable to creatures—in the Deity as it transcends being, unity, truth, goodness, intelligence, and love. For in all these absolute perfections creatures can participate naturally, whereas participation in the Deity is possible only through sanctifying grace, which is a participation in the divine nature not simply as intellectual life, but as a life strictly divine and the principle of that immediate vision and of that love which God has for Himself.[17]

---

[16] Council of Quiersey, A. D. 853 (Denzinger, 318): *Deus omnipotens omnes homines sine exceptione vult salvos fieri* (I Tim. 2: 4), *licet non omnes salventur. Quod autem quidam salvantur, salvantis est donum; quod autem quidam pereunt, pereuntium est meritum.*

[17] By their very nature both human souls and angels participate in the intellectual life and as such bear an analogical resemblance to God in so far as He is intelligent. Sanctifying grace, however, is a resemblance to God not simply as He is intelligent, but precisely as God; it is a participation in the Deity as such, or, if you will, in the divine intellectuality as it is divine. This is our reply to a question put to us by Père Gardeil in his excellent work, *La structure de l'âme et l'expérience mystique*, (I, 388), where he treats of the relation between sanctifying grace and the formal constituent of the divine nature. Sanctifying grace is a partici-

That we may perceive how the two principles of which we are speaking are intimately reconciled with each other, we must have immediate vision of the divine essence. The more certain we are of the truth of these two principles, the more striking by contrast is the obscurity, the light-transcending obscurity, enveloping the heights of God's intimate life in which they are united. They are like the two extremities of a dazzling arc disappearing above into what the mystics call the great darkness, which is none other than that light inaccessible in which God dwells (I Tim. 6: 16).

This, though very imperfectly expressed, is to our mind the subject of Augustine's speculation, or rather let us say of his contemplation, and it is the constant source of inspiration to St. Thomas in these difficult questions. The divine obscurity here mentioned is far beyond the reach of speculative theology; it is the proper object of faith (*fides est de non visis*), of faith illumined by the gifts of understanding and wisdom (*fides donis illustrata*).

From this higher standpoint, the contemplation of this terrible yet gracious mystery brings peace. Penetrated through and through with this doctrine, Bossuet writes as follows to one tormented with all sorts of ideas about predestination:

When such thoughts come into the mind, when all our efforts to dissipate them have proved vain, we should end by abandoning

pation in the divine nature considered not simply as being or as intellectual, but as strictly divine; grace is a physical and formal, though analogical participation in the *Deity* as such, whose formal concept transcends in its absolute eminence the concepts of being, unity, etc., in all of which it is possible for creatures to participate naturally. So also says Cajetan in his commentary on Ia, q.39, a.1 (n. 7): *Deitas est super ens et super unum,* etc. We have explained ourselves at some length on this point elsewhere (*God, His Existence and His Nature,* tr. by Dom Bede Rose, O.S.B., Vol. II, chap. 1, n. 42; chap. 3, n. 54). Père Gardeil himself speaks in the same sense (I, 246, 287).

ourselves to God, with the assurance that our salvation is infinitely more secure in God's hands than in our own. Only thus shall we find peace. All teaching about predestination should end in this; this should be the effect produced in us by our sovereign Master's secret, a secret we should adore without pretending to sound its depths. We must lose ourselves in the heights and impenetrable depths of God's wisdom, must cast ourselves into the arms of His immense loving kindness, looking to Him for everything, yet without unburdening ourselves of that care for our salvation which He demands of us. . . . The result of this tormenting must be the abandonment of yourself to God, who by reason of His loving kindness and the promises He has made will then be bound to watch over you. This, while the present life lasts, must be the final solution to all those questions about predestination which beset you; henceforth you must find your repose not in yourself but solely in God and His fatherly loving kindness." [18]

Bossuet, speaking in the same strain in one of the finest chapters of his *Méditations sur l'Evangile* (Part II, 72d day), says:

The proud man fears that unless he retains his salvation in his own hands, it is rendered too insecure; but in this he deceives himself. Can I find any security in myself? O my God, I feel my will escaping me at every moment, and even wert Thou willing to make me the sole master of my fate, I should refuse a power so dangerous to my weakness. Let it not be said that this doctrine of grace and predilection will bring pious souls to despair. How can anyone imagine he will give me greater assurance by throwing me back upon myself, by delivering me up to my own inconstancy? No, my God, I will have none of it. I can find no security except in abandoning myself to Thee. And this security is the greater when I reflect that those in whom Thou dost inspire this confidence, this complete self-

[18] *Lettres de direction* (Œuvres, XI, 444).

THE GRACE OF A HAPPY DEATH

abandonment to Thee, receive in this gentle prompting the highest mark of Thy loving kindness that can be had here on earth.

As we have shown elsewhere,[19] this to us seems to be the true mind of St. Augustine at its loftiest, when finally he soars above all reasoning, and comes to rest in the divine obscurity where the two aspects of the mystery, to all appearances diametrically opposed, must at last be reconciled. As formulated in the two principles—God never commands the impossible; no one would be better than another, were he not more beloved of God—these two aspects of the mystery are as two stars of the first magnitude shining brightly in the dark night of the spirit, yet wholly inadequate to reveal to us the uttermost depths of the firmament, the secret of the Deity.

Until we are given the beatific vision, grace by a secret instinct allays all our fears as to the intimate reconciliation of infinite justice and infinite mercy in the Deity, and this it does because it is itself a participation in the Deity, the light of life far surpassing the natural light of either the angelic or the human intellect.

Doubtless the whole of our interior life, every one of our actions, are shrouded in mystery; for every salutary act presupposes the mystery of grace from which it proceeds, and all sin is a mystery of iniquity, presupposing the divine permission that evil shall exist in view of some higher good purpose which will often escape us and will be clearly seen only in heaven. But in this obscurity characteristic of faith and also of contemplation here on earth, we are reassured when we

[19] "La volonté salvifique chez S. Augustin," in *Revue Thomiste*, 1930, pp. 473–487. Also *Dictionnaire de théologie catholique*, art. "Prédestination," conclusion.

remember that God's will is to save, that Christ has died for us, that His sacrifice is perpetuated in substance on the altar, and that our salvation is more secure in His hands than it would be in ours, since we are more certain of the rectitude of the divine intentions than of our own, even the best of them.

Let us abandon ourselves in all confidence and love to His infinite mercy: there can be no better way of ensuring His condescending mercy toward us at this moment and above all at the hour of our death.

Let us frequently call to mind those beautiful words of the psalm, recurring each week in Thursday's office of Tierce: "Cast thy care upon the Lord, and He shall sustain thee: He shall not suffer the just to waver forever" (Ps. 54: 23).

Let us call to mind the beautiful canticle of Tobias: "Thou art great, O Lord, forever, and Thy kingdom is unto all ages. For Thou scourgest, and Thou savest: Thou leadest down to hell, and bringest up again. He hath chastised us for our iniquities: and He will save us for His own mercy" (Tob. 13: 1).

In this self-abandonment we shall find peace. As our Lord hung dying for us, He experienced in His holy soul the keenest suffering our sins had caused, yet likewise the profoundest peace. So, too, in every Christian death, as in that of the good thief, there is suffering, a holy fear and trembling before the infinite justice of God, and a profound peace, a most intimate union prevailing between them. Nevertheless it is peace, the tranquillity that comes of true order, which predominates, as is apparent from these words of our Lord as He died: 'It is consummated. . . . Father, into Thy hands I commend My spirit" (Luke 23: 46).

CHAPTER XXVIII

Providence and Charity Toward our Neighbor

In the preceding chapter we saw how one of the greatest means in the workings of providence is charity toward our neighbor, by which all men should be united for their mutual aid in their progress toward the common goal, eternal life.

This subject is always of the greatest interest and we should often revert to it, especially in this age when charity toward others is summarily rejected by individualism in all its forms and completely distorted by the humanitarianism of the communist and internationalist.

Individualism aims at nothing higher than the search for what is useful and pleasurable to the individual or at most to the restricted group to which the individual belongs. Hence the bitter strife arising sometimes among members of the same family, but especially between classes and races or nations. Hence arise jealousy and envy, discord and hatred, and the most profound disruptions. It implies a complete disregard for the common good in its different degrees and an almost exclusive assertion of individual or particular rights.

In opposition to this, communist and internationalist *humanitarianism* lays so much stress on the rights of humanity as a whole, which in some degree is identified with God in a pantheistic sense, that the rights of individuals, families, and nations disappear altogether. On the pretext of promoting unity, harmony, and peace, the way is prepared for appalling confusion and disorder, like that which has prevailed in Russia since the revolution. To desire that all the parts in an organism shall have the perfection of the head, or to do away with the head because it is more perfect than the members, is to destroy the organism altogether.

Obviously the truth lies within these two extreme errors, yet transcends them. Equally remote from both individualism and communism, it affirms the rights inherent in the individual, in families, and in nations, and at the same time the claims of the *common good,* which is above every particular good. Thus a right estimation of things will safeguard the *welfare of the individual* through two kinds of justice: commutative, regulating the mutual dealings between one private party and another, and distributive, which sees to a fair distribution of general utilities and burdens. Also it will safeguard the common good through legal justice providing for the enactment of just laws and their observance, and again through equity, which looks to the spirit of the law in those exceptional cases where the letter of the law cannot be applied.

Admirably differentiated by Aristotle and well developed by St. Thomas in his treatise *De justitia* (IIa IIae, q. 58, 61, 120), these four kinds of justice (commutative, distributive, and legal or social justice, and equity) suffice in a way to preserve the just mean between the opposing errors of individualism and communist humanitarianism. St. Thomas' teaching on this question is too little known and might well be made the subject of a series of interesting and useful studies.

However perfect this fourfold justice may become, even

when enlightened by Christian faith, it can never attain the perfection that distinguishes charity toward God and our neighbor, the formal object of which is incomparably on a higher plane.

Let us recall what the primary object of charity is and what is its secondary object. We shall then see how we are to practice charity toward our neighbor and what part it plays in the fulfilment of the plan of Providence.

The primary object and formal motive of charity

The primary object of charity is something far above the distinctive good of the individual, far above the good of the family, of country, even of humanity. It is God, to be loved above all things, even more than ourselves, since His goodness is infinitely greater than our own. That is the first commandment: "Thou shalt love the Lord thy God with thy whole heart and with thy whole soul and with all thy strength and with all thy mind" (Luke 10: 27).

To this supreme commandment, all the other commandments and all the counsels are subordinate. Though it belongs to the supernatural order, nevertheless it corresponds to a natural inclination, to the primordial inclination of nature both in ourselves and in a certain sense in every creature.

Of course, innate in us is the instinct for self-preservation, the instinct, too, for the preservation of the species, the inclination to defend family and country, to love our fellows. But deeper still, as St. Thomas has shown (Ia, q. 60, a. 5) in our nature is the inclination prompting us to love more than ourselves God the very author of our nature. Why should this be? Because whatever by its very nature belongs to another, as the part belongs to the whole, the hand to the body, is naturally inclined to love that other more than itself: thus the hand will voluntarily sacrifice itself to protect the body. Now every creature, and in all that it is, is necessarily dependent upon God the Creator and Conserver of our being; hence every creature is inclined naturally, each after its own fashion, to love its Creator more than itself.

Thus the stone tends toward the center of the earth for the cohesion, for the very welfare of the universe, which is itself a manifestation of God's goodness radiating externally. Again, to use our Lord's own illustration, we know that the hen will gather her chickens under her wings to defend them from the hawk, sacrificing her own life if necessary for the welfare of the species, which in its turn contributes to the good of the universe.

In men and angels this primordial natural inclination is illumined by the light of intelligence, and thus we are led *to love God* the author of our nature *more than ourselves,* but with a love in some degree conscious.

No doubt this natural inclination has been enfeebled by original sin; but in spite of this weakening it persists, imperishable as is this spiritual faculty, our will.

This natural inclination is sublimated by the supernatural or infused virtue of charity, of an order infinitely transcending nature, whether of men or of angels. Illumined by infused faith, charity inclines us to love God more than self, more than all else, but now as the author of grace and not simply of our nature. This is God who "hath first loved us" (I John 4: 10) by bestowing on us over and above existence, life, and intelligence, the supreme gift of sanctifying grace, the germ of eternal life, a germ that one day is to flower into the immediate vision of the divine essence and a most holy, supernatural love which nothing thenceforth shall be able to destroy or diminish.

Such is the primary object of charity: God who has first loved us and has communicated to us a share in His own intimate life. For this reason charity is a friendship between God and us.

The formal motive why we must love God, is His own infinite goodness, a goodness infinitely greater than ours, infinitely greater than any gift He can confer upon us.

If we do not constantly dwell upon this, the primary object of charity and its formal motive, we shall not in the least understand the sort of love that must be given to its secondary object.

There are not two virtues of charity, one relating to God, the other to our neighbor. It is one and the same theological virtue from which these two acts of love proceed, one being essentially subordinated to the other.

Charity can desire nothing except in relation to God and for the love of God, as the power of vision cannot be exercised except through color and in relation to color, as the power of hearing can hear nothing except sound and what emits sound. For the love of God we are bound to love everything that is in any way related to Him.

The secondary object of charity

Expressed for us in the second commandment: "Thou shalt love thy neighbor as thyself for the love of God," it includes first of all *ourselves,* in the sense that we must love self with a holy love, desiring salvation that we may give glory to God eternally. It includes in the second place *our neighbor,* to be loved as we love ourselves, for God's sake;

which means that we must desire for our neighbor all the gifts necessary for salvation and salvation itself, so that with us also he may give glory to God eternally. This love of our neighbor the Savior puts before us as the necessary consequence, the radiation and the sign of our love for God: "By this shall all men know that you are My disciples, if you have love for one another" (John 13: 35). And St. John himself tells us: "If any man say: I love God, and hateth his brother, he is a liar" (I John 4: 20).

Evidently this charity toward our neighbor is infinitely removed from that natural inclination which prompts us to do good in order to please, to love our benefactors, to hate those who do us any harm, and to remain indifferent to the rest of men. Natural love makes us love our neighbor for his naturally good qualities and the benefits we receive from him. The motive that inspires charity is something quite different, the proof being that we must "love our enemies, do good to them that hate us, and pray for them that persecute and calumniate us" (Matt. 5: 44; Luke 6: 27, 35).

Charity, too, surpasses justice, not only commutative and distributive justice, but also that legal justice and equity which command respect for the rights of others out of love for the common good of society.

Charity constrains us to love our neighbor, even our enemies, for the love of God and with the same supernatural, theological virtue of love we have for Him. But how is it possible for us to have for men a love that is divine, when for the most part they are so imperfect and in some cases sinners?

Theology replies with a very simple illustration which St. Thomas explains in this way: One who has an intense love for a friend will love with the same love his friend's children; he will love them because he loves their father and will wish them well for his sake. Again, for the sake of his friend he will, when necessary, come to the assistance of these and, if he is offended, will forgive them. If, then, all men are the children of God, are at least called to be so, we must love them all, even our enemies, in the measure that we love their common Father.[1]

But that we may love our neighbor with this supernatural love, we must look on him with the eyes of faith and say to ourselves: Here is one very different from me perhaps in temperament and character, who yet is "born not of blood, nor of the will of the flesh, nor of the will of man," but like myself is "born of God" (John 1: 13), at least is called to be so and to participate in the same divine life, in the same beatitude. This is how members of the same family should regard one another, those too who are united in the same society and are citizens of the same country. This truth applies especially to all those who are of the Church universal which, while respecting the legitimate and inevitable differences between one country and another, unites them all in order to bring their children into the kingdom of God.

And so we can and indeed should say of everyone with whom we live, even of those with whom we are not naturally in sympathy: Here is a soul which, even if it is not in the state of grace, has undoubtedly been called to be God's child, or to become His child once again, to be the temple of the Holy Ghost and a member of Christ's mystical body. Perhaps

[1] See in the *Summa* of St. Thomas (IIa IIae) the two great questions 25 and 26 on the extent of charity and the order it should observe. They will be summed up in what follows.

it is nearer to the heart of our Lord than I am, a living stone upon which He is working, more elaborately, it may be, than upon others, in order to fit it into its place in the heavenly Jerusalem.

This being so, how is it possible for me not to love that soul if in very truth I love my God? And if in fact I do not love this person, if in fact I have no desire for his welfare and his salvation, then my love for God is a lie. On the other hand, if, in spite of differences in temperament, character, and upbringing, I really do love him, this is a sign that I really love God. I can truly give to that person the same essentially supernatural and theological love I have for the three divine Persons, because my love for him is directed to that participation in the intimate life of God which he either possesses already or is at least called to receive. And my love is directed to the realization of the divine plan that presides over his destiny, and to the glory he has been called to render to God.

But the unbeliever raises an objection. Is this really to love men, he asks? Is it not simply to love God and Christ in man, as a diamond is admired in its setting? Man wants to be loved for his own sake; in that case he cannot ask for a love that is divine. It was by way of reaction against this egoistic tendency that Pascal uttered what was intentionally a paradox: "I have no desire to be loved by anyone."

In reality it is not only to God-in-man that the love of charity is directed, but to man-in-God: *man is loved in himself but for God's sake*. After all, charity loves what man is destined to be, an imperishable member of Christ's mystical body, and it does everything possible to bring heaven within his reach. It loves besides what man is already by grace, and if grace is absent it will love his very nature, not precisely as fallen nature, wounded and hostile to grace, but as capable of receiving it.

It is indeed to man himself that charity is directed, but for God's sake, for the sake of the glory he is called to render to God, a glory which is nothing less than the manifestation, the radiation of the divine goodness.

Charity toward our neighbor, or fraternal charity, is in essence the love of God extended so as to embrace all whom God Himself loves.

From this consideration we derive the characteristics of fraternal charity. *It must be universal,* knowing no limits whatever. None may be excluded, whether on earth, in purgatory, or in heaven. It stops only at hell. Only the damned we cannot love, for no longer is it possible for them to become God's children, nor have they the slightest wish to be raised up again; pride and hate smother the very thought of asking for pardon. But apart from those whose damnation is certain—and who can be certain that a soul is lost?—all have a claim on our charity, which knows no limits but those imposed by that love which is seated in the very heart of God.

Here is something incomparably sublime, and the more profound the gulf that, humanly speaking, separates souls, the more sublime does charity appear. Once during the World War a little French soldier as he lay dying was unable to finish the Hail Mary he was reciting and it was finished for him by a young German who was himself dying there by his side. Our Lord and the Blessed Virgin brought these two brethren together at the very moment when the rupture between their two countries was complete. Such are the mighty victories won by charity.

For charity to be universal, it need not necessarily be given everywhere in the same degree. It respects and sublimates the order dictated by nature itself. We must love God in the first place more than all else, even more than ourselves, and with a love founded at least on a right estimation of values (*appretiative*). Though we may not always experience for God the sensible yearning of our hearts, nevertheless our love for Him should ever be increasing in intensity. Next after God we should love *our own souls,* destined to give glory to Him eternally, then *our neighbor,* and lastly our *bodies,* for these must be sacrificed where the salvation of a soul is at stake, especially when it is our bounden duty to watch over its welfare. Among our fellows greater love should be given to those who are holier and nearer to God, to those, too, who are nearer to us by blood, by marriage, by vocation, or by friendship. The nearer a soul is to God, the more it deserves our esteem; the closer the ties that bind it to us, the more sensible is our love for it, and the more whole-hearted should be the devotion we show in all that concerns family, country, vocation, and friendship.[2] Thus, instead of destroying patriotism, charity exalts it, as we see in the case of St. Joan of Arc or St. Louis.

This, then, is the order to be observed in charity. God desires to reign in our hearts, but He excludes no affection that can be subordinated to what is due to Himself. On the contrary, He exalts and quickens it, inspiring it with a greater dignity and generosity. This is the way we must love even the

[2] Cf. St. Thomas, IIa IIae, q. 26, a. 8.

enemies of the Church and pray for them. But, on pretext of showing a certain pity, to have for the Church's enemies a greater love than for certain of her children who are laboring side by side with us, and of whom perhaps we are a little jealous, is completely to reverse the order dictated by charity.

Lastly, fraternal charity, like the love we have for God, must be effective, not simply affective, must be beneficent as well as benevolent. "Love one another as I have loved you" (John 13: 34), our Lord tells us, and He has loved us even to the death of the cross. Him the saints have imitated, and their lives are one continuous act of radiant charity, bringing great peace and a holy joy. Such is fraternal charity, an extension of that charity we must give to God.

The practice of fraternal charity and the watchfulness of Providence

In the *Dialogue,* St. Catherine of Siena often notes the wide diversity of qualities which Providence has bestowed on one and another. Thus we have opportunities to promote one another's welfare and perfection, and we have abundant occasions to practice fraternal charity.

Nor have we far to seek for opportunities of failing in this respect. Even where a deeply Christian spirit prevails we have to acknowledge that, side by side with admirable virtues, there is notable moral weakness. Even if we could rid ourselves of all our shortcomings, the possibility of discord and irritation would persist owing to differences of temperament and character, differences also in intellectual bent, inclining some to speculation and others to more practical things, for some opening wide views, while inspiring in others an attention to detail rather than to general effect. Again, there arise further occasions of friction through the influence of him who loves to create divisions in order to spoil God's work, to frustrate especially those things that are most sublime, most divine, and most beautiful. Only in heaven will all occasion of friction disappear, for there, illumined by a divine light, each one of the blessed sees in the Word what his desires and wishes must be.

Surrounded as we are with all sorts of difficulties, *how are we to practice fraternal charity?* In two ways. In the first place *by benevolence,* viewing our neighbor in the light of faith, so as to discover in him the life of grace, or at any rate a certain aspiration to that life. And secondly, *by beneficence,* by giving our service, by bearing with the failings of others, even returning good for evil, by avoiding jealousy, and by frequently asking God to effect the union of minds and hearts.

First of all *benevolence.* We must be clear-sighted and keen to discover in our neighbor, sometimes beneath a coarse exterior difficult to penetrate, the presence of a divine life, or at least certain latent aspirations to that life, the fruit of prevenient actual graces which every man receives at some time or other. But, to look thus into the soul of our neighbor, we must be detached from self.

Very often what provokes and irritates us in him is not some serious fault in the sight of God, but simply a defect in temperament, a twist of character, which is quite compatible with very real virtue. We would be ready enough perhaps to tolerate a sinner utterly estranged from God, but of a lovable nature, whereas a soul that is fairly advanced we will sometimes find trying. We must be careful, then, to regard those with whom we live in the light of faith, so as to detect in them just what makes them pleasing to God, and love them as He does.

The great obstacle to this benevolence is *rash judgment.* This is something more than a simple impression; it consists in affirming the presence of evil on nothing more than slight evidence. People make things out to be twice as bad as they are, usually through pride. If the matter is grave and there is full deliberation and consent, a judgment of this sort is a serious failure in justice and charity; a failure in justice, because our neighbor has a right to his good reputation, a right which, after that of doing his duty, is one of the most sacred he has, far more so than the right to his property. There are many who would not think of stealing five dollars, yet they will rob their neighbor of his good reputation by rash judgments without any solid foundation in fact. More often than not, the judgment is false. How are we to estimate truthfully the interior intentions of one whose doubts, difficulties, temptations, good desires, and repentance are unkown to us? And even if the rash judgment is true, it falls short of justice, since in thus passing sentence we arrogate to ourselves a jurisdiction that does not belong to us. God alone can judge of the intentions of the heart so long as they are not made sufficiently clear externally.

Rash judgment is also wanting in charity, because it *proceeds from ill will,* though often framed under a mask of kindliness, a few faint praises leading up to that characteristic "but . . ." Instead of looking on our neighbor as a brother, we regard him as an adversary, a rival to be supplanted. For this reason our Lord tells us: "Judge not that you may not be judged. For with what judgment you judge, you shall be judged: and with what measure you mete, it shall be meas-

ured to you again. And why seest thou the mote that is in
thy brother's eye; and seest not the beam that is in thy own
eye?" (Matt. 7: 1.)

But supposing the sin is patent. Does God mean us to
delude ourselves? He does not; but He does forbid that
murmuring which springs from pride. In some cases, in fact,
He imposes on us in the name of charity the obligation of
fraternal correction to be carried out with kindliness, humility, gentleness, and discretion. Where this private correction
is impossible or has been unsuccessful, it may be necessary
humbly to refer the matter to the superior whose duty it is to
watch over the welfare of the community. In any case, as
St. Catherine of Siena says, where the sin is evident the perfect way consists not in murmuring, but in showing compassion before God, laying the blame to some extent at least upon
ourselves, after the example of our Lord who took upon Himself the sins of us all and who has bidden us "love one another
as I have loved you" (John 13: 34). This is one of the sublimest features of the providential plan.

Therefore, to check rash judgment, we must acquire the
habit of looking upon our neighbor in the light of faith.

But we must love him, too, with a love that is real, efficacious, practical: *our charity must be beneficent,* not merely
benevolent. In what way? By giving our service where necessary and when it is in our power to do so. By bearing also
with our neighbor's failings, this being one way of rendering
him service and leading him to self-correction. In this connection we should remember that frequently what most irritates us in our neighbor is not a serious fault in the sight
of God, but a defect in temperament. This may be a certain
nervousness, for instance, which makes him slam doors, a

certain narrowness in his views, a way of generally doing the wrong thing, a constant eagerness to push himself forward, and other like failings. Let us in all charity bear with one another and not become irritated at what after all is simply an evil permitted by God to humble the one and try the patience of the other. We must not allow ourselves to develop a bitter zeal, and if we must complain of others, we should never imagine that we ourselves have reached the ideal. Our prayer must not be the prayer of the Pharisee.

Again, we must be able to recognize the right moment to put in a kindly word—another means Providence has put in our way of helping others. A religious who is overwhelmed with difficulties will often take fresh courage through a few simple words from a superior wishing him many consolations in his ministry and just enough trouble to enable him to undergo purgatory here on earth.

Needless to say, if we are to love our neighbor effectively, we must be careful to avoid jealousy, and therefore, as Bossuet somewhere remarks, *we must take a holy delight in the good qualities God has bestowed on others* and which we ourselves do not possess. Thus there has been a distribution of labor and functions in the Church, for the beauty of the Church and of religious communities. As St. Paul says, the hand is not jealous of the eye; the light which the eye receives is for the benefit of the hand also. So should it be with us: far from being jealous of one another, we should rejoice in the good qualities we find in our neighbor, for they are also ours; we and our neighbor are all members of the same mystical body, in which everything should contribute to the glory of God and the salvation of souls.

Not only must we bear with one another and avoid jealousy, we must also return good for evil, by prayer, by good example, and by mutual help. One way of entering into St. Teresa's good graces, it is said, was by causing her to suffer. She thus put into practice the counsel given by our Lord: "If a man will take away thy coat, let go thy cloak also unto him" (Matt. 5: 40). Prayer for our neighbor at a time when we are suffering because of him is of special efficacy. Such was the prayer of St. Stephen the first martyr and of St. Peter Martyr for their executioners.

And lastly, for the proper practice of fraternal charity we must often ask God *that minds and hearts be in unison.* The first Christians in the infant Church "had but one heart and one soul" (Acts 4: 32). Men said of them, "See how they love one another." Our Lord had declared: "By this shall all men know that you are My disciples" (John 13: 35), and by the light of faith every Christian family, every Christian community should recognize here that charity so characteristic of the Christians in the infant Church. Then will be forever realized the prayer of Christ: "Not for them only [the Apostles] do I pray, but for them also who through their word shall believe in Me. That they all may be one, as Thou, Father, in Me, and I in Thee; that they also may be one in Us: that the world may believe that Thou hast sent Me. And the glory which Thou has given Me, I have given to them: that they may be one, as We also are one" (John 17: 20–22).

Thus, mightily yet sweetly charity contributes to the working out of the providential plan: thus human beings truly help one another as they journey on to eternal life. Herein also is a proof of the divine origin of Christianity, for obviously charity such as this cannot come from a world that builds upon egoism, self-love, and divided interests; its own particular associations quickly fall asunder, those high-sounding words, solidarity and fraternity, being often no more than a cloak to cover the deepest jealousy and hatred.[3]

The Savior alone can deliver us, and it was for this He came. "Who for us men and for our salvation came down from heaven. . . . And He was made man" (Nicene Creed).

[3] This is the place to recall those words of Pascal's to be found equivalently in St. Augustine and St. Thomas: "The infinite distance between matter and mind symbolizes the infinitely more infinite distance between mind and charity; for charity is supernatural. . . . The whole universe of matter and mind, with all their products, cannot equal in value the least movement of charity, which belongs to an order infinitely more exalted." *Pensées,* ed. E. Havet, pp. 266, 269.

CHAPTER XXIX

PROVIDENCE AND THE COMMUNION OF SAINTS

Nowhere is the kindliness and majesty of Providence and the divine governance more clearly seen than in the communion of saints. We have already said that although Providence disposes all things, even the least of them, immediately, yet in the divine governance, in the execution of the providential plan, its action extends to the lower orders of beings through the higher,[1] and thus it is that through the angels and saints in heaven it assists men in their journey to eternity and the souls that are in purgatory. This is clearly brought out in the dogma of the communion of saints: "I believe in the Holy Ghost, the holy Catholic Church, the communion of saints" (Apostles' Creed).

This dogma expresses the communion or mutual relations existing between the various members of the Church militant, suffering, and triumphant, and their participation in the merits of Christ and the saints. There is a reciprocal communication of the merits of the just.

Protestants have attacked this dogma as being an alien growth. Some have even maintained that, by giving worship to the saints, Catholics look upon them as so many gods and thus fall into a sort of polytheism. Others have chosen to see in this reciprocal communication of the merits of the just a

[1] Cf. St. Thomas, Ia, q. 22, a. 3.

mere mechanical system whereby sinners may be justified without any co-operation on their part.

A clear statement of the dogma suffices to show what a travesty of it such an interpretation is. It is not an alien growth, but a synthesis of the principal truths of faith: the dogmas on the Trinity and the indwelling of the three divine Persons in the souls of the just, the dogmas relating to Christ the head of the Church militant, suffering, and triumphant: the dogmas on grace, on works of merit and satisfaction, and on prayer. Let us see in what this communion of saints consists according to the Scripture, and then consider in particular what are the relations souls have with God and Christ, and with one another.

The communion of saints according to Holy Scripture

This dogmatic truth may be expressed as follows: There is a communion of saints whereby all the members of Christ are closely united through Him and in Him, participating in varying degrees in the same spiritual gifts.

The Gospels make this point clear when they speak of *the kingdom of God*. This kingdom is something more than the external visible society of the Church militant instituted for the salvation of souls; it *is a spiritual society* embracing, besides the faithful on earth, the holy souls of the departed and the saints and angels in heaven, all united through Christ with God, living by the same truth, the same charity. Charity is presented as the bond of perfection, that spiritual bond which unites one soul with another by uniting them all with God.

What the Gospel says on this point is clear. Our Lord, after declaring His intentions and preparing the way, at length establishes the kingdom of God, in which all the members, united through charity, are to form one family with God as their Father. To that family the angels also belong, for the Gospel speaks of their joy at the conversion of sinners.

It will be enough to recall Christ's words as recorded in St. Matthew and as a rule in St. Mark and St. Luke also.

First, St. John the Baptist admonishes his hearers to "do penance, for the kingdom of God is at hand." [2]

Later on, the Savior, before sending forth His Apostles to preach the Gospel, tells them: "He that receiveth you, receiveth Me: and he that receiveth Me receiveth Him that sent Me." [3]

And a little later He says: "If I by the Spirit of God cast out devils, then is the kingdom of God come upon you." [4]

All the faithful are brethren, since all are the children of God and in their prayer are to address Him as "Our Father, who art in heaven." [5] Again, our Lord tells us: "Pray for them that persecute and calumniate you: that you may be the children of your Father who is in heaven, and who maketh His sun to rise upon the good and bad." [6]

This dogma is expressed even more clearly in our Lord's sermon after the last supper as recorded in St. John: "I am the vine: you the branches. He that abideth in Me, and I in him, the same beareth much fruit: for without Me you can do nothing." [7] A little further on He says: "Not for them only [the Apostles] do I pray, but for them also who through their word shall believe in Me. That they all may be one,

---

[2] Matt. 3: 2.
[3] Matt. 10: 40.
[4] Matt. 12: 28.
[5] Matt. 6: 9.
[6] Matt. 5: 44.
[7] John 15: 5.

as Thou, Father, in Me, and I in Thee." [8] It is with this in mind that St. John says in his First Epistle (1:3): "That which we have seen and have heard, we declare unto you: That you also may have fellowship with us and our fellowship may be with the Father and with His Son Jesus Christ." Here we have the true doctrine of the communion of saints.

St. Paul declares it again and again, and explains it by showing how the risen and ever-living Christ is the head of a mystical body of which we are the members. [9]

The relation of the members with Christ the Mediator and with God

As in our own organism there is a physical influence exerted by the head upon the members, communicating their appropriate movements to them through the nervous system, so also in the mystical body virtue goes out from our Lord's humanity upon all the faithful, upon all the members composing this body, imparting to them the life of grace, of faith, hope, and charity, and at the same time giving to the blessed in heaven that consummation of grace which we call glory and which can never be lost. In this way *our Savior applies the fruits of His merit to us,* passing on all the graces He has obtained for us on the cross. This transmission of graces is effected through His humanity as an instrument inseparably united to His divinity, the source of all grace, and again through the sacraments as detached instruments vibrating as it were at Christ's touch and so able to affect and quicken our very souls. But first and foremost this communication of graces is made daily through the holy mass perpetuating in substance the sacrifice of the cross, applying the merits of

8 John 17: 20.
9 Rom. 12: 4, 5; I Cor. 12: 12–27; Ephes. 1: 22; Col. 1: 18; 2: 19.

that sacrifice to us and permitting us to participate in it by
holy communion. Souls are thus able to grow daily in the
life of grace as they journey toward eternity.

The supernatural influence exerted upon us by God and
Christ is principally one of illumination and love, since to
the faithful on earth and the souls in purgatory it imparts
the light of faith and the gifts of the Holy Ghost together
with the love of charity, while to the blessed in heaven it
communicates the light of glory which is the source of the
beatific vision, and a love of charity that nothing henceforth
can destroy or diminish.

The supernatural life which the members of the mystical
body thus receive by this supernatural inpouring of illumination and love must be made to ascend once again to the Most
High, being the same supernatural life, the same knowledge
and love, praising the glory of God by acknowledging His
infinite goodness.

And so from the souls of all the just on earth, in purgatory,
and in heaven there ascends to God a love in which the
sovereign good is preferred to all else. In the faithful on
earth this act of love illumined by faith inspires a homage of
adoration, supplication, thanksgiving, and reparation, especially during the time of mass. These are the four ends of
sacrifice.

Thus the supernatural influx of illumination and love coming down from God through Christ the Redeemer upon the
souls of men on earth, in purgatory, and in heaven, ascends
again to God as a hymn of grateful acknowledgment and
brings them peace by keeping them there within the radiance
of the divine goodness. There lies the purpose of Creation;
almighty God has created all things for the manifestation of

His goodness, and His glory is simply this goodness radiating externally.

The relations of the members with one another

Such being the ties binding the souls of the just upon earth, in purgatory, and in heaven to Christ the Mediator and to God, the ultimate source of all grace, we are given the explanation of the relations existing between one member and another, and particularly between the Church triumphant on the one hand and the Church militant and suffering on the other.

The blessed in heaven intercede for the faithful here on earth and the souls in purgatory, and to that intercession we may have recourse in all confidence, especially to the intercession of Mary Mediatrix, as the Church constantly does in the Hail Mary and the Litany of Loreto. As St. Paul wrote to the Hebrews (12: 22): "You are come to Mount Sion and to the city of the living God, the heavenly Jerusalem, and to the company of many thousands of angels, and to the Church of the first-born who are written in the heavens, and to God the judge of all, and to the spirits of the just made perfect, and to Jesus the Mediator of the New Testament, and to the sprinkling of blood which speaketh better than that of Abel."

Every one of the saints in union with Christ, makes intercession for us when we invoke them.[10] The angels also come to our assistance, for they too are subject to Christ. St. Paul delights in telling the Colossians how even the most exalted

[10] If we ask holy persons here on earth to pray for us, as people used to ask the Curé of Ars, then surely, whatever Protestants may say, it is right to ask the saints in heaven to intercede for us. These are now in the fulness of light and know better than we do what may rightly be asked on our behalf.

of creatures are subject to the Word made flesh: "In Him were all things created in heaven and on earth, visible and invisible, whether thrones, or dominations, or principalities, or powers. All things were created by Him and in Him. . . . And He is the head of the body, the Church" (1:16). To the Church triumphant the angels also belong, inferior only to Jesus and Mary in the intensity of their charity and the light of glory.

But there are also close ties linking the Church militant with the Church suffering. *It is our duty to pray for the souls in purgatory,* to have masses said for their deliverance, to gain indulgences for them, which means that we obtain for them the application of the fruits of our Savior's merits and the merits of the saints. And the works of charity we perform in their behalf (the prayers we offer for them, the crosses we take upon ourselves to alleviate their sufferings) God will certainly reward. The Church has always prayed for the dead: in the Second Epistle to Timothy (1:8) we read of St. Paul begging God's mercy for the repose of the soul of his friend Onesphorus.

And lastly, no less intimate are the ties that bind the faithful on earth with one another. They can assist one another by prayer and good works, works of merit and satisfaction. One who is in the state of grace can merit in the wide sense for his neighbor also, and in the same sense can make satisfaction for him, can take upon himself the penalties due to his neighbor's sin. United as they are with Christ, God regards the merits and sufferings of the just and has mercy on the sinner. God said to Abraham: "If I find in Sodom ten just within the city, I will spare the whole place for their sake" (Gen. 8: 26, 32).

It is to these spiritual relations existing between the faithful on earth that St. Paul is referring when he tells us:

There are diversities of graces, but the same Spirit. And there are diversities of ministries, but the same Lord. And there are diversities of operations, but the same God, who worketh all in all.[11] . . . One body and one Spirit: as you are called in one hope of your calling. . . . One Lord, one faith, one baptism. One God and Father of all, who is above all, and through all, and in us all.[12] For the body also is not one member, but many. If the foot should say: Because I am not the hand, I am not of the body: is it therefore not of the body? And if the ear should say: Because I am not the eye, I am not of the body: is it therefore not of the body? If the whole body were the eye, where would be the hearing? . . . The eye cannot say to the hand: I need not thy help. Nor again the head to the feet: I have no need of you. . . . And if one member suffer anything, all the members suffer with it: or if one member glory, all the members rejoice with it. Now you are the body of Christ and members of member.[13] . . . Bear ye one another's burdens: and so you shall fulfil the law of Christ. . . . Whilst we have time, let us work good to all men, but especially to those who are of the household of the faith.[14]

Were we to behold the mystical body as we behold a multitude of persons, we should discern an immense gathering of men, women, and children, and within them a hungering for God more or less intense, more or less conscious, temptation too, and pain. Here are souls very generous in their sufferings, there are the humdrum Christians; lower down the line are souls on the point of yielding to the temptations

[11] See I Cor. 12: 4–6.
[12] Ephes. 4: 4–6.
[13] See I Cor. 12: 14, 26–27.
[14] Gal. 6: 2–10.

of the senses, others about to lose their faith, and there are the aged who are near the grave. Then we should realize how true Christians living by prayer must have the same attitude toward souls as a mother bending over the cradle of her child.

Further, let us remember that, as St. Thomas says (Ia IIae, q. 89, a. 6), when a child, even though not baptized and still in unbelief, comes to the full use of reason, he is bound to choose between the right and the wrong road, between duty and pleasure, between the true last end, though but vaguely recognized, and whatever is opposed to it. If there is no resistance to the grace then offered him, he loves above all things God thus vaguely recognized and is thereby justified, so as to enter into the mystical body. "If he then direct himself to the due end, he will, by means of grace, receive the remission of original sin" (*loc. cit.*).

Now the precious blood of our Savior has been put at our disposal that with Him we may offer it up for the many souls who as yet know Him not or who have turned their backs upon Him.

Among all the faithful, therefore, charity should reign, which is the bond of perfection, uniting us with God and with Christ the Redeemer and with Mary.

In this age of revolt, no longer confined to Europe but worldwide, when atheistic "Leagues of the Godless," the spawn of Russian Bolshevism, are multiplying throughout the nations and the way is being prepared for a terrible conflict between the spirit of Christ and the spirit of the Evil One, now more than ever must we live by this mystery of the communion of saints.

We feel the urgent need of rising above the violent opposition that prevails between an international communism, materialist in its inspiration, which tramples underfoot the dignity of the human person, of family and country, and a nationalism which, when no longer simply for defense but for offense, develops in one way or other into an idolatrous nation-worship. Though we should entertain a real and if necessary heroic love for our country, it is absolutely imperative for us to direct our thoughts even more to that City of God which has its beginnings here on earth, to be consummated in that heavenly and enduring country in which the peoples of all nations should one day be united.

Believers living in the different countries of Europe and throughout the world must unite without delay in fervent prayer, especially in the holy sacrifice of the mass, that the peace of Christ may reign among the nations.

It is the same body and blood of the Savior that is offered on every altar throughout the world, in Rome and in Jerusalem, in every Catholic church of the five continents. It is the same interior, ever living oblation in the heart of Jesus that animates all the thousands of masses celebrated daily wherever the sun is rising.

We must pray and pray with all earnestness that the kingdom of God may come, placing our petitions in the hands of Mary Mediatrix to present to her Son, to whom at the beginning of this century His Holiness Leo XIII consecrated the whole human race.

Embracing as it does those who are still in unbelief, this consecration of the whole human race brings down upon them new graces. It is by living this mystery of the communion of saints more intensely and above all by having masses said for the conversion of unbelievers, that the way is prepared for the missionary apostolate. As Père de Foucauld realized, we must prepare for the apostolate by bathing, so to speak, the souls of unbelievers in the blood of Christ, which has been given to us and which we are able to offer daily with Him.

Through the communion of saints the chalice of superabundant redemption is put into our hands, that by our prayers and sacrifices it may be made to overflow upon souls that, all unconsciously perhaps, are hungering for God and are dying far from Christ.

To the doctrine we are explaining here, this objection has been raised: How is it that, with so many thousands of saints in heaven, confirmed now in grace, more sinners are not converted by them?

A certain contemplative has correctly answered:

Though inseparable, heaven and the Church on earth are nevertheless distinct. Although there is enough heat in a single star to melt every particle of ice on the earth, yet we have still to submit to the rigors of winter. To raise a heavy weight with a powerful lever, we still need a fulcrum. Similarly, it is God's will that every action exerted from heaven on this world shall have its fulcrum here below. That fulcrum is to be found in the saints who are still pursuing their pilgrimage in this life. The incomprehensible might of heaven will not have its full efficacy on earth except through one who is really in communion with Christ, through one who is in immediate contact with Calvary and the cross.

As Père de Foucauld wrote, "Has not a man riches enough, happiness enough, when he possesses Jesus?" Though all abandon him, he still has the one thing necessary, which by prayer and sacrifice he is able to pass on to others.

The practical consequences of this mystery of the communion of saints are numberless. Bossuet has given us a summary of them in his *Catechisme de Meaux*.[15] Every spiritual gift is the common property of all the faithful: the graces each one receives and the good works each one performs are for the benefit of the whole body and every other member of the Church, by reason of their close union. And so, when one member of the Church possesses some gift or other, let the others rejoice instead of giving way to jealousy; when one member suffers, all should show their compassion instead of closing their hearts to him. What are the vices incompatible with the communion of saints? They are all enmities and jealousies. Those who entertain jealousy, sin against this article of the Creed, the communion of saints.

Finally, we realize why in this dogma the faithful are called saints: because they are called to be holy, because, too, they have been consecrated to God through baptism.

Who are they to whom the term "saint" is especially applicable? The term applies to those who in perfect faith lead also a holy life.

From this we see what a misfortune it is to be deprived of the communion of saints; so the Church by her excommunication deprives notorious sinners of the sacraments, the source of their life, until such time as they show a sincere desire to repent.

This mystery of the communion of saints shows with special clearness how the Christian life is the beginning here on earth of life eternal, since it is primarily by sanctifying grace and charity that we have in very truth the seed of glory within us. Thus we are given a wonderful insight into

---

[15] *Œuvres complètes*, XII, 417.

the supreme end and purpose to which all things have been ordered by Providence, and the meaning and implications of these words in our Lord's sacerdotal prayer: "That they who believe in Me may be one, as Thou, Father, art in Me, and I in Thee" (John 17: 21).[16]

[16] In connection with Providence and the communion of saints, we should notice that in order to undertake any sort of work in the Church it is necessary to have a mission and to preserve the spirit of that mission, a point well brought out by Père Clerissac, O.P., in that excellent work, *Le Mystère de l'Eglise,* chap. 7, "La Mission et l'esprit." Thus it was with the founders of the religious orders.

A striking example of this law in the order of grace is to be found in the Life of Mother Cornelia Connelly, Foundress of the Society of the Holy Child Jesus, 1809–1879. Formerly a Protestant, married to a Protestant, and the mother of a family, she was converted to Catholicism at the same time as her husband. When later on her husband recognized that he had a vocation to the priesthood and was ordained, Mother Connelly herself, following the advice given her by Gregory XVI, founded a religious congregation in America. Unfortunately her former husband took it for granted that he would have the direction of this congregation, a task for which he had no mission whatever. This lost him the grace of his own vocation and he left the Church, while Mother Connelly, in the midst of incredible difficulties, finally succeeded in carrying through the work almighty God had entrusted to her.

CHAPTER XXX

The End and Purpose of the Divine Governance

We have said it is the divine governance that presides over the execution of the providential plan, its purpose being to manifest the divine goodness, which bestows upon the just and maintains within them forever a life that is eternal. Concerning this end and purpose, let us see what the Old Testament with its incomplete revelation has to tell us, and then we shall be able to appreciate better the full light given us in the Gospels. This was the method used by St. Augustine, particularly in his work on providence or the divine plan: the City of God, its progressive building up here on earth and its full development in eternal happiness.

The incomplete intimation

In the Old Testament the ultimate purpose of the divine governance was expressed in a manner as yet imperfect, often merely symbolic. The Promised Land, for instance, was the symbol of heaven. The whole system of worship with its sacrifices and varied rites, and in a greater degree the prophecies, proclaimed the coming of the promised Redeemer, who was to bring light and peace and reconciliation with God.

The announcement of the future Redeemer thus contained in a vague way the promise of eternal life, which was to be given us through Him. That in the Old Testament, prior to the fulness of light contained in the Gospels, so little enlightenment should have been given on this matter of eternal beatitude, is easily explained; it was because, until Christ had suffered and died, the souls of the just had to wait in limbo for the gates of heaven to be opened to them by their Savior.[1]

Nevertheless, as we have already seen, *the Prophets* occasionally contain sublime and most significant passages on the magnificent reward God has in store for the just in the next life, passages that state more clearly what was already said before them.[2]

Thus the psalmist said: "As for me, I will appear before Thy sight in justice: I shall be satisfied when Thy glory shall appear." Job spoke in a similar strain.[3]

Speaking of the New Jerusalem, *Isaias* said (60: 19): "The Lord shall be unto thee for an everlasting light, and thy God for thy glory. Thy sun shall go down no more. For the Lord shall be unto thee for an everlasting light: and the days of thy mourning shall be ended."

Daniel wrote (12: 3): "But they that are learned [in the things of God, and are faithful to His law] shall shine as the brightness of the firmament: and they that instruct many to justice, as stars for all eternity." Nor is it a question here of the just who will appear on earth in the years to come; the reference is to those still living or who have already died: the reward promised them is eternal.

More explicit still, as we have seen, is the Second Book of *Machabees* (7: 9), where we are told how with his last breath

---

[1] Cf. St. Thomas, IIIa, q.52, a.5.

[2] Gen. 5: 24; 17: 8; 26: 24; 35: 29; 47: 9; 49: 18, 29–33; Num. 20: 24; 27: 13; Deut. 25: 8, 17; 32: 50.

[3] Job. 14: 13–25; 19: 25–27; cf. also Ps. 11: 7; 15: 10–12; 48: 15 ff.; 72: 24; Prov. 10: 30; 11: 7; Ecclus. 1: 13; 11: 28; 18: 24, etc.

one of the martyrs addressed his executioners: "Thou, indeed, O wicked man, destroyest us out of this present life: but the King of the world will raise us up, who die for His laws, in the resurrection of eternal life."

Again, it is of eternal bliss that the Book of Wisdom speaks when it says:

The souls of the just are in the hands of God: and the torment of death shall not touch them. . . . The just shall shine, and shall run to and fro like sparks among the reeds. They shall judge nations, and rule over people: and their Lord shall reign forever . . . for grace and peace is to His elect. . . . The just shall live for evermore: and their reward is with the Lord, and the care of them with the most High (3: 1; 5: 1 ff.).

Eternal life according to the New Testament

In the fulness of revelation contained in the New Testament, eternal bliss is spoken of in terms within the reach of all. Indeed, Christ has now been given us. Whereas everything that preceded Him pointed to His coming, henceforth He Himself proclaims to all peoples the establishment of the kingdom of God and leads souls to eternal life.

This is expressed again and again in our Savior's sermons recorded in the first three Gospels. There it is said of the reward in store for the just: "Neither can they die any more: for they are equal to the angels and are the children of God, being the children of the resurrection" (Luke 20: 36); "The just shall go into life everlasting" (Matt. 25: 46; Mark 10: 30). It is not merely the future life spoken of by philosophers like Socrates and Plato, but an everlasting life, a life participating in God's eternity, transcending time, past, present, and future.

Elsewhere, in a passage recalling the prophecy of Daniel (12:13), Jesus exclaims: "Then shall the just shine as the sun in the kingdom of their Father" (Matt. 13:43). "Then shall the king [the Son of man] say to them that are on His right hand: Come, ye blessed of My Father, possess you the kingdom prepared for you from the foundation of the world." Here we have truly the ultimate purpose of the divine governance. "For I was hungry, and you gave Me to eat: I was thirsty, and you gave Me to drink: I was a stranger, and you took Me in: naked, and you covered Me: sick, and you visited Me" (Matt. 25:34).

In the *Sermon on the Mount*, Jesus had said: "Blessed are the clean of heart: for they shall see God. . . . Be glad and rejoice, for your reward is very great in heaven" (Matt. 5:8–12). Here indeed is the true Promised Land of which the Old Testament scarcely spoke except in symbols. The souls of men were too conscious of their profound need of redemption to be ready for the full enlightenment.

In the *Gospel of St. John*, Christ speaks of eternal life more frequently still. Thus to the Samaritan woman: "If thou didst know the gift of God. . . . He that shall drink of the water that I will give him shall not thirst forever. But the water that I will give him shall become in him a fountain of living water, springing up into life everlasting" (John 4:10–14).

Several times in the Fourth Gospel Jesus repeats the phrase: "He that believeth in Me hath everlasting life" (cf. 3:36; 6:40, 47). That is, one who believes in Me with living faith combined with the love of God has already within him the beginnings of eternal life. And why? Because, as He tells us later in His sacerdotal prayer, "this is eternal life: that they may know Thee, the only true God, and Jesus Christ, whom Thou hast sent" (John 17: 3); "Father, I will that where I am, they also whom Thou hast given Me may be with Me: that they may see My glory which Thou hast given Me, because Thou hast loved Me from the creation of the world" (*ibid.*, 17: 24). To look upon Christ in His glory we must be there where Christ was even then present in the higher regions of His holy soul: that is, in heaven, as He Himself said: "No man hath ascended into heaven, but He that descended from heaven, the Son of man who is in heaven" (John 3: 11-13).

In the same sense Jesus said: "Amen, amen, I say to you: If any man keep My word, he shall not see death forever" (John 8: 51). And again at the tomb of Lazarus He said: "I am the resurrection and the life: he that believeth in Me, although he be dead, shall live: and everyone that liveth and believeth in Me shall not die forever" (John 11: 25-26).

Here is the fulness of that revelation heralded in the distant past by Job and the psalmist, by Isaias, by Daniel, in the Book of Machabees, and again in the Book of Wisdom. Then it was no more than a little stream; now it is a vast river moving onward and losing itself in the infinite ocean of the divine life.

Elsewhere Jesus speaks of the narrow gate and the strait way (of self-abnegation) that leads to life,[4] that immeasurable way that leads to God. The Lord calls all men to labor in His vineyard, giving them as recompense, even to the laborers of the eleventh hour, His own eternal happiness

[4] Matt. 7: 14.

(Matt. 20: 1–6). The recompense He gives is Himself, though according to the merits and degree of charity each one has attained, for "in His Father's house there are many mansions" (John 14:2).

Our Lord's teaching is still more clearly expounded in the Epistles of St. Paul and of St. John.

St. Paul refers to eternal happiness when he says (I Cor. 2:9): "Eye hath not seen, nor ear heard: neither hath it entered into the heart of man, what things God hath prepared for them that love Him. But to us God hath revealed them, by His Spirit. For the Spirit searcheth all things, yea, the deep things of God."

Still more distinctly St. Paul says in another passage of the same Epistle (13:8):

Charity never falleth away: whether prophecies shall be made void or tongues shall cease or knowledge [imperfect knowledge] shall be destroyed. For we know in part, and prophesy in part. But when that which is perfect is come, that which is in part shall be done away. . . . We see [God] now through a glass in a dark manner: but then face to face. Now I know in part: but then I shall know [Him] even as I am known [by Him],

with a knowledge that is immediate and perfectly distinct; I shall behold Him as He beholds Himself, face to face, and no longer as in a mirror, obscurely, confusedly.

St. John speaks in the same sense in his First Epistle (3:2): "Dearly beloved, we are now the sons of God: and it hath not yet appeared what we shall be. We know that when He shall appear we shall be like to Him: because we shall see Him as He is." The Church has defined that this revealed teaching must be understood of an immediate vision of the divine essence with no created thing intervening as medium previously known.[5] In other words, through intellectual vision we shall see God more clearly than we see with our bodily eyes the persons with whom we are conversing, for we shall see Him distinctly as something more intimately present to us than we are to ourselves. Here on earth our knowledge of God is in the main confined to what He is not. We say that He is not material, not subject to change, not limited or confined. Hereafter we shall see Him as He really is, in His Deity, in His infinite essence, in that intimate life of His, common to the three Persons, of which grace, and especially its consummation in glory is a participation, since it is through grace that it will be granted to us to see and love God as He sees and loves Himself, and thus we shall live by Him eternally.

Such is the teaching of revelation on eternal life as the manifestation of the divine goodness and the ultimate purpose of God's governance. Let us now glance briefly at what theology has to add, haltingly always, in an endeavor to give us a better understanding of the mystery.

The beatific vision and the love for God of which it is the source

Theology throws a certain amount of light on this subject by contrasting a purely natural happiness with that happiness which only grace in its consummation can bring.

[5] Benedict XII (Denzinger, n. 530): "We define . . . that . . . even before the resurrection of their bodies and the general judgment . . . the souls of all the saints . . . in whom, when they departed this life, there was nothing to be cleansed . . . behold the divine essence with intuitive vision, face to face, in such wise that nothing created intervenes as object of vision, but the divine essence presents itself to their immediate gaze, unveiled, clearly and openly." Cf. also the Council of Florence (Denzinger n. 693).

Had God created us in a purely natural state, with a mortal body and an immortal soul but without the supernatural life of grace, our final destiny, our happiness, would still have consisted in knowing God and loving Him above all things, for our intellect was made to know truth and above all the supreme truth, our will was made to love and desire the good and beyond all else the sovereign good.

Had we been created without the supernatural life of grace, the final reward of the just would indeed have been, so to say, from without, through the reflexion of His perfections in creatures, as the great philosophers of antiquity knew Him. This would have been a knowledge more certain than theirs, and without any admixture of error, but still an abstract knowledge, obtained through the medium of things, in the mirror of things created. We should have had a knowledge of God as the first cause of spiritual and corporeal beings, we should have numbered His infinite perfections as they are known analogically from their reflexions in the created order. Our ideas of the divine attributes would still have been like tiny bits of mosaic, incapable of reproducing without hardening the spiritual features of God.

Similarly we should have loved God as the author of our nature, doubtless with a love of admiration, reverence, and gratitude, but without that gentle, simple familiarity which God's children experience in their hearts. We should have been the servants of God, not His children.

Such a destiny, however, would still have been of a very high order. It could never have palled upon us any more than our eyes can ever tire of beholding the blue skies. It would have been a spiritual destiny, moreover, and unlike material things the spiritual can be enjoyed fully by each one without detriment to the enjoyment of others and the consequent risk of jealousies.

But in this abstract and indirect knowledge of God, many obscurities would have remained, particularly as to the manner in which the divine perfections are reconciled with one another. We should always have been asking how an omnipotent goodness can be reconciled with the divine permission of evil, how infinite mercy can be intimately harmonized with justice.

The human mind would have been forced to exclaim: "Would that I might behold this God, the fount of all truth and of all goodness, whence steals forth the life of creation, the life of intellect and of will!"

But what reason even at its highest cannot discover, has been made known to us through revelation. Here we are told that *our final destiny consists in beholding God immediately,* face to face, and as He really is, in knowing Him no longer simply from without, but intimately, even as He knows Himself; that it consists also in loving Him even as He loves Himself. It tells us that we are now predestined "to be made conformable to the image of His Son: that He might be the first-born among many brethren" (Rom. 8: 29). In creating us, God was not bound to have us *partakers with Himself in His intimate life,* to invite us to this immediate vision of Him, but it was in His power to do so by making us His adopted sons, and this out of pure loving kindness He has willed to do.

It is our destiny therefore to see God not merely as mirrored in creatures, no matter how perfect, not even in that radiation of Him in the angelic world, but to behold Him immediately, without any creature intervening, and more distinctly than we behold ourselves with the eyes of sense. Being wholly spiritual, God will be intimately present to our intellect, illuminating and invigorating it and so giving it strength to look upon Him. (Cf. St. Thomas, Ia, q. 12, a. 2.)

This exclusion of any intermediary between God and ourselves extends even to the idea. No created idea could ever represent, as it really is, that purely intellectual and eternally subsisting flash which is God. No word of ours, not even an interior word, will be adequate to express what we are contemplating: thus even now when we are absorbed in gazing at some sublime spectacle, we cannot express what we see. Only one word can utter what God really is in Himself— His own eternal, substantial Word.

This vision of God face to face infinitely surpasses the most sublime philosophy. No longer will there be mere concepts of the divine attributes, these concepts reminding us of tiny bits of mosaic. Part of the destiny to which we are called is to behold all the divine perfections intimately reconciled, nay, identified in their common source, the Deity, the intimate life of God; to behold how the tenderest mercy and an absolutely inflexible justice proceed from one and the same infinitely generous and infinitely holy love that possesses a transcendent quality in which these apparently conflicting attributes are in fact identified; to behold how justice and mercy combine in all the works of God. Part of our destiny is to behold how this love, even when the freest good pleasure, is yet identified with pure wisdom, how in this love there is nothing that is not all-wise and in this wisdom nothing that is not transformed into love. Our destiny is to behold how this same love is identified with the sovereign good forever loved from all eternity, how divine wisdom is identified with the supreme truth forever known, and how all these perfections are but one with the essence of Him who is.

Our destiny is to contemplate in God this transcendent simplicity of His, absolute in its purity and holiness; to behold the infinite fecundity of the divine nature flowering in three Persons; to contemplate the eternal generation of the Word, "the brightness of the Father's glory and the figure of His substance" (Heb. 1:3); to behold the ineffable *spiratio* of the Holy Ghost, the term of the mutual love between Father and Son, uniting them eternally in this most exhaustive outpouring of themselves. "Goodness is essentially diffusive of itself" in God's interior life, and freely it scatters its riches abroad.

No one can express the joy begotten of such a vision, or the love that will spring from it, a love so mighty, so perfect, that nothing henceforth shall be able to weaken, far less destroy it. It is a love born of admiration and reverence and gratitude, but of friendship most of all, with all the simplicity and holy familiarity that friendship implies. Filled with this love, we shall rejoice first and foremost that God is God, with His infinite holiness, His infinite justice, His infinite mercy; we shall adore every decree of His providence, whose sole purpose is the manifestation of His goodness. And in all things we shall be subject to Him.

Wholly supernatural, such a knowledge and love will be made possible only through grace sublimating our faculties, and there at the very root of them, in the very essence of the soul, remaining a divine engrafting that can nevermore be lost to us. This consummation of grace, which we call glory, will in very truth be *an enduring participation in the very nature of God,* in His intimate life, since it will enable us to behold Him and to love Him even as He beholds and loves Himself.

Such, though very imperfectly expressed, is eternal life, a life to which we may all aspire, since through baptism we have already received it in germ, in sanctifying grace, which is the *semen gloriae.*

Herein lies the purpose of the divine governance, to show forth that divine goodness which is one day to bestow an eternal happiness upon us and maintain it forever within us. Then indeed will these words be realized: "God hath pre-destined us to be made conformable to the image of His Son: that He might be the first-born among many brethren" (Rom. 8: 29), that He who is Son by His very nature might be the first-born among many brethren, the children of God by adoption. It will be the perfect fulfilment of these words of Jesus: "Father, I will that where I am, they also whom Thou hast given Me may be with Me: that they may see My glory which Thou hast given Me, because Thou hast loved Me before the creation of the world" (John 17: 24). Christ's glory is the supreme manifestation of the divine goodness, for Him and for us unending happiness, the measure of which is the measure of God's own happiness, which is something transcending time, being no less than the unique instant of changeless eternity.

Let us conclude with St. Paul: "For which cause we faint not: but though our outward man is corrupted, yet the inward man is renewed day by day. For that which is at present momentary and light of our tribulation worketh for us above measure exceedingly an eternal weight of glory" (II Cor. 4: 16–17).[6]

[6] In times of great affliction not a few interior souls have found peace and even joy, though circumstances continued to give immense pain, when through God's inspiration they have conceived the idea of making a vow of self-abandonment to Providence.

When a soul is prompted by grace to make such a vow and is firmly resolved not to divorce self-abandonment from fidelity to daily duties, the following form may be used. It should be renewed daily during the prayer of thanksgiving:

"Whenever the will of God is expressed in a cross, I will yield myself to it entirely and with a note of joy, paying no regard to what was instrumental in bringing it about. In difficulties that in any way distress me I will avoid all self-probing, introspection, and idle preoccupations; I will steep myself more deeply in confidence, and seek to solve my difficulties through the action of grace. I will take up this attitude of mind and heart and plunge myself in God the instant something occurs to wound me. And all this I will do with an exceeding great love."

This self-abandonment should be accompanied by close fidelity to grace and the illuminations received in prayer.

INDEX

Abraham: intercession of, 364; self-abandonment of, 232 f., 234; trial of, serves a higher purpose, 184, 227

Agent, finality of, 23 f.

Angel, a finite good, 44

Animals, instinct of, 21: not result of chance, 21 f.

Aristotle, his principle of finality, 46

Augustine, St.: on the gift of wisdom, 245 f.; on gratuity of grace, 318 f.; on perfect happiness, 42; two principles, how reconciled, 319 f.

Author of life, contact with, 16 f.

Baldad, sin the cause of Job's trials, 178

Beatific vision: and the human intellect, 126; nature of, 98, 122 f., 376 f., 379 f.; source of, 377 f.; two principles reconciled in, 336

Benedict XV, and a happy death, 331

Boethius, definition of eternity, 112

Book of Wisdom: and eternal bliss, 373; on future reward of the just, 186 f.; praise of wisdom, 134; trials of good and wicked contrasted, 189

Bossuet: condescension of Jesus, 88; on expressed will of God, 218 note 6; on predestination and self-abandonment, 337 f.; on simplicity in creatures, 84

Catherine of Siena, St.: charity the basis of Christian perfection, 270 f.; on experimental knowledge, 279 f.; the general call, 283 f.; on infused knowledge, 277 f., 280; interpretation of *Dialogue* not forced, 287;

on merit and discretion, 272; on passive purifications, 281 f.; praise of, 269; repentance of sinners, 310 f.; sign of perfect love, 285 f.; the supreme commandment, 274 f.; the unrepentant sinner, 296; vocal and mental prayer, 276 f.

Catholic hospitals, and conversion of sinners, 310

Causality, final and efficient, 46 f.

Caussade, Père de, the divine operation in the soul, 249 f.: in simple souls, 264

Chance: is accidental, 21 f.; not first cause of order, 22 f.

Chardon, O.P., the divine action in simple souls, 266

Charity: characteristics of fraternal, 349 f.; formal motive of, 345; practice of fraternal, 351-357; primary object of, 343-345; secondary object of, 345 f.; unbeliever's objection to, 348

Church, relations between members of, 333 f.

Communion of saints: according to Scripture, 359 f.; not an alien growth, 358 f.; objection answered, 368; practical consequences of, 369 f.

Conscience, its relation to good, 54 f.

Cornelia Connelly, missionary spirit of, 370 note 16

Cottolengo, St., self-abandonment of, 236 note 16

Creation: a free act, 148 f.; of man, 306 f.

Curé of Ars, spiritual discernment of, 241 note 4

present moment, 247-251; of salvation, 306
Grou, Père, self-possession of Jesus, 89 f.

Happiness, natural desire for: its purpose, 47 f., 377 f.; not chimerical, 45 f.; summary of its proof for God's existence, 53; what it demands, 49 f.
Humanitarianism, communist: what it stresses, 341 f., 366 f.
Humiliation, acceptance of, 229 f.

Individualism, purpose of, 341
Infinity: of perfection, differs from indetermination of matter, 92; quantitative and qualitative, 92
Injuries, forgiveness of, 304 note 16
Intellect: not formal constituent of divine nature, 69 f.; range of human, 96 f.
Isaias, glories of New Jerusalem, 186, 372

Jansenism, errors of, 320
Jesus Christ: betrayal of, 297; birth of, and Providence, 262 f.; Canaanite woman praised by, 209; defense of Providence, 28; on eternal life, 373 f.; fidelity in little things, 251 f.; on general call to perfection, 284 (see also Catherine, St.); gentleness and fortitude of, 87 f.; on goodness of Providence, 208; Holy Spirit our guide, 250; the kingdom of God, 360; on love of neighbor, 346; love for us, 153; message of peace, 51 f.; the mystical body of, 361 f.; patience in persecution, 196 f.; prayer for unity, 356; presence of God in, 104 f.; promise of the Paraclete, 248; proof of Providence, 195, 198; severity of final judgment, 244; simplicity and innocence of, 85 f.; soul in arms of, 236; on

the supreme commandment, 274; the Truth, 26; universal redemption by, 310; urges watchfulness, 199 f.; on the way to pray, 195
Job: belief in a future life, 179; clue to Book of, 183 f.; humble confession of, 183; our Lord's final answer to question of, 29; purpose of Book of, 28; replies to his friends, 177 f.; trials of, 175 f.
John of the Cross, St.: the beaten track, 203; infused contemplation of, 278
Joseph, St., self-abandonment of, 225
Joseph (patriarch): and the designs of Providence, 262; purpose of his trial, 185
Judgment: general, 303; particular, 300; rash, 353 f.
Judith, on patience in tribulation, 188
Justice, kinds of, 342

Kant, his view of God's love, 144 f.
Knowledge: experimental, of God's dealings, 240 f.; kinds of, 280

Leonori, A., trial of, 294 note 3
Liberty, not formal constituent of divine nature, 68

Machabees, belief in future life, 187 f., 197, 372 f.
Maritain, J., on the two tendencies in life, 316 note 13
Mercy: prayer of, 308; relation to justice, 305 f.
Merit: condign, and final perseverance, 325; congruous, not principle of final perseverance, 326 note 10; principle of, 324 f.
Micheas, on mercy of God, 189
Motion, proof of God from. See Existence
Mover, First: characteristics of, 14 f.; must be spiritual, 13 f.; practical conclusions, 15 f.
Mozart, his conception of a melody, 114

If you have enjoyed this book, consider making your next selection from among the following . . .

Prices subject to change.

Moments Divine—Before the Blessed Sacrament. *Reuter* 8.50
Miraculous Images of Our Lady. *Cruz* 20.00
Miraculous Images of Our Lord. *Cruz* 13.50
Raised from the Dead. *Fr. Hebert*................................ 16.50
Love and Service of God, Infinite Love. *Mother Louise Margaret* 12.50
Life and Work of Mother Louise Margaret. *Fr. O'Connell* 12.50
Autobiography of St. Margaret Mary............................. 5.00
Thoughts and Sayings of St. Margaret Mary....................... 5.00
The Voice of the Saints. *Comp. by Francis Johnston* 7.00
The 12 Steps to Holiness and Salvation. *St. Alphonsus*................. 7.50
The Rosary and the Crisis of Faith. *Cirrincione & Nelson* 2.00
Sin and Its Consequences. *Cardinal Manning* 6.00
Fourfold Sovereignty of God. *Cardinal Manning*..................... 5.00
Dialogue of St. Catherine of Siena. *Transl. Algar Thorold* 10.00
Catholic Answer to Jehovah's Witnesses. *D'Angelo* 12.00
Twelve Promises of the Sacred Heart. (100 cards)..................... 5.00
Life of St. Aloysius Gonzaga. *Fr. Meschler* 12.00
The Love of Mary. *D. Roberto*.................................. 8.00
Begone Satan. *Fr. Vogl*.. 3.00
The Prophets and Our Times. *Fr. R. G. Culleton*.................... 13.50
St. Therese, The Little Flower. *John Beevers* 6.00
St. Joseph of Copertino. *Fr. Angelo Pastrovicchi*.................... 6.00
Mary, The Second Eve. *Cardinal Newman*......................... 3.00
Devotion to Infant Jesus of Prague. *Booklet*........................ .75
Reign of Christ the King in Public & Private Life. *Davies* 1.25
The Wonder of Guadalupe. *Francis Johnston*....................... 7.50
Apologetics. *Msgr. Paul Glenn*................................. 10.00
Baltimore Catechism No. 1...................................... 3.50
Baltimore Catechism No. 2...................................... 4.50
Baltimore Catechism No. 3...................................... 8.00
An Explanation of the Baltimore Catechism. *Fr. Kinkead*.............. 16.50
Bethlehem. *Fr. Faber*... 18.00
Bible History. *Schuster*.. 13.50
Blessed Eucharist. *Fr. Mueller* 9.00
Catholic Catechism. *Fr. Faerber*................................. 7.00
The Devil. *Fr. Delaporte* 6.00
Dogmatic Theology for the Laity. *Fr. Premm*...................... 20.00
Evidence of Satan in the Modern World. *Cristiani* 10.00
Fifteen Promises of Mary. (100 cards)............................. 5.00
Life of Anne Catherine Emmerich. 2 vols. *Schmoeger* 37.50
Life of the Blessed Virgin Mary. *Emmerich* 16.50
Manual of Practical Devotion to St. Joseph. *Patrignani* 15.00
Prayer to St. Michael. (100 leaflets) 5.00
Prayerbook of Favorite Litanies. *Fr. Hebert*....................... 10.00
Preparation for Death. (Abridged). *St. Alphonsus*................... 8.00
Purgatory Explained. *Schouppe* 13.50
Purgatory Explained. (pocket, unabr.). *Schouppe* 9.00
Fundamentals of Catholic Dogma. *Ludwig Ott*..................... 21.00
Spiritual Conferences. *Tauler*................................... 13.00
Trustful Surrender to Divine Providence. *Bl. Claude* 5.00
Wife, Mother and Mystic. *Bessieres*.............................. 8.00
The Agony of Jesus. *Padre Pio*.................................. 2.00

Prices subject to change.

Prices subject to change.

Prices subject to change.

At your Bookdealer or direct from the Publisher.
Call Toll-Free 1-800-437-5876.

Prices subject to change.

Explains the entire Catholic tradition on the spiritual life. . .

THE THREE AGES OF THE INTERIOR LIFE

by Fr. Reginald Garrigou-Lagrange, O.P.

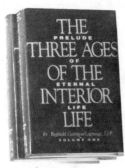

No. 1073. 1,166 Pages.
2 Volumes.
Sewn Hardbound.
Impr. ISBN-2477.

48.00
(Price subject to change.)

The Three Ages of the Interior Life is one of the greatest Catholic classics on the spiritual life, and it is the masterpiece of Father Reginald Garrigou-Lagrange, O.P. (1877-1964), whom many consider the greatest theologian of the 20th century. Both instructive and inspiring, this book is based squarely on the teachings of St. Thomas Aquinas and St. John of the Cross. Fr. Garrigou-Lagrange has organized and clarified the rich spiritual doctrine found in Sacred Scripture and in the great saints and other Catholic mystical writers. Among the topics covered:

• Infused contemplation as being in the normal way of sanctity • The degrees of contemplative prayer • Discovering one's predominant fault • Healing pride and acedia (spiritual sloth) • Spiritual direction • The active and passive purification of the senses, intellect and will • Retarded souls • The 3 successive "ways" of the interior life—Purgative, Illuminative and Unitive • Understanding the language of mystical writers • The dark nights of the senses and spirit • "Heroic virtue" • The inspirations of the Holy Ghost • The development and flowering of Sanctifying Grace and the 7 Gifts of the Holy Ghost • The spiritual fruits of chastity • The discerning of spirits • The errors of Modernism, Naturalism, Americanism, Jansenism and Quietism and how they deform the spiritual life • The role of spiritual childhood and of True Devotion to Mary • The fruits of Confession and Communion • The charisms (visions, stigmatization, etc.) • Private revelations • True mystical phenomena vs. false or diabolical phenomena.

This work is clear, complete, orthodox and inspiring! A masterpiece in every sense of the word!

U.S. & CAN. POST./HDLG.: If total order = $1-$10, add $2; $10.01-$20.00, add $3; $20.01-$30, add $4; $30.01-$50.00, add $5; $50.01-$75, add $6; $75.01-up, add $7.

FR. REGINALD GARRIGOU-LAGRANGE, O.P.

Fr. Garrigou-Lagrange, O.P.
1877-1964

Fr. Reginald Marie Garrigou-Lagrange, O.P. (1877-1964) was probably the greatest Catholic theologian of the 20th century. (He is not to be confused with his uncle, Père Lagrange, the biblical scholar.) Fr. Garrigou-Lagrange initially attracted attention in the early 20th century, when he wrote against Modernism. Recognizing that Modernism—which denied the objective truth of divine revelation and affirmed an heretical conception of the evolution of dogma—struck at the very root of Catholic faith, Fr. Garrigou-Lagrange wrote classic works on apologetics, defending the Catholic Faith by way of both philosophy and theology. Fr. Garrigou-Lagrange taught at the Angelicum in Rome from 1909 to 1960, and he served for many years as a consultor to the Holy Office and other Roman Congregations. He is most famous, however, for his writings, producing over 500 books and articles. In these he showed himself to be a thoroughgoing Thomist in the classic Dominican tradition.

Fr. Garrigou-Lagrange was best known for his spiritual theology, particularly for insisting that all are called to holiness and for zealously propounding the thesis that infused contemplation and the resulting mystical life are in the normal way of holiness or Christian perfection. His classic work in this field—and his overall masterpiece—is *The Three Ages of the Interior Life,* in which the Catholic Faith stands out in all its splendor as a divine work of incomparable integrity, structure and beauty, ordered to raise man to the divine life of grace and bring to flower in him the "supernatural organism" of Sanctifying Grace and the Seven Gifts of the Holy Ghost—the wellsprings of all true mysticism. Among his other famous theological works are *The Three Ways of the Spiritual Life, Christian Perfection and Contemplation* (a forerunner of *The Three Ages of the Interior Life*), *The Love of God and the Cross of Jesus, The Mother of the Saviour and our Interior Life,* and *Christ the Saviour.* His most important philosophical work was *God, His Existence and Nature: A Thomistic Solution of Certain Agnostic Antinomies.*

The works of Fr. Garrigou-Lagrange are unlikely to be equalled for many decades to come.